WORKING WITHOUT COMMITMENTS

Working Without Commitments

The Health Effects
of Precarious Employment

WAYNE LEWCHUK, MARLEA CLARKE,
ALICE DE WOLFF

McGill-Queen's University Press
Montreal & Kingston • London • Ithaca

© McGill-Queen's University Press 2011
ISBN 978-0-7735-3827-6 (cloth)
ISBN 978-0-7735-3828-3 (paper)

Legal deposit first quarter 2011
Bibliothèque nationale du Québec

Printed in Canada on acid-free paper that is 100%
ancient forest free (100% post-consumer recycled),
processed chlorine free.

This book has been published with the help of a grant
from the Canadian Federation for the Humanities and
Social Sciences, through the Aid to Scholarly Publications Programme, using funds provided by the Social
Sciences and Humanities Research Council of Canada.

McGill-Queen's University Press acknowledges the
support of the Canada Council for the Arts for our
publishing program. We also acknowledge the financial
support of the Government of Canada through the
Canada Book Fund for our publishing activities.

Library and Archives Canada Cataloguing in Publication

Lewchuk, Wayne A
    Working without commitments : the health effects of pre-
carious employment / Wayne Lewchuk, Marlea Clarke,
Alice De Wolff.

Includes bibliographical references and index.
ISBN 978-0-7735-3827-6 (bnd)
ISBN 978-0-7735-3828-3 (pbk)

    1. Precarious employment – Health aspects – Canada.
2. Precarious employment – Social aspects – Canada.
3. Job stress – Canada. I. De Wolff, Alice, 1947-
II. Clarke, Marlea III. Title.

HD5854.2.C3L49 2011   331.25'7290971   C2010-905725-2

This book was typeset by True to Type in 10.5/13 Sabon

Contents

Acknowledgments

We would like to thank the many individuals who took the time to fill in our surveys and to talk with us about their experiences in the contemporary labour market. As we hope the following chapters demonstrate, in addition to providing us with data, their insights into their experience as workers contributed greatly to the development of our theoretical framework and to our understanding of what it means to be working both with, and without, commitments.

A number of our colleagues were closely involved with this project at various stages and will recognize their valuable contribution to his volume. In particular, Andy King (department leader in Canada of the United Steel Workers Canadian National Health, Safety and Environment Office), joined our research group in its early stages, and worked closely with us for several years. He was a key participant in our discussions about how to deal with the relationship of precarity to health, and played an important role in shaping our initial thinking. Michael Polanyi was also involved in many of those early discussions, and provided useful comments on the research as the project unfolded. This study originated in a research project on precarious employment housed at York University and lead by Leah Vosko which provided a supportive environment for some of our ideas. Cindy Gangaram was instrumental in coordinating our work during this initial period, and suggesting we use a Canada Post service for distributing surveys to workers in particular Toronto neighborhoods. As the study grew, a number of honours and graduate students at McMaster University worked with us on the survey and interview components of the research. Special thanks go to them, especially to Sarah Declerk and Emily Watkins who helped administer the survey and Josephine Eric, Holly Gibbs, Laura McCready, Erika Mieto, Guo Qian, Ashley Robertson, Ester Rootham, Meaghan Ross, and Kirandeep Sibia, who helped code the surveys and transcribe the interviews. Diego Benavides set up our web survey for us and provided ongoing digital assistance. Esther Rootham assisted with identifying the postal areas for the survey drop and C. Lin and T. Sathyan helped in translating our surveys into Mandarin and Tamil. We are also grateful to the Workers' Action Centre in Toronto for providing a space in which to conduct many of our interviews. Thanks to Michael Quinlan, Katherine Lippell, and Robert Storey, who engaged us in discussions of the work and often read early drafts of our articles and chapters. The Social Sciences and Humanities Research Council, the Workplace Safety and Insurance Board, and the Lupina Foundation provided funding. Lewchuk thanks his colleagues in the School of Labour Studies for providing a stimulating academic community and the members of the Work and Health Research Unit at the University of Sydney and members of the Australian School of Business, University of New South Wales, for hosting him during an extended stay while completing this manuscript. Susan Glickman provided editorial advice during the final preparation of the manuscript.

Last but not least, we thank Dale Brown, who generously read and commented on the manuscript, Danielle Lewchuk for her help coding surveys, and Stephen Lewchuk for his assistance in keeping our computers running. Catherine Schissel commented on earlier drafts and shared her own insights about sustainability when "working without commitments." Cori Sandler provided graphics expertise and was an appreciated resource as we conducted neighbourhood outreach. We thank her for her support, which was based on long experience with the strains that are the focus of this study.

WORKING WITHOUT COMMITMENTS

1

Working Without Commitments: Employment Relationships and Health

There is a trend to completely eliminate full-time employment and to just have people like me working for contracts, because it is very beneficial for the companies. They are not responsible for anything that happens to me; like, if I am sick, they don't pay me, it's my responsibility. If they don't want me anymore, they just tell me 'we don't need you anymore,' once the contract is over. So, the shorter term the contract, the better it is for them because the more flexibility they have, the better off they are (Valdez #5542).

INTRODUCTION

Valdez's situation typifies that of a class of workers who are in less-than-permanent relationships with their employers. The contemporary Canadian labour market includes a large and growing number of workers like him whose employment relationships may be considered precarious (Vosko 2006). Canada is not unique in this regard. In many countries, less permanent forms of the employment relationship are growing faster than overall employment. For Valdez, the security associated with a long-term relationship with a single employer who provides decent wages, benefits, and career opportunities, has been replaced by a short-term employment contract that is insecure, is constantly being renegotiated, and is shaped by short-term market forces.

Valdez is "working without commitments": because his employers make few commitments to him beyond paying his salary, it makes little sense for him to make commitments to his employers beyond accomplishing work assigned to him; in addition, he and his colleagues have little connection with each other, hence few or no mutual commitments. Others have referred to this situation as "fragmented work," and discussed it as a product of the shift from large hierarchical organizations with internalized employment relationships to networked organizational structures where firms focus on core-competencies and contract out other activities (Marchington et al. 2005). Throughout this book, our focus on *commitments* will emphasize the changing balance in the "give and take," the transfer of effort, and the risks and responsibilities in employment relationships that are the result of the fragmentation of employment.

Working Without Commitments examines the connections between the working conditions and stresses that Valdez and workers like him experience, and the consequent increased risks to their health and the health of their households and, ultimately, their capacity to participate in their communities. Less permanent employment relationships qualitatively and quantitatively transform the economic, social, and political commitments that link employers to workers and workers to each other, and this transformation affects workers' health. The connections are not completely straightforward: some permanent workers experience significant employment stress and poorer health, some contract workers are in stable and rewarding employment situations, while many others are in precarious employment relationships that are unsustainable and toxic. This book exposes the pathways from the presence or absence of commitments in the employment relationship to the health of workers. Because working without commitments is a growing phenomenon that is of concern to our whole society, the final chapter explores pragmatic policy solutions.

Around one-quarter of all Canadian workers are currently in less permanent forms of employment relationships, including short-term contracts, self-employment, and employment through temporary employment agencies. While it is too soon to predict what impact the financial crisis of 2008–09 will have on employment,[1]

---

[1] Some argue that the financial crisis *itself* is a product of the spread of less permanent employment. Households under increased financial stress due to

preliminary evidence suggests that sectors of the North American and European economies where permanent employment is most prevalent have been the hardest hit in terms of job losses and concession contracts. In Canada, many of those who have lost their jobs are either resorting to temporary work in the non-union, low paid, low benefit service sector, or to self-employment (Vrankulj 2010). The dramatic and steady growth of newly self-employed people is especially troubling, given the tendency for this type of work to be characterized by low wages and few, if any, benefits. Employment shifts over the last several decades, combined with emerging shifts associated with the recession, make it imperative that workers, unionists, researchers, and policy analysts have a clear understanding of the characteristics of these employment relationships and the economic and social implications of working without commitments. What is their impact on workers' quality of life and, in particular, their health? What impact do less permanent employment relationships have on the well-being and health of other family members? How do they affect the social reproduction of existing social structures, traditions and citizenship? These are some of the questions that *Working Without Commitments* explores.

The economic and social bonds between employers and workers in less permanent employment relationships can be very different from those in permanent full-time employment relationships. Without being nostalgic about the past, it is important to remember that the system of permanent full-time employment that emerged after

---

stagnant compensation packages and irregular income flows turned to the financial sector to sustain living standards. The financial sector, especially in the United States, was liberated from the regulations first put in place in the 1930s to protect against the sort of melt-down experienced in late 2008, and was more than ready to make loans. Initially, low interest rates, and some dubious financial promotions, reinforced the willingness of households to borrow. Financial institutions discounted the risks of default, in part because the new environment allowed loans to be secured by third parties, which removed the risk from the initial lenders' bets that households could pay. Ferguson points out that rather than reallocating risk to those who could bear it, risk was allocating to those who could not understand it (Ferguson 2008: 269). When economic conditions began to deteriorate in early 2008, the weight of these loads became unmanageable and the global economy was driven into an unprecedented financial crisis.

World War II went some way to decommodifing labour. The exchange of workers' time for money was increasingly governed by customs and traditions that transcended short-term economic concerns, unlike the exchange of other inputs into the production process. As a result, workers expected to be placed on an organization's payroll and provided with benefits such as health care, paid sick leave, and a pension. Labour market regulations developed since World War II, and the rules enshrined in collective labour agreements, provide most workers in permanent employment relations some protection from arbitrary dismissal, discrimination, and unsafe working conditions. Consequently, these workers' jobs *are* permanent in the sense that they can be terminated only through a layoff with notice, or by dismissal following a recognized mechanism of due process. Permanent employment relationships are also more likely to be embedded in a set of social norms and practices that implies a longer-term commitment between employer and worker, and between workers themselves, that goes beyond contractual securities. Employers invest in the well-being of their workers through a range of activities and programs, such as employer-supported training and work-life balance provisions, and workers can expect opportunities to advance within their organizations. Social activities such as seasonal parties and retreats are symbolic of a relationship that is more than contractual and implies a long-term commitment between employer and worker.[2] Correspondingly (or in turn), many workers invest in friendships with co-workers, and in collective forms of representation, such as trade unions, and engage in collective bargaining to promote their long-term interests with their employers.

This "standard employment relationship" became prevalent after World War II in North America in sectors of the economy such as manufacturing, and for certain classes of workers, particularly white males. But workers in less permanent employment relations, those we describe as "working without commitments" are less likely to be included in the medium and long-term plans of their employer and hence may have less access to training and career development. These workers are less likely to be covered by

---

2 The history of the emergence of this form of the employment relationship can be found in Kaufman 2008.

employer pension plans or other benefits, and their terms and conditions of work are open to renegotiation at the start of any new contract. Existing labour market regulations are generally less effective in protecting workers on short-term contracts, and provide few rights to further employment once a contract is over. In Canada, changes to the unemployment insurance system in the 1990s dramatically reduced the ability of those in short-term employment to benefit from the program, and the rules regulating the formation of unions continue to discriminate against workers who are not in permanent full-time positions. They are often excluded from workplace social functions and are less likely to develop on-going relations with either their employers or co-workers. They have less incentive to invest in collective labour organizations such as unions, and are less able to exercise rights embedded in workplace health and safety regulations (Quinlan 2000 and 2006; Lewchuk, Clarke, and de Wolff 2009). It is sometimes unclear who their employers are, or who is responsible for managing their work (Frade and Darmon 2005). They are free agents in a lightly regulated labour market: their labour has been recommodified and exposed to the short-term pressures of impersonal market forces.

THIS STUDY OF CHANGES
IN CANADIAN LABOUR MARKETS

Working Without Commitments is based on a case study of the labour market of a single region in a developed economy. It was conducted in the Greater Toronto region of Canada, but it speaks to a global phenomenon that has implications for workers in both developed and developing countries. It not only describes in detail what it means to work in less permanent forms of employment relationships, it also provides a framework to understand the health implications of the employment relationship, and in particular its impact on stress and mental health. It is the end result of a six-year study by a team of university and community researchers. The team represents the range of employment relationships explored in what follows: one is employed on a full-time permanent basis, one is employed on a short-term contract but on a path to permanent full-time employment, and one makes a living through short-term temporary contracts. We are based in the School of Labour Studies at

McMaster University, and take an interdisciplinary approach to the subject. Our research backgrounds are also varied and related to the project: Lewchuk came to this study after a career of studying permanent full-time workers in the automobile sector, Clarke had just completed a major study of temporary employment relationships in South Africa and is now based in the Political Science Department at the University of Victoria, and de Wolff has a long history as a feminist and labour community researcher and activist.

The study examines workers' uncertainties over future employment, uncertainty over valued characteristics of future employment, their strategies to reduce this uncertainty, and the social relationships that buffer individuals from this form of uncertainty. Our conceptualization of the employment relationship focuses on the employment-related effort of finding, securing, and keeping employment; rights to future employment and influence over the setting of its terms and conditions; control over where and when work is done; social relations at work, such as levels of support from employers and co-workers; and the costs and benefits of having multiple employers, work-sites, sets of co-workers, and supervisors. We argue that both the form of contractual arrangements between employer and worker and – even more importantly – the assumptions regarding the contracting parties' long-term commitments are in transition.

We have drawn heavily on the work pioneered by Robert Karasek and his notion of "job strain," but have expanded it to include the effort of sustaining an employment relationship and of finding support associated with different forms of employment that extended into household and community relationships. Our analysis of the interactions between these components has created the Employment Strain Model to identify workers who are at highest risk of stress and poor health because of their employment relationship. This framework makes it possible to disentangle the heterogeneity underlying contractual arrangements and provides an explanatory framework that links employment relationships to health outcomes.

Our consideration of employment relationships will explore three related areas of contention. The first is the debate over the benefits of flexible labour markets. Economies such as Britain, the United States, Australia, and Canada responded to the economic crisis of the 1970s by easing labour market regulations, assuming that these changes would benefit individual enterprises and national economies (OECD 1994; OECD 1997). In the process, however, the capacity of unions to organize and bargain for workers was reduced, safety nets such as unemployment insurance were weakened, labour standards were revised, and much of the regulatory infrastructure was dismantled, with the goal of making employment more flexible and these economies more attractive to investment. Some employers made greater use of short-term contracts and employment through third parties, including temporary employment agencies. France's attempt to follow this path during the summer of 2006 led to widespread rioting, but did not prevent the candidate in favour of what came to be called "flexibilization" from winning the presidential election in 2007. Temporary employment relationships have played an important role in the emergence of China as an industrial power, but growing concern over the social implications of this form of employment led the Chinese government to pass new labour laws in the summer of 2007 requiring employers to provide workers with written contracts and limiting their ability to hire workers on a temporary basis (*Globe and Mail*, June 2007; Kahn and Barboza 2007). Policy makers have focused on the efficacy of flexibilization as a strategy for generating employment in the short-run and holding down inflation. Less has been written on its long-term effects on the quality of work life (Heery and Salmon 2000). This is a gap that *Working Without Commitments* explores.

A second and closely related concern is the impact of less permanent forms of employment on workers' health. While there are indicators that an increase in employment insecurity can lead to increased stress, and that the disorganization associated with the shift away from full-time permanent employment hampers attempts to regulate workplace health and safety, several empirical studies found only a weak relationship between less permanent forms employment and health (Letourneux 1998; Benavides and Benach 1999; Quinlan et al. 2001; Ferrie et al. 2002; Goudswaard and Andries 2002; Virtanen 2005). *Working Without Commitments* explores why this is the case and, through a new approach to occupational health and safety, offers a way of understanding the pathways from the employment relationship to health.

Health and safety research has traditionally focused on exposures to stress, toxins, and other dangerous working conditions once inside the factory gates or the office door. *Working Without Commitments* argues that exposure to employment-related stress begins *before* workers even arrive at the workplace, and is particularly prevalent amongst workers employed in short-term relationships. While it is sometimes argued that workers in less permanent relationships may be forced into accepting more physically hazardous work, or increased exposure to toxins, this is not the core of our argument. Rather, we argue that there is a limit to how much employment uncertainty and risk can be downloaded to individuals – at some point workers become stressed, and the employment relationship itself becomes toxic. This can have significant health impacts on workers and other household members,[3] and upon any household's capacity to sustain and reproduce the workforce.

The final subject to be explored is how the erosion of permanent employment relationships might impact the interface between work and home and the process of social reproduction. Authors such as Daniel Pink (2001) celebrate the spread of alternative forms of employment and see them as a liberating force with potential to enhance the quality of life of workers. Others caution that the erosion of full-time permanent employment will have broad social implications for society and families (Beck 1992; Sennett 1998; Beck 2000). These impacts include the persistent imbalance between family and work demands, the resulting stress and time pressure experienced by many families, and the possible contribution to declining fertility/birth rates in advanced economies (Golsch 2005; Crompton 2006; Corman and Luxton 2007). *Working Without Commitments* explores the advantages and disadvantages of these alternative forms of employment from the perspective of workers and begins to assess the impact of the decline of full-time permanent employment on men and women, and on the processes that shape social structures and traditions.

---

3 Giatti et al. 2008 have shown that living in a household that includes someone engaged in an informal employment relationship results in poorer health for household members, regardless of individual factors and the socio-economic characteristics of the household.

COMMITMENT

The concept of "commitment" is critical to our understanding of the changes taking place in contemporary labour markets and how they affect health. Commitment is a broad set of social factors that reflect the extent to which workers and employers have entered a long-term relationship that engenders support and concern for both the enterprise and the social and economic development of an individual. It is the human side of the employment relationship and is generally stronger in situations where the employment relationship has been decommodified. In short-term employment, the levels of commitment between employers and workers generally decline as they are increasingly shaped by impersonal market forces. As argued by others, developing community and commitment between individuals takes time – which is itself in short supply in less permanent relationships (Marglin 2008).[4] The "invisible hand" that is supposed to drive the efficient allocation of resources in a market economy has little interest beyond short-term financial performance. We argue that commitments between employer and worker, and between workers themselves, are important determinants of health because they buffer individuals from the stress inherent in a market-based economy. Further, we argue that the commitments implicit in the "standard employment relationship" are in transition, and that this is having an effect not only on social relations at work but also on relations within households and within communities. However, rather than trying to return to the era associated with the "standard employment relationship," we suggest a bold new path for economic development where workers take more direct control of their relations with employers.

IS EMPLOYMENT BECOMING LESS PERMANENT?

If – and to what degree – employment is becoming less permanent and more insecure remains a contentious issue in North America

---

4 The importance of community to individual well-being has been the subject of a recent book by Stephen Marglin (2008), who is also critical of the individualistic orientation of relations in advanced market economies. Our approach focuses on the employment relationship, but has implications for forms of community outside the workplace, including the household and civil society.

and elsewhere. If we examine only the *form* of the employment relationship, it is clear that permanent full-time employment remains the most common form in most western countries, including Canada. However, there is substantial evidence that less permanent forms have become increasingly widespread since the late 1970s. Until the early 1970s, most temporary employment relationships filled transitory fluctuations in labour demand. Vidal and Tigges (2009) suggest this is no longer the case and, increasingly, temporary employment has become a component of employers' search for a flexible labour supply. As a result, at an increasing number of workplaces, temporary workers are permanently filling core positions. In Canada, the prevalence of permanent full-time employment fell from sixty-eight percent of total employment in 1989 to sixty-four percent in 2007. The percentage of workers who are either temporary part-time, temporary full-time, or solo self-employed,[5] has increased by fifty percent in the same period and now represents over one in five Canadian workers (Kapsalis and Tourigny 2004: 6; Vosko 2009: 30). Data from the Canadian Labour Force Survey shows that temporary work has become more prevalent amongst new hires in the private sector. In fact, the percentage of workers with less than two years of seniority in temporary jobs nearly doubled between 1989 and 2004 (Morissette and Johnson 2005).

A similar pattern can be found in other countries (Heery and Salmon 2000); Burchell, Ladipo and Wilkinson 2002; Campbell et al. 2009; Gottfried 2009; Jonsson and Nyberg 2009). Campbell and Burgess reported that between 1983 and 1998, temporary employment increased in twelve of the fifteen OECD countries and in four (Australia, France, the Netherlands and Spain) the increase exceeded fifty percent (Campbell and Burgess 2001: 173). In most of these countries, self-employment, employment through temporary employment agencies, casual employment, and short-term contract employment, have become more prevalent. OECD data indicates a gradual increase in the prevalence of temporary employment from around five percent for men and seven percent for women in Europe in 1983 to around fifteen percent for both men and women by 2006. Much of this increase occurred in the 1980s and 1990s,

---

5 Solo self-employed workers operate their own businesses, but do not hire other employees.

and appears to have slowed since 2000 (Goudswaard and Andries 2002: 11; OECD nd.; Benach et al. 2004: 316). Australia has seen a particularly strong trend towards less permanent employment. Between 1992 and 2007, full-time permanent employment, as a share of all employment, fell almost ten percent. Full-time casual employment was the fastest growing form of employment over that same period, more than doubling, and growing at three times the rate of total employment in the economy (Louie et al. 2006; Campbell et al. 2009;). Casual work plus self-employment increased from twenty-eight percent of all employment in 1982 to forty percent in 1999 (Burgess and de Rutyer 2000). Even in Sweden, where legislation requires employers to place workers on permanent contracts once they have completed fourteen months of temporary contract work in the preceding five years, the percentage of temporary workers has been increasing. Between 1987 and 2007, the proportion of women in temporary positions increased by almost one-third to nearly nineteen percent of all female employees, and increased for men by nearly thirty percent to thirteen percent of all male employees (Jonsson and Nyberg 2009).

During the same period, self-employment also increased in many economies (Arum and Müller 2004). In reality, many self-employed workers are reliant on a single client for most of their work and for direction on how to complete their assignments, and therefore their relationships differ little from those in contract or temporary employment. Between 1979 and the late 1990s, the average share of self-employment in non-agricultural employment in OECD countries increased from 9.8 to 11.9 percent. In a number of countries including Britain, Canada, Finland, Iceland, New Zealand, Portugal, and Sweden, the share increase exceeded fifty percent (OECD 2000: 158). Between 1979 and 1998, the average rate of growth of self-employment in OECD countries was more than sixty percent faster than the growth of overall employment (OECD 2000: 159). This rate appears to have slowed since the late 1990s, but it still shows an upward trend. Self-employment represented 12.8 percent of non-agricultural employment in all OECD developed economies between 2000 and 2007, and 13.2 percent in non-European developed economies (OECD 2009: Table 2). In Canada, the incidence of self-employment has almost tripled since the 1970s and in Australia is has almost doubled (OECD 2009: Table 2).

This shift in the prevalence of different forms of the employment relationship may mark the end of a brief period when, at least for some workers, jobs were becoming more permanent and the commitments between employers and workers were increasing (Cappelli 1999; Vosko 2006). Even those in so called "permanent" jobs may be experiencing a shift in their employment relationships as the line is blurring between the core labour market, which has traditionally had greater security, and the less secure secondary labour market. Evidence of this change can be found in a study by Hallock (2009) who reviewed the reasons given by Fortune 500 firms for job losses as published in the *Wall Street Journal* between 1970 and 2007. He argues that "slumps in demand" have become less important as a reason for laying off workers. Instead, firms are using layoffs as a normal strategy in response to competitive pressures. His conclusion is that the implicit contract by which employers guarded senior workers from unnecessary layoffs and workers returned the favour by showing some loyalty to their employers has frayed. This suggests a new role for public policy: "This erosion of the implicit employment contract suggests that if employers have become less involved with cushioning the blow of unemployment and avoiding layoffs where possible, then public policy might have a role to play in spreading the burden of a down labor market so that the burden is not borne so heavily by those who lose their jobs entirely" (Hallock 2009: 70). Sennett suggests that the modern employment relationship threatens to undermine the mechanisms that "bind human beings to one another and furnishes each with a sense of sustainable self" (Sennett 1998: 27). As suggested by Cappelli, "The old employment system of secure, lifetime jobs with predictable advancement and stable pay is dead" (Cappelli 1999: 17). Some argue that this shift is also spelling the end of the "standard employment relationship" as the norm in western labour markets (Vosko 2000).

A significant body of research argues that such changes also imply an overall increase in employment insecurity. For instance, Beck, writing from a European perspective, discusses the emergence of the "Risk Society" and Hacker, writing about trends in the United States, refers to the "Great Risk Shift" (Beck 1992; Beck 2000; Hacker 2006a). Sennett uses the term "Flexible Capitalism" to describe a set of economic relations wherein "workers are asked to behave nimbly, to be open to change on short notice, to take risks continually, to become ever less dependent on regulations and formal procedures" (Sennett 1998: 9). He points to the decline in commitment and loyalty as a result of the increasingly short-term nature of employment relationships (Sennett 1998: 24). In a similar vein, Smith, studying the "New Economy" in the United States, argues that "uncertainty and unpredictability, and to varying degrees personal risk, have diffused into a broad range of postindustrial workplaces, services and production alike ... Opportunity and advancement are intertwined with temporariness and risk" (Smith 2001: 7). Osterman concludes that in the United States, "the ties that bind the workforce to the firm have frayed ... new work arrangements, captured by the phrase 'contingent work,' imply a much looser link between firm and employee" (Osterman 1999: 3-4). Others argue that the increased rate of involuntary job losses is another indicator of the erosion of the "standard employment relationship." Since 1976 in the US, there has been a steady decrease in the likelihood that someone employed at the beginning of a year will be with the same employer at the end. While senior workers are more likely to remain than those having low seniority, their advantage has declined appreciably since 1976 (Valetta 1999; 2007).

Other research indicates that the association between changing forms of employment and worker insecurity is more complex than suggested by authors such as Beck and Sennett. Green and others argue that, despite the popular impression to the contrary, there has *not* been an increase in overall employee insecurity since the 1980s. Their research focuses on Britain and the United States, where they contend that average job tenure has changed very little and that employee perceptions of job loss and difficulty finding new employment continue to be correlated with broader macro economic factors such as unemployment rates rather than major structural changes in how labour markets function (Doogan 2001 and 2005; Green 2006; Fevre 2007). Their basic finding is supported by Canadian data that shows that average job tenure actually increased by over ten percent between 1976 and 2006 (Lowe 2007: 13).

The apparent contradiction between those who claim that employment has become less secure, including many popular commentators, and data that suggests job tenure has not changed dramatically since the mid-1980s, can be explained by several factors. One is that aggregate data provides a limited view of what is going on in the economy and masks important differences taking place within different age cohorts and different sectors of the labour market. Faber (2008a; 2008b; 2008c) uses data from the US Current Population Survey from 1973–2006 to report on age-adjusted changes in tenure, job churning (jobs lasting less than one year), and long-term employment (jobs lasting at least ten years). He reports important differences in the labour market experiences of men and women, and of private and public sector workers. At all ages, the mean job tenure of men has decreased. At age fifty, the mean job tenure of men declined from 13.6 years in the early 1970s to 11.8 years in the early 2000s. However, for women the trend has been in the opposite direction. At age fifty, mean job tenure increased from 8.9 years in the early 1970s to 9.7 years in the early 2000s (Faber 2008a: 7).

Faber also reported sectoral differences. At age fifty, mean job tenure has declined for men in the private sector, has remained unchanged for women in the private sector, but has increased for men and women in the public sector (Faber 2008a: 7–11). Similar findings are reported for the incidence of long-term employment (measured as tenure of at least ten years or tenure of at least twenty years). Again, the incidence of age-specific long-term tenure is declining for men in the private sector, unchanged for women in the private sector, and higher for men and women in the public sector (16-18). There is also evidence of an increase in the prevalence of jobs that last one year or less for men in the private sector, but a decline of such jobs for women in the public sector. Overall, Faber concludes that in the United States, age-specific job tenure and the incidence of age-specific long-term employment relationships has declined since the 1970s. As a result, "The structure of employment in the private sector in the United States has become less oriented toward long-term jobs ... young workers today will be less likely than their parents to have a 'life-time' job" (Faber 2008a: 20).

Another reason why aggregate measures of insecurity may mask substantial changes in the structure of labour markets is that some industrial sectors have adopted less permanent employment relationships more vigorously than others. We have already reported above important differences between the public and private sector in the United States, and that the trend away from long-term employment has been most prevalent for men in the private sector. Frade and Darmon (2005) report findings for three different sectors (call centers, care for the elderly, performing arts) in five different European countries, and show wide differences in the overall prevalence of less permanent employment contracts and the specific form those contracts take. They conclude that in the sectors they examine labour had been "recommodified." British data suggests that in the service and manufacturing sectors, employment may actually have become *more* secure in the 1980s, in contrast to higher paid occupations and professions, which reported greater insecurity (Burchell 2002). Similarly Fraser (2001) argues that in North America, white collar work, once the bastion of the "standard employment relationship," has fundamentally changed since the 1990s and become less secure.

Case studies of specific sectors and specific firms also points to the uneven spread of insecurity in different labour markets. Marchington et al. (2005) studied the UK labour market and the shift away from the hierarchical firm to networked organizations and the spread of "fragmented work." With this shift, employers gain greater labour supply flexibility, but also open themselves to other types of vulnerability as they become more dependent on workers in temporary positions and on suppliers beyond their direct control. They conclude that the shift away from a single employer to an inter-organizational multiple employer-multiple client model affects different workers in different ways. For many, especially those doing contracted-out work that is not considered "core" to the operation, the increase in labour flexibility will generally be associated with a reduction in bargaining power as labour is made increasingly disposable and subject to short-term market discipline. Their employment becomes less secure and subject to the "whip" of the market and potential loss of contracts (Marchington et al. 2005: 12). However, other workers might gain from this shift. Employers seeking secure and dependable relations between firms along extended supply chains may empower some classes of workers and enhance their ability to demand more secure and better working conditions. Employers are likely to treat core skilled workers and "boundary spanners" – workers who act as bridges and decision-makers between companies – more favourably. In the long run, who will gain from the shift to "fragmented work" remains to be determined, as does the possibility that, from the perspective of labour, winners will outnumber losers.

Lazonick, in his study of the US information and communication technology sector, describes the transition from an old model where labour had long-term employment relationships to a new model which is more reliant on inter-firm labour mobility and less continuous employment. He makes the important point that changes in employment insecurity resulting from changes in employment relations are not constant over time. For firms like IBM that pioneered permanent full-time employment, the new model meant a reversal of human resources strategies and the increasing reliance on short-term contracts. IBM workers were discouraged from thinking of their relationship with the company as lifetime employment but this did not lead immediately to increased insecurity. During boom years, the insecurity of short-term employment was balanced by ease of mobility between firms. However, with the end of the dot-com boom in the 1990s, workers experienced increasing insecurity. This was particularly true for higher-paid senior staff with skill-sets that quickly became dated in a sector known for rapid technical change (Lazonick 2009).

The final explanation of why aggregate measures of insecurity have changed relatively little is that job-tenure and fear of job loss may be misleading indicators of insecurity (Robinson 2000; Tompa et al. 2007). Workers may respond to insecurity in labour markets by changing jobs less frequently, preferring to stay in a less than optimal relationship rather than risk moving to a new job that may not work out at all. Of course, fear of job loss represents just one aspect of employment insecurity. A more comprehensive measure would include loss of control over other characteristics of employment, such as those Burchell refers to as "valued job characteristics," including training and promotion opportunities, the pace of work, the nature of work, work schedules or future pay and benefit improvements. Burchell's study found that forty percent of workers who reported that it was unlikely they would lose their jobs still did not feel secure (Burchell 2002: 70).

While accepting that changes in employment insecurity have not been uniform in all countries, or in all segments of the economy, the weight of evidence does point to a shift away from permanent full-time employment in most countries and for many types of workers since the 1970s. There is some evidence that those most affected by this trend are men in the private sector, workers in new economy sectors (including computer-based work and sectors focusing on the processing and generating of information), white collar workers, and professionals. Even within affected sectors, employers may treat different workers differently as they deal with the labour supply problems created by the shift to less permanent employment relationships. As Cappelli concluded, "The new employment relationship is an uneasy dance between an open-ended relationship and the pull of the market, with the parties constantly renegotiating their commitments. Pressures from the labor market are now the important forces shaping the nature of the relationship" (Cappelli 1999: 3).

The Canadian labour market has witnessed major international pressures that add to this sense of labour insecurity. Free trade agreements have opened Canadian markets to Mexican and American companies. Protections such as the Auto Pact, that once shielded an important component of the Canadian manufacturing sector from unrestricted foreign competition, have largely been gutted. Foreign ownership continues to be an important characteristic of the Canadian economy and a series of recent takeovers of major Canadian employers has continued this trend, leaving decisions about Canadian employment in foreign hands.[6] These new employers are demanding radical changes to existing employment practices that have resulted in several prolonged strikes and raised uncertainty about the future of Canadian manufacturing and mining operations. The internationalization both of markets for Canadian goods and services and of corporate ownership structures exposes workers to new forms of competition. The resulting requirement for increased competitiveness may lead to the disappearance of jobs, painful workplace reorganizations, or changes in the terms and conditions of employment to protect jobs. At the same time, union density has fallen and recent changes in labour legislation

---

6 In the last few years much of Canada's steelmaking capacity (STELCO and DOFASCO), mining (ALCAN, INCO, Falconbridge), high tech (NORTEL), retail (Hudson's Bay), services (Four Seasons Hotel), and large sections of western timber and tar sand capacity have fallen into foreign hands.

and workplace organisation are making it more difficult for unions to organize and represent workers. These changes may not reduce job tenure, the length of time individuals spend with an employer. However, they certainly create doubts in the minds of many workers regarding the security or their employment and the nature of the commitment of their employer to a long-term relationship.

Working Without Commitments argues that the increase in the prevalence of less permanent forms of the employment relationship is an indicator of fundamental labour market changes associated with less secure employment and weaker commitments between employers and workers. Nonetheless, not all workers who participated in this study felt they would be better off in a permanent full-time relationship. About one sixth of those employed through a temporary employment agency or on short-term contracts indicated they were not interested in a more permanent job. For this small segment of the workforce, less permanent employment has improved their quality of life and freed them from some of the demands and constraints implicit in long-term full-time relationships with a single employer. Some of these individuals were exploiting demand for a scarce skill. Others were able to benefit from the flexibility associated with less permanent relationships because they could draw on the support of friends, family, or previous employers, or the state. However, this was not the case for the majority of those we interviewed who were in less permanent forms of employment. They reported uncertainty over access to future employment and its terms and conditions, were more likely to be concerned about ongoing evaluations of their performance, were more likely to report various forms of discrimination in getting new jobs, and expended considerable effort finding and keeping employment. Using our broader definition of insecurity, the majority of those in less permanent employment do face insecurity. They adapt to this uncertainty with new strategies around job search, training, and workplace behaviour. At the same time as they were trying to adjust to new employment relationships, they also reported limited support at work from co-workers and management, and from their households. Even for the small group that had benefits from less permanent employment, there were questions whether this was sustainable if the private and public supports they were drawing on came under attack.

WHAT IS AN EMPLOYMENT RELATIONSHIP?

We define an employment relationship as the set of rules, laws, customs, and practices that regulate exchanges between the buyers and sellers of labour time. It influences how people acquire employment, how they keep employment, how its terms and conditions are set, the social relations between workers, and that between workers and employers. While the employment relationship is implicitly associated with a specific job, it is largely independent of that particular job's characteristics. That is to say that the employment relationship and the job itself need not be closely associated with each other. "Bad" jobs can be associated with both secure and insecure employment relationships. Workers in less permanent employment may be more vulnerable to exposure to hazards, but they also may find it easier to leave hazardous jobs and search for something different. An employment relationship can be little more than a short-term relationship that defines an exchange of time for money, or it can be a complex long-term relationship that shapes employment rights, career development, and future earnings and benefits.

Any job's short-term characteristics are embedded in a legal contract that defines the terms of exchange between the buyer and seller of labour time. The International Labour Organization (ILO),[7] for instance, recently defined the employment relationship as: "A legal notion widely used ... to refer to the relationship between a person called an employee ... and an employer for whom the employee performs work under certain conditions in return for remuneration. It is through the employment relationship ... that reciprocal rights and obligations are created between the employee and the employer" (ILO 2006:3). Broadening the scope of the employment relationship to include not only the mechanisms through which workers find and keep jobs but also their expectations of long-term employment and career growth requires expanding this analysis beyond the formal contract. More often it is customs and practices, and the unwritten norms implicit in an employment relationship, that influence how contracts are entered

---

7 The LIO, based in Geneva, brings together employers, worker representatives, and government representatives to study labour trends and to suggest policies to improve the lives of workers.

into and ended, the future rights of sellers and buyers of labour time, the codes of conduct that shape how buyers and sellers are expected to behave given contractual obligations, and the assumptions regarding their long-term interests. The relationship changes depending on whether sellers of labour time seek employment directly or through an intermediary such as an employment agency, and whether the contract is an individual contract or one negotiated collectively through a union. It is shaped by assumptions about the long-term commitments between buyers and sellers of labour time and whether they view their relationship as a permanent one or a short-term exchange of time for money. Critical to understanding the broader implications of an employment relationship are the rules and practices regulating who gets to work and who gets to keep working. Is the labour contract open-ended or for a fixed period of time? How does the buyer or seller of labour time end a contract? What protection does the seller of labour time have from unfair dismissal? What is the entitlement to continuing employment once a contract is entered into? And finally, how are the terms and conditions of employment periodically renegotiated? Is this done collectively or based on short-term market conditions? A number of scholars have turned their attention to these broader characteristics of the employment relationship, and to the entitlements associated with different regulatory and legal frameworks that create protections for all workers regardless of their specific contractual arrangement (Lippel 2006; Bernstein 2006).

It is our contention that some of the most significant differences between those in permanent employment relationships and those in less permanent relationships are not found in labour contracts themselves, but rather in changes to the customs and practices and the unwritten norms regarding how individuals become employed and their rights to remain employed. When employers weaken their commitments to their workers, workers may have to search for work on their own time, engage in unpaid training, or perform tasks for employers beyond those defined in their written contracts. Contracts of employment can be revised on relatively short notice. At the same time, insurance against the risk of economic uncertainty becomes increasingly individualized. Workers are forced to plan for their own retirement and make individual provisions for illness and injury. They are forced to look to their households and the broader community for the support needed to buffer them from the insecurity of a market economy. In turn, those households and communities are affected by changes in employment relationships.

To help readers understand what we mean by an employment relationship, we have constructed two different examples, one "permanent" and one "less permanent," each drawing on the characteristics of several individuals interviewed during the project. At one extreme is Kim, who is in a permanent employment relationship, and at the other is Pat, whose employment relationship is much more precarious. What is most significant is that both are doing essentially the same job.

Kim has had a permanent full-time position with the same company for ten years. She has some influence over where she works, with whom, and when. She is working steady days and has a pretty good idea what she will be doing six months from now. Kim's company is unionized, provides reasonable benefits, and has a pension plan. She and her partner just had their third child, and she is just returning from a year's paid maternity leave; she feels so secure in her position that she is thinking of taking on a bigger mortgage to add more space to her house. She works in quality control, dividing her time between checking things on the factory floor and processing data at her desk. It's a good job even if it is a bit repetitive, and she hasn't thought about looking for work somewhere else for quite a while. She has gained the respect of her employer, who is sending her on a training course with the expectation she will move into a more responsible position in the near future. She likes her fellow workers and looks forward to occasional drinks with them after work, as long as this does not interfere with coaching her older daughter's ball team. She doesn't like her supervisor much and lets him know it. She's not concerned about him retaliating because she is protected from unfair dismissal by both the collective agreement and existing labour laws. She heard that the union is looking for improvements in pension benefits and education allowances in the current round of collective bargaining. The company is asking again for more flexibility in scheduling and the right to hire more temporary contract workers. She has also heard rumours that things are not going that well for the company, but with ten years' seniority, she is not really worried this will affect her. As long as the company stays in business and keeps this plant open and she performs her job in a reasonable way, she is unlikely to lose this job anytime soon. Kim is worried about her daughter though; she would like to work here but the only openings are temporary positions recruited through an employment agency.

Pat, who shares a desk with Kim in quality control, is one of those temporary workers, employed full-time on a six-month contract. He graduated from university ten years ago but has been unable to find a permanent position, so he finds work through an employment agency. This is his third contract with Kim's company. Quality control is a new job for him and he likes it, even though he is not doing what he thought he would be doing when he was first hired. This week he is working nights but he is not sure when he will be scheduled next week. He gets on okay with the other workers, but they are a bit suspicious of temporary hires and seem reluctant to help him. The pay is lower than he would like – about two-thirds of what Kim is paid – and he gets no benefits. He has the option of paying for his own benefits through the employment agency but cannot afford to do so. There are a lot of rumours going around the workplace that sales are down and some workers are going to be let go. Four workers from the same employment agency did not have their contracts renewed last month. He needs to keep this job. Pat is worried because he has had some problems with his supervisor (the same as Kim's), but he tries to get along. Because he doesn't belong to the union, complaining about his supervisor might reduce his chances of getting another contract and there is no legal recourse if his contract is not renewed.[8] He needs to keep this job, but to stay here he might have to take a position in another

---

8 The legal rights of contract and temporary workers to further employment vary from country to country. In Japan, the "doctrine of abusive dismissal" offers some protection to workers who are employed on repeated contracts with the same employer (van Dresser 1999). In Quebec and the Netherlands, long-term temporary workers have some legal recourse should their contracts not be renewed (Grnell 2001; Bernstein 2006). In Britain, contract workers' rights are severely limited upon the ending of a specific contract unless it can be shown that there is a "mutuality of obligation" that implies the employer has an overriding obligation to offer further contracts and the employee has an obligation to accept these contracts (Department of Trade and Industry 2007). In most jurisdictions, even if these rights exist, they are difficult to enforce (Bernstein et al. 2006).

part of the plant, where he has heard that people do not get along well. It would almost certainly mean a pay cut and would also involve more weekend work. In addition, changing his schedule might make it impossible for him to continue taking courses to improve his computer skills. Now that he works nights and some weekends, and even spends time after work looking for other jobs in the area just in case he loses this one, he hardly ever sees his partner. They are thinking about starting a family but would like more security first. His partner is also working on contract with a schedule that is equally irregular. He would like to buy a house, but the bank is reluctant to lend him money as they are worried that he does not have a permanent position.

While Kim and Pat are fictional, they are representative of the two opposing dynamics playing out in many labour markets across the globe. They have similar jobs in the same workplace but are in two different forms of the employment relationship. How they relate to their employer and to the other workers is radically different. Kim has some control over what she does at work and, more significantly, some control over whether she will continue to have a job with her current employer. She also has an understanding of how the terms and conditions of her employment are likely to change and be renegotiated from time to time. The company has at least some commitment to Kim and is willing to invest in upgrading her skills. Pat's position is more precarious. His continued employment is contingent on the company being willing to issue a new contract. There are no guarantees that this will happen or that the terms and conditions will remain the same. Some of the other workers see him as a threat to their positions, which creates some tension. It is up to Pat to ensure his employability. Kim's household is thriving while Pat's is full of uncertainty. He is much more vulnerable than her, despite the superficial similarity between their jobs.

THE EMPLOYMENT RELATIONSHIP AND HEALTH

The basic question explored in what follows is how the employment relationship affects workers' health and well-being. We are also interested in how employment insecurity is affecting households and the process of social reproduction. Kim and Pat essentially do the same work and so are exposed to many of the same health and safety risks as defined by traditional health and safety studies. Yet in other ways Kim and Pat are quite different: how they acquire work, how they keep work, how they negotiate the terms and conditions of work, and how they relate to their employer and the other workers, are all significantly affected by their different employment relationships. Can this difference affect their potential health outcomes?

As we developed questions and indicators for the *Working Without Commitments* survey, we used a broad set of measures to identify who was employed in a permanent or less than permanent employment relationships, and who was working without commitments.[9] The analysis began in part with measures of precariousness that include employment type, the degree of regulatory protection, income and benefit levels, and control over the labour process. The components we used to construct these measures draw on the work of others, including Vosko (2006) and Vosko, MacDonald and Campbell (2009). These measures make it possible to identify a continuum of precariousness that is based on a single dimension with multiple components, but the continuum analysis does not adequately isolate the stress that leads to health problems and therefore was not sufficient for this study.

Throughout the book we use the term "less permanent employment relationships" to describe short-term and temporary employment relationships. It is intended to keep ourselves and our readers open to the extent to which different dimensions of the employment relationship interact to create negative health effects for workers. We tend not to use the term "precarious employment relationships" because it generally has a negative connotation and does not acknowledge that some *permanent* employment relationships exhibit many of the characteristics of precariousness and are also associated with negative health effects. An important finding of this study is that on their own, neither the form of the employment relationship nor precariousness is a strong indicator of health outcomes.

---

9 For an extended discussion of the multi-dimensional characteristic of precarity and labour market insecurity, see Vosko, MacDonald, and Campell 2009.

A significant body of research based on the Karasek "Job Strain" model has influenced our approach (Karasek 1990). This model examines the interaction between control, effort, and support at work on health. It has provided convincing evidence that the combination of high effort loads, low control over how work is done, and low support are stressful and damaging to health. The "job strain" model focuses on the characteristics of the work one does once employed. *Working Without Commitments* extends this analysis to the employment relationship and the broader social context in which employment is embedded.

In order to understand how the employment relationship and the changing allocation of employment risks impact health, we have developed a set of indicators to measure the characteristics of employment. We have used these to construct a model that follows the pathways from how people find, keep, and negotiate employment to health outcomes. These indicators provide an alternative to using the form of the employment relationship (e.g. temporary employment, part-time employment, and full-time employment) as proxies for the different characteristics of employment relationships. The lack of detail provided by using these forms limits their potential to identify specific characteristics of an employment relationship that might be affecting health outcomes, making it difficult to design interventions. In addition, such a procedure assumes that everyone employed in a particular form of employment faces similar issues; something our research suggests is unlikely to be true. This is why we have developed a model that differentiates employment relationships along three broad dimensions: *employment relationship uncertainty, employment relationship effort*, and *employment relationship support*. Interaction between these three dimensions of the employment relationship influence exposure to *"employment strain."* We call this the *Employment Strain Model*, whose basic components are presented in Diagram 1.1.

The first dimension, *employment relationship uncertainty*, measures the level of control individuals have over work schedules, future employment, and the terms and conditions of such employment. The level of *employment relationship uncertainty* tends to increase as employment relationships become less permanent. The end of a contract and reassignment by an employment agency are both moments when future employment is uncertain, as are its

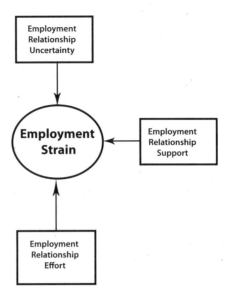

Diagram 1.1: The employment strain model

terms and conditions. This is not to suggest that those in permanent employment never face *employment relationship uncertainty*, only that it tends to be more pronounced for individuals in less permanent positions and for those frequently moving between jobs or contracts.

The *employment relationship effort* dimension measures the effort workers expend on keeping employed, effort balancing the demands of multiple employers or multiple work locations, and effort expended to gain good references for future employment. In less permanent employment relationships, the effort needed to ensure that one has future employment increases. Here effort is broadly defined to include not only effort intensification on the job, a point made by Burchell et al. (2002), but also increased job search, self-funded training, and more frequent exposure to harassment and discrimination. While those in permanent employment relationships have some rights to future employment with the same employer and are generally protected from unfair dismissal by labour laws and contract provisions, this is less likely to be the case for those in less permanent employment. Those who buy their time generally have control over further employment, and protection from "unfair non-contract renewal" is either non-existent or difficult to enforce. Hence, those in less permanent employment are aware that they are constantly being assessed for future employment and that, at the end of one contract and the start of another, they may be especially vulnerable to discrimination based on race, age, or sex. The end of a contract is also a moment of significant uncertainty and limited control over future outcomes. A critical point of our study is that while workers may be employed in less permanent employment relationships and hence be more insecure, this need not translate directly into an increased fear of unemployment or shorter job tenure if strategies are adopted to compensate for the eroded rights to employment with an existing employer. Most of these strategies will imply increased *employment relationship effort*.

The *employment relationship support* dimension measures the support a worker receives at work whether from formal organizations such as unions or simply from other workers, and outside the workplace from friends and family. Less permanent employment relationships can result in transitory social relations between employers and workers, and between workers. Employers are less likely to make a long-term commitment to less permanent workers, and this may result not only in weaker personal relationships at work but also in less investment in training by employers, as well as fewer long-term benefits. At the same time, those in permanent positions may view those in less permanent employment with suspicion and concern, while the less permanent workers may see permanent workers as privileged. The potential for conflict between them is likely to increase. In her study of precarious forms of employment, Smith noted: "The temporaries often identified with their managers more than with their co-workers because managers informally cultivated and mentored them, and often led them to desire permanent membership in the CompTech community ... An individualistic approach to work and employment seemed to mute the turmoil, stress, or unpredictability of flexible workplaces" (Smith 2001: 171–2).

Independently, each dimension of the employment relationship may affect health. Those who spend a lot of time looking for work or who are constantly aware they are being evaluated on the job or who feel lack of support in the workplace may feel stress and strain. The dimensions of the employment relationship may also interact to create *employment strain*. Workers who are uncertain about future job prospects and expend effort looking for employment in a context of limited support may experience heightened stress. *High employment strain* is defined as the combination of high levels of *employment relationship uncertainty* and *employment relationship effort* that may or may not be buffered by high levels of *employment relationship support*.

In what follows, the health effects of less permanent employment relationships are examined using the three broad dimensions of the *Employment Strain Model*. We argue that there is a limit to how much employment uncertainty and risk can be downloaded to individuals – at some point they become overloaded, and the employment relationship becomes toxic. We are interested in how this process is gendered and racialized. Do men and women, or white workers and individuals from different racialized groups, experience precariousness and the weakening ties between employers and workers in the same way? Which groups in society have the resources to handle this downloading of stress? How are households and social reproduction affected by the concomitant transfer of risks and costs? What is the role, if any, of public programs to assist households in this increasingly insecure society?

This study seeks to understand whether, through their employment, workers are entitled to health benefits, a predictable source of income, and income replacement in the case of illness and old age, and how the lack of some or all of these elements affects health outcomes. In most societies, employment is not the only source of such benefits. Many societies provide some of these supports through publically funded health care, unemployment insurance programs, and pension systems. Canada, where this study is based, does provide all of these benefits, to a greater or lesser extent, through public programs. In particular, Canada has a publically funded universal health care system that covers most, but not all, hospital and doctor expenses (It does not cover drug, dental, or vision expenses.) Canada also provides some insurance against unemployment, and a limited, publicly funded pension plan. To the extent that these benefits are available to workers irrespective of their employment relationship, the potential negative health effects of working without commitments may be less dramatic in Canada than in jurisdictions with less generous public supports.

DATA SOURCES

The chapters that follow draw data from a project on changing employment relationships in the Greater Toronto area. Phase One began with a pilot survey in 2002, followed by focus groups with homecare workers, university staff, and service sector workers (Lewchuk et al. 2006a and 2006b). Phase Two began in the fall of 2005 and winter of 2006 and involved a random population-based survey of individuals living in Toronto and nearby communities. A total of 3,244 surveys were received. The survey asked participants to describe the characteristics of their employment relationship, what they did at work, and indicators of their health. Approximately two-thirds of respondents were employed in relationships with most of the characteristics of a "standard employment relationship": relationships that were permanent and full-time. Over a quarter were in less permanent or precarious forms of employment, including employment through temporary employment agencies, working on fixed-term contracts of less than one year in duration, and self-employment without any employees. The remaining survey participants were in permanent part-time positions. A number of survey respondents were selected for further interviews approximately six months after the survey. They were chosen to represent the experiences of workers in different types of less permanent employment, and those in full-time employment who reported high levels of *employment strain*. Eighty-six individuals were interviewed. The final phase in early 2007 involved repeat interviews with about half of those interviewed during 2006 to assess any changes in their situation.[10]

OUTLINE OF THE BOOK

The book is divided into two sections. The first section (chapters 1 to 5) focuses on measuring the different characteristics of employment relationships and how they affect health outcomes. The second

---

10 Details of the project can be found in the methods appendix.

section (chapters 6 to 9) focuses on individuals in less permanent employment, their experiences working without commitments, and the strategies they adopt when faced with economic insecurity. The current chapter serves as an introduction to the whole book as well as to the first section; the next, chapter 2, examines the evolution of employment relationships including pre-capitalist relationships, early forms of market-based relationships, the emergence of the "standard employment relationship" in the twentieth century, and its recent decline. It explores the historical roots of commitments between employers and workers, and ends with a discussion of the nature of the employment relationship in contemporary economies. Chapter 3 begins the analysis of the survey data and presents findings on the overall characteristics of different employment relationships in the Greater Toronto labour market. Chapter 4 examines the gender and racial dimensions of contemporary employment relationships. It focuses on these two questions: Are women or workers from racialized groups employed in relationships with different characteristics? And, how are changes in employment relationships affecting the process of social reproduction? Chapter 5 develops the Employment Strain Model and uses it to examine how the characteristics of the employment relationship shape health outcomes.

The second section of the book, chapters 6 through 9, makes use of the qualitative data gathered during focus groups and interviews. Chapter 6 analyzes encroaching uncertainties in the experience of those in relatively permanent and full-time employment. It concludes that, even for individuals who are employed in what looks like a "standard employment relationship" conditions have changed, and their employment is becoming less secure and less rewarding. The next three chapters explore three different clusters of individuals in less permanent employment relationships. Chapter 7 examines a group who are in less permanent employment but see this as a sustainable arrangement in the long term. While no longer employed in a "standard employment relationship," they have succeed in either recreating some of the commitments associated with permanent relationships or have been successful in accessing support that buffers them from the insecurity of less permanent employment relationships. All are quite happy with their current situation and are benefiting from the flexibility associated with this employment relationship. Chapter 8 focuses on individuals who view less permanent employment as a transition phase to a more permanent and secure position. Although some are satisfied with this form of employment in the short-term, most are not happy with being in less permanent relationships and all workers in this cluster do not want or expect to be in this type of employment indefinitely. Chapter 9 discusses the experience of individuals who feel they have been forced into less permanent employment relationships and despite viewing their situation as unsustainable, are not optimistic that something more permanent will become available.

Chapter 10 concludes this book by examining the role that policies play in shaping employment relationships and the health outcomes of working without commitments, and by outlining both the types of policies that might mitigate some of the negative aspects of less permanent employment, and options for more comprehensive reforms.

Working Without Commitments advances five key claims:

- To fully understand the transition under way in employment relationships, one needs to assess both the contractual nature of the employment relationship and the social norms and practices associated with each form;
- This broader definition of the employment relationship provides a fuller understanding of insecurity associated with both permanent and less permanent employment relationships and reveals why workers may feel more insecure despite no clear trend in survey data on average tenure;
- The correlation between forms of the employment relationship and levels of insecurity is not perfect. Not all workers employed in less permanent employment relationships face increased insecurity;
- Understanding the nature of insecurity associated with the employment relationship provides a new way of understanding the pathways from employment and work to health; and
- The spread of less permanent employment and the transition to the dual insecure earner household is changing the role of households in production and social reproduction.

2

A Short History of the Employment Relationship: Control, Effort, and Support

I call it like an employer's market where there's just so many of us. It's like they're sharks in the water and there's just hoards of fish, they just grab whatever one because there's so many of us, you know. Just pay them very little, don't have to offer them anything because, if they quit well, there's like a million others they can get of us (Dalton #5449).

As we argued in the previous chapter, there is growing evidence that labour markets in many developed[1] economies are in transition. Labour market flexibility has become fashionable, leading to an increase in the prevalence of less permanent forms of employment and, we would argue, weaker commitments between employers and workers. This is a reversal of the "standard employment relationship" and the "male breadwinner model" common during much of the twentieth century: a period that witnessed not only the growth of large-scale mass producers but also increased labour market stability. During that time, employers and workers were linked into longer-term relationships through paternalistic forms of economic organization, which Jacoby (1997) refers to as the "Modern Manor." Initially offered predominantly to male white-collar work-

---

1 Labour markets in many countries in the Global South have also undergone significant changes over the last several decades, including the growth of less permanent employment relationships and the expansion of employment in service industries and informal sectors. Given the diverse set of factors shaping labour market changes in much of the Global South, this book focuses on industrialized countries and on Canada in particular.

ers, this new form of the employment relationship spread to male unionized blue-collar workers after World War II and to public sector workers in the 1960s and 1970s. The result was a deepening of long-term commitments between employers and workers, and a greater sense of control over their own employment for workers (Kaufman 2008).

Today, it is widely argued that the commitments that tie employers to employees are deteriorating (Marchington et al. 2005; Lazonick 2009; Pupo and Thomas 2010). The walls of the "Modern Manor" that insulated workers from some of the economic risks associated with a market-based economy while ensuring a company's access to qualified labour are being broached by a new managerial ideology of "flexibilization": the spread of networked organizations, increased reliance on extended globalized supply chains, and "new economy business models." Contracting work out to third parties is becoming more common, and employment through arms-length employment agencies more widespread. At many workplaces, internal career ladders are either being torn down or are only accessible to core employees. If IBM and Ford were the symbols of twentieth century employment relationships, Manpower Inc. and Labor Ready are the symbols of twenty-first century employment relationships. This chapter discusses these changes in detail and focuses on their impact on *employment relationship uncertainty, effort, support,* and health outcomes.

PRE-CAPITALIST EMPLOYMENT RELATIONSHIPS

Throughout Europe, both the employment relationship and the exposure of workers to economic insecurity were very different prior to the emergence of capitalism three hundred years ago. Until then labour markets, where workers contracted with employers, barely existed, so it is not really meaningful to refer to workers as "employees" before this period. Ancient Greek and Roman societies were predominantly agrarian, and the working population was divided between relatively free small landowners, an independent artisan class, and a significant population of slaves. Estimates suggest that from one-quarter to one-half of the population in these societies worked as slaves (Wood 1995: 182–7). Under slavery, labour was bought and sold as a commodity. Workers had no say if, when, or to whom they would be sold. Slave-owners controlled who got to work, the terms and conditions of work, and its organization. In exchange for their time, most slaves received little more than a subsistence wage: just enough to protect their owners' investment. This was a highly insecure existence subject to arbitrary decisions by the slave-owner. Job search as we know it did not exist, while support between slaves, and between slaves and masters, was shaped by the masters' ownership and the masters' economic interests. Workers responded to this insecurity with a combination of subservience and resistance.

A less restrictive model of labour exchange emerged in Europe under feudalism, partially in response to the labour shortages created by the Black Death in the fourteenth century. Workers were no longer the legal property of their masters, but they still had very limited control over who they worked for, and were not free to sell their time to the highest bidder. In Britain, the 1351 Statute of Labourers set rates for most types of labour and, more importantly, forced workers to accept a master's offer of work at the going rate. According to Leeson, "[the Statute] was intended to make labour in town or countryside stand still and take the rate of pay offered" (Leeson 1980: 38). Around the same time, the trades came to be regulated by the practice of apprenticeship, which tied young apprentices to masters for seven years until the age of twenty-four. This represented a significant portion of the short life-spans of medieval workers. These practices were formalized by the Statute of Apprentices in 1563. Access to the trades was restricted to children from households with an annual income of at least twenty shillings, more than most rural households earned, and the ratio of apprentices to journeymen was capped to minimize economic insecurity (Leeson 1980: 59–62).

In medieval society, nearly all decisions regarding one's occupation and master were largely settled at birth. Most workers were still involved in agriculture and therefore bound to the land on which they were born and to the lord who controlled the land through the monarch. Workers were obligated to provide services to their lord in the form of labour and of taxes paid out of the income they derived from farming small plots of land. The obligations the lord had to his subjects was to protect them both physically and spiritually in ways that went beyond the economic self-interest inherent in slavery. The lord was expected to keep the peace locally, provide military resources to defend the nation, and to support the church for the use of local workers. There were considerable restrictions on the mobility of non-agricultural labour. Artisans were bound to their trades for life and the freedom to change occupations or masters was restricted. An important feature of this employment relationship was that "economic life was stable ... the basic rhythms and techniques of economic existence were steady and repetitive" (Heilbroner and Thurow 1987: 13). While life was full of insecurity because of the possibilities of war and crop failure, the economic exchange between those who needed to work for a living and those who employed them for economic gain was stable. Buyers and sellers of labour time were bound to each other, and supported each other through a dense web of social, spiritual, and economic institutions. Marglin notes that "community" was a central feature of economic organization in this period, and that "mutual dependence, power, affection and reciprocal obligation were taken for granted" (Marglin 2008: 81). Workers had little control over what they did for a living or how their work was organized, and they were subject to exploitation and harsh treatment, but they had acquired rights that limited the insecurity they faced and offered a degree of social support. In other words, economic relationships were full of "commitments."

EARLY CAPITALIST LABOUR MARKETS
AND "FREE" WAGE LABOUR

About three hundred years ago, a new model of economic organization began to take shape, one that we now call "capitalism," and with it, the concept of free wage labour slowly emerged.[2] While market-based exchanges were common in earlier periods, they differed under capitalism in two ways. First, many more exchanges were mediated through markets, with prices reflecting more closely

---

2 As late as 1800, more than half of workers who were economically active in Britain were self-employed as small artisans and small landowners. In the United States, the transition was slower. In 1800, eighty percent were still self-employed, falling to twenty percent by 1920, and only eight percent in 1984 (Beder 2000; 62 and 71).

the forces of supply and demand. For the first time in history, there was a market involving buyers and sellers of labour time in which workers were free to contract and employers were free to rid themselves of unneeded labour. The master and servant relationship was drifting towards an employer and employee relationship. Second, tradition, custom, and practice became less important in shaping economic decisions while competition – and the goal of maximizing profits – became more important. Decisions regarding the level of economic activity were increasingly dictated by the rules of exchange and profit rather than more broadly defined societal needs.

The impact of these changes on workers was mixed. On the one hand, many gained new freedoms: the legal freedom to work or not, to move as they pleased, and to contract employment with whom they pleased. However, the regulations passed during the medieval period that protected workers from some elements of economic insecurity and obliged landowners and masters to support their workers were gradually swept aside. Gone were the rules that bound workers to a piece of land, to a master, or to an occupation. The stability of the master and servant relationship was replaced by a market relationship that was inherently insecure. The ties that bound buyers and sellers of labour time were loosened and a new form of the employment relationship emerged, one based on market individualism. The magnitude of the change is obvious in how Sir Walter Scott, a contemporary commentator, described it: "A man may assemble five hundred workmen one week and dismiss them the next ... without having any further connection with them than to receive a week's work for a week's wages, nor any further solicitude about their future fate than if they were so many old shuttles" (Cited in Beder 2000: 56).

While the gains in living standards linked to the shift from feudalism to capitalism continue to be debated, what is not open to debate is the insecurity workers now faced. For many, employment became impersonal, casual, temporary, and short-term. The risks associated with changing market conditions, of suffering a deterioration in the terms under which labour time was sold, of not having a job, of injury, and of old age, were increasingly borne by workers as individuals – and also by their households. Equally significant, employers gained new rights to control who would be employed and under what conditions. Labour time had become a tradable commodity, and the relationship between worker and employer was increasingly shaped by short-term profit calculations. The social upheavals that spread through eighteenth and nineteenth century Europe were, at least in part, a response to the insecurity and lack of control workers faced, and their growing reluctance to bear the risks associated with the economic cycle, the loss of income due to work-related injury, illness, or old age, and the risks associated with arbitrary treatment by employers. Workers not only faced increased insecurity, they also had to invest effort in job search, and experienced a deterioration in support as their land-based communities were replaced by less personal urban social relations.

This transition was not uniform. In regions such as the southern United States, slavery remained a dominant form of employment for black agricultural workers until the middle of the nineteenth century. Unease with the social implications of the new models of economic organization led utopian socialists like Robert Owen and Saint Simon to promote, with limited success, alternative economic models and employment relationships that were based less on markets, competition, and individualism (Hodgson 1999: 18). The emerging labour markets also created problems for employers who searched for ways to stabilize their access to labour and to limit workers' new-found right to sell their time to the highest bidder. The rules of most apprenticeship programs were weighted in favour of the employer and tied young workers to their masters for a lengthy period. Regulations such as the Master and Servant Acts fined employers who did not live up to the terms of employment contracts, but threatened workers with criminal proceedings if they abandoned their employers. Employers also experimented with complex contracting arrangements such as the putting-out system in textiles and the gang system and internal contracting in manufacturing. These forms of the employment relationship often resulted in an arm's length relationship between worker and employer.[3]

---

3 Under putting-out, small artisans took work on behalf of their extended family and/or several helpers. The putter-out received raw materials and agreed to return finished product to a merchant. Under the gang system and internal contracting, employers contracted with gang bosses for the delivery of so many pieces, or so many employees (Melman 1958).

In North America, indentured labour became common. Impoverished European and Asian workers had their way paid to North America in return for agreeing to serve a master for a fixed period of time.

By the end of the nineteenth century, more and more workers entered direct employment relationships with a company. In its earliest form, this was still a relationship firmly rooted in market exchanges and therefore full of insecurity for the worker. The relationship between worker and company was often through a foreman who had the power to hire and fire, and might do so on short notice. Workers had little long-term security and were vulnerable to shifts in economic fortunes largely outside of their control. For most, employment had become insecure and temporary. Less permanent employment relationships became the new norm by the end of the nineteenth century in many sectors and countries (Cappelli 1999: 4; Vosko 2006). While labour had been freed from the restrictions associated with feudalism, workers were increasingly on their own in terms of finding and keeping work, having lost much of the support associated with the earlier period. If feudalism can be described as a system where labour was integrated into a community by birth, the early phase of capitalism was a period when labour was on its own.

Workers responded to the loss of land-based communities and the security they provided by creating new types of urban communities such as mutual benefit societies. In Europe, workers demanded – and increasingly won – the right to form unions, and to bargain collectively with employers within a framework that represented a more equitable balance of power. Skilled workers were generally more successful in shielding themselves from economic insecurity through collective organizations than the less skilled. In Canada, industrialized centers like Hamilton exhibited a dense network of mutual aid organizations, labour bodies, and social clubs (Palmer 1979).

By the end of the nineteenth century, workers had found a political voice, forming their own parties in countries like Britain and, in others, transforming existing parties. Growing disenchantment with their treatment led many workers to view more favourably the radical political and economic solutions put forward by socialists who promised both greater security and worker control over work arrangements. In Russia, worker unrest resulted in the overthrow of the existing order. In Britain, the manufacturing sector became a breeding ground for socialist movements, and in Canada, the need for greater security led workers to demand the right to organize, a demand leading to a series of general strikes after World War I (McKay 2008). This growing unrest contributed to Bismarck's decision in 1883 to implement paternalistic labour policies designed to stabilize the employment relationship and to shield workers from some of the economic insecurity associated with economic downturns, injuries, and old age, in the new German Empire. The reforms included obligatory health, accident, old-age and disability insurance programs. Other states followed, implementing protective labour market legislation and social insurance schemes that partially protected workers from unemployment, workplace risks, and loss of income in old age. Labour market regulations began limiting the freedom of employers to treat workers as commodities. Research suggests that those economies best able to shield workers from the insecurity associated with a market-based economy were also the most productive (Huberman and Lewchuk 2003). Nonetheless, despite the emergence of new worker-initiated communities, employment remained insecure, and workers and their households were exposed to the short-term swings of the market with few, if any, protections.

EARLY WELFARE CAPITALISM
AND NEW MODELS OF WORKING WITH COMMITMENTS

As the nineteenth century drew to a close, the ongoing tension and instability associated with free wage labour and individualized employment relationships mediated through labour markets was creating problems for employers as well. The advantages of a stable supply of workers became more obvious to employers as companies became more complex and multi-unit organizations replaced single unit operations. Cappelli argues: "As it became more efficient to internalize the business transactions that had in the past been performed by the market, it also became more efficient to transform the employment relationship, moving from an arm's-length relationship that relied on the labour market for governance to one that was internalized in the firm ... Companies internalized employment, moving away from the market, to make the supply of skills and labor more predictable" (Cappelli 1999: 60).

Edwards refers to this period as one of "research, experimentation and trial" (Edwards 1979: 90). A number of companies began employing a new form of the employment relationship: one that offered employers and workers more stability by encouraging long-term commitments between buyers and sellers of labour time. The basic contours of what came to be known as "welfare capitalism" and the "standard employment relationship" began to emerge. Management became more bureaucratic and, in a sense, more professional. A new class of factory managers – many with some formal training – took greater direct control over production operations, while relations with workers were centralized in human resource departments where administrative rules and some semblance of due process in dealing with workers was encouraged. One goal was to limit the arbitrary treatment of workers by untrained foremen (Nelson 1975; Edwards 1979). Long-term commitments between employers and workers were deepened, and casual and temporary employment relationships were converted into more permanent relationships that offered pensions, benefits, and the potential to advance up a career ladder.[4] Jacoby (1997) argues that employers were creating "Modern Manors." In exchange for accepting managerial direction at work and delivering acceptable service to employers, workers were offered some protection from economic insecurity and arbitrary treatment. Rather than relying exclusively on the fear of job loss to discipline workers, employers invested in worker loyalty and sought to mould workers in the service of higher profits. In return, they were willing to share some of those profits with workers and to bear some of the insecurity associated with a market economy. For workers, the overall level of economic insecurity was reduced, and supports were offered for those injured on the job or too old to work. Managers who practiced welfare capitalism viewed it as an "efficient alternative to market individualism: training would be cheaper and productivity higher if employees spent their work lives with a single firm instead of seeking their fortunes on the open market" (Jacoby 1997: 4). Kaufman

---

4 In 1914, the National Civic Federation in the United States listed 2,500 companies offering some type of welfare benefits (cited in Jacoby 1987: 13).

views the main change in this period as one where "the rise of formally designated and professionally staffed HR departments" resulted in the "displacement of external labour markets coordinated by the invisible hand of demand and supply with internal labour markets coordinated by the visible hand of management" (Kaufman 2008: 4). Accordingly, there was a shift from treating "employees as a commodity, and short-run cost, and the employment relationship as a zero-sum game" to seeing "employees as human assets and the employment relationship as a positive-sum game" (Kaufman 2008: 3).

These changes represented a deepening of commitments between buyers and sellers of labour and the reconstruction of some of the mutual obligations implicit in pre-capitalist forms of employment. They also represented an alternative to worker-initiated communities that were under construction by the end of the nineteenth century. In this early variant of welfare capitalism, the employment relationship was still highly contingent. Those who management decided were not holding to their half of the bargain were summarily dismissed, and workers were only partially shielded from economic insecurity that could lead to job loss or skill redundancy. Initially, this new employment relationship was extended mainly to managerial, white-collar, and skilled workers. Offering longer-term employment had the advantage of making it easier for employers to recoup the cost of training and to retain organizational knowledge acquired through time on the job. In addition, the incentive of career ladders provided a low-cost mechanism for instilling company loyalty (Cappelli 1999: 4). While some of these benefits were offered to some of the less skilled, most continued to work in employment relationships where they bore the brunt of labour market insecurity with little, if any, support.

These changes in the nature of the employment relationship are reflected in changes at an ideological level and the emerging view that labour markets should function differently than markets for other commodities. The Treaty of Versailles that brought World War I to an end included a Labour Charter whose core principle was "Labour is not a commodity." This principle shaped the activities of the ILO after 1919, and was reasserted in the ILO's famous Philadelphia declaration at the end of World War II (Standing 2002: 9). The ILO sought to ensure that workers retained the rights they had won during the transition from feudalism to capitalism, including the freedom to contract and move in the economy, while at the same time softening the outcomes of insecurity in an economy guided by the principles of competition and employer control over access to employment. This was a period when social and economic policies were increasingly viewed as tools to reduce economic and social inequality with the ultimate goal of sustaining peace between nations (Standing 2002: 22).

IBM was one of the earliest companies to adopt this new form of the employment relationship. Under Thomas J. Watson, the company encouraged "company pride and loyalty" to IBM. Watson is said to have argued that "Loyalty saves the wear and tear of making daily decisions as to what is best to do" (Quoted in Sennett 1998: 122). During the depression, Watson kept his staff employed on new projects as well as building equipment for inventory. A group life-insurance plan was implemented in 1934, survivor benefits in 1935, and paid vacations in 1936 (Knowledge Socialization Project, nd). This was followed with corporate-owned golf courses, childcare, and subsidized mortgages (Sennett 1998: 123). "(IBM) provided a lifetime ladder of employment, all the stages of a career laid out for people who were expected to stay and to climb" (Sennett 1998: 123). By the 1940s, Putnam reports that "World War II veterans joining IBM were instructed to consult with their wives before taking the job because 'once you came aboard you were a member of the corporate family for life'" (Putnam 2000: 88). IBM boasted that in its first forty years of business as a computer company, it had never laid anyone off (Cappelli 1999: 71). It did this in part by employing a fringe of non-core IBM workers who would come and go in response to market ups and downs.

WELFARE STATE CAPITALISM AND WORKING WITH COMMITMENTS AS AN EMPLOYMENT NORM

This first wave of welfare capitalism largely collapsed as a result of the economic pressures created by the depression that started in 1929. Both David Brody and Stuart Brandes argue that its collapse had little to do with labour rejecting the new form of the employment relationship and more to do with the reluctance of employers to fund benefit plans and offer secure employment in the face of an economic crisis (Brody 1968; Brandes 1984). Abandoned to the vagaries of market individualism, workers in most industrialized capitalist economies turned to collective organization and new forms of worker-initiated communities to alter the outcomes associated with increased economic insecurity. This was facilitated by a growing willingness by the state to implement policies that provided minimum levels of protection from the risks associated with a market-based economy.

In Canada, as in many other countries, rapid industrialization during and after World War II created opportunities for workers to push for a new form of the employment relationship and gave the state the fiscal capacity to fund social welfare programs. With the passage of new regulations in 1944, the Canadian state recognized collective bargaining: that is, the right of workers to select their own representatives and to participate in shaping their own labour agreements. Unions became the norm for the new mass production industries. They demanded employment relationships for both skilled and less skilled workers that included a degree of employment permanency, decent wages, sick benefits, pensions, vacations, and some protection from arbitrary management decisions. In North America, workers acquired new rights based on seniority, including protection from lay-offs, access to preferred jobs, higher pay, and extended vacations. This created a disincentive to change employers. The "normal" job came to be defined as full-time, full-year work with a single employer at a single worksite. Of critical importance to what follows, while employers were still the dominant party in labour exchanges, workers had acquired some rights to future employment with an employer and entitlement to some participation in setting the terms and conditions of employment.

As unions demanded changes to the nature of the employment relationship, ideological developments contributed to a shift in the public's expectations of government, and a corresponding change within public office about the role of government in the economy. The economic collapse that started in 1929 suggested that an unregulated capitalist market could not be counted on to provide the kind of economic reliability needed to ensure sustained profits and a stable socio-political regime. The writings of intellectuals such as John Maynard Keynes following the collapse suggested that the state ought to be an agent of social and economic stability. To

Keynes, stability was the key to increasing efficiency, and to heading off the collapse of market-based economic organization. As
well, after the experience of state-directed full employment during
World War II, the working class had come to expect a better standard of living than they had experienced prior to the war. The stage
was set for the state to legislate labour-market regulations, and to
provide insurance against the instability left by the collapse of welfare capitalism.

As companies increased their investment in expensive fixed-capi-
tal equipment, and as mass production became the norm in many
sectors, employers increasingly appreciated the economic rationale
of social and labour stability. From this emerged, in a more complete form, the "standard employment relationship" that came to
be viewed less as a compromise with workers and more as an efficient model of social and economic organization. The "[standard
employment relationship's] essential elements came to include an
indeterminate employment contract, adequate social benefits that
complete the social wage, the existence of a single employer, reasonable hours and full-time, full-year employment, frequently, but
not necessarily, in a unionized sector" (Vosko 2000: 24). The state's
role was to provide the context in which this employment relationship could thrive. Rights to unionize, entitlements to unemployment insurance, state-sponsored pension plans, training, and eventually workplace health and safety regulations, all favoured those in
"normal" forms of the employment relationship while offering
fewer benefits to those in less permanent forms, those dominated by
women and racialized groups. This approach to economic insecurity reflected the intellectual thought of authors such as William
Haber and Wilbur Cohen who, in the late 1940s, made the case for
greater state involvement in regulating economic relationships.
They drew their inspiration from the earlier work of J. Douglas
Brown of Princeton University, who had argued at the beginning of
the century that "the survival of democratic capitalism will depend
upon the genius of man in combining three ingredients – individual
incentive, mutual responsibility, and an effective framework of protection against the corroding fear of insecurity" (Haber and Cohen,
1948: v quoted in Wallulis 1998: 50).

This new approach to organizing labour markets is best reflected in the United States by the Roosevelt-inspired "New Deal,"

and the implementation of the Social Security Act in 1935 that provided some insurance against the insecurity associated with modern industrial life (Hacker 2006a: 43). Large companies, many of which had initially resisted publicly-funded insurance schemes, soon realised the advantages of using public benefits as a minimum level of insurance and started extending improved pensions, health care insurance, and insurance against temporary job loss to their workers (Hacker 2006a: 43). By the end of the 1960s, companies like Kodak had implemented employment security and a benefit package that provided unprecedented insurance for their workers. Influential policy advisors to the US government argued that it was only a matter of time before the same generous benefit package would be made available to *all* workers through a combination of public and private benefit plans (Hacker 2006a: 46). In 1965, the National Association of Manufacturers was advocating that, "Private employee benefit plans with their inherent flexibility to adapt to the almost infinite requirements of employees and employers should be encouraged to grow and prosper within a favorable government policy climate" (quoted in Hacker 2006a: 45).

State policy initiatives in response to the Great Depression were designed to stabilize the economy, labour demand, and the employer and worker relationship. New labour laws encouraged employers to recognize unions as bargaining agents as a way of ensuring that wage increases and purchasing power kept pace with increased productivity, and as a means of containing more radical demands by workers. Government spending was employed to balance changes in private demand, and new labour standards regulated the ability of employers to treat labour as a commodity. As Standing argues, this was an era when the economics profession was advocating security from the worst ravages of labour market instability as a way of improving productivity (Standing 2002: 4). The term "efficiency wage" was developed to capture the idea that paying workers more and treating them better would ensure that they would be more productive. This implied an important reversal of causation: rather than productivity and the ability to pay determining wages, which is the case in standard economic models, wages were seen as determining productivity and the ability to pay. Henry Ford's "Five Dollar Day," introduced in 1913, doubled the real wages of unskilled workers overnight, and was seen widely as an innovative strategy to boost labour productivity.

The "standard employment relationship" became the new norm, but not necessarily the most prevalent form of the employment relationship. In North America, its ascendancy was marked by the landmark agreement in the 1950s between General Motors (GM) and the United Automobile Workers (UAW). In return for accepting managerial control of decision making, GM offered the UAW recognition as the legitimate representative of the workforce. It also agreed to provide workers a share of future productivity gains in the form of an Annual Improvement Factor as well as protection from inflation through a Cost of Living Formula. Equally important, seniority rights played a growing role in regulating who got to work and at what job. Similar struggles in steel and other mass production industries forced employers to accept the "standard employment relationship" in most North American goods-producing sectors. By the 1960s, unions in the public sector were winning similar contracts.

For a privileged few, particularly white males in the developed economies and in the new mass production industries, this was a period of significant protection from labour market insecurity. Corporate strategies, state policies, and social values were all based on the ideal of full-time permanent employment. At least for core workers, many of the insecurities associated with capitalist labour markets had been tempered, although of course they were never eliminated. Once workers found a job, their need to search for further employment was reduced, and they could expect significant support from their unions, from their employers, and from the state. They could form households and expect a reasonable quality of life for their families. However – and of critical importance to interpreting *current* levels of economic insecurity – the "standard employment relationship" (SER) was never generalized to the entire working class. The SER was very much a normative model, and masked high levels of insecurity for the majority of workers who had the misfortune of working outside of the core labour market: in particular women, new immigrants, racialized groups, the disabled, and the elderly.

Gordon, Edwards, and Reich identified three segments of the North American labour market in the post-World War II period:

Independent Primary Market, Subordinate Primary Market, and Secondary Market. Only the first two offered the sort of security associated with the "standard employment relationship." The Independent Primary market was made up of middle-level managers, accountants, and bookkeepers doing jobs with general skills. The Subordinate Primary Market was made up of individuals in the mass production industries for whom unions won the kinds of security the Independent Primary market had long had (Gordon et.al. 1982: 16). This represented an historic compromise. Unions agreed to let management manage (the origin of "right to manage" clauses in most union contracts in North America), while workers received improved job security, the assumption of long-term employment, and generous benefits. As a result, the threat of dismissal became less of a disciplinary mechanism for management, and the labour market less of a source of insecurity for workers (Edward, 1979: 181). Workers in the Secondary Market never gained these securities. "Here labor comes closest to being treated simply as a commodity unfettered and unencumbered by any job structure, union, or other institutional constraints" (Edwards 1979: 167). The allocation of workers to these sectors of the labour market had both a racial and a gender dimension. In North America, white men dominated the primary markets while women and workers of colour were more likely to end up in the secondary market.

The "standard employment relationship" also served employers' interests in social reproduction and a continuing supply of able-bodied workers (Vosko 2000: 21). For example, Henry Ford's "Five Dollar Day" was offered only to his male workers, with the understanding that female partners would provide a home environment that permitted Ford to extract maximum effort from those male workers (Meyer III 1981). This dependence on a single wage-earner was reinforced by the structure of social benefits that were provided by the state to families rather than individuals, but almost always through a principle wage-earner (Christie 2000; Cameron 2006). To gain access to these benefits, the household needed a permanent, full-time, wage-earner. The nuclear family increasingly took the form of a male breadwinner engaged in paid employment and a female caregiver working at home without pay. As Standing noted, "The national insurance social security system was the cornerstone of the postwar consensus ... It was based on two key premises: full or near-full employment and the norm of a man in a regular full-time job with a wife and children outside the labour force" (Guy Standing, cited in Wallulis 1998: 79).

Beck refers to this era as the first modernity "characterized by collective lifestyles, full-employment, the national state and the welfare state, and an attitude of heedless exploitation of nature" (Beck 2000: 18). It was the heyday of the Fordist regime of mass production, mass consumption, and mass labour. Employers, unions, and the state all accepted a growth strategy according to which a significant class of workers had a degree of security and improved living standards, employers experienced a robust demand for their products, and the state benefited from a degree of social cohesion and political stability. Unions such as the United Automobile Workers and the United Steel Workers gained both recognition and the power to insulate their members from the worst aspects of labour market insecurity (Gindin 1995). The regime was based on an assumption that growth would bring prosperity to all. "Thus, under the conditions of Fordism, institutionalized expectations of constant economic growth, rising consumption, public affluence and social security constituted the 'social cement' of the regime" (Beck 2000: 69). Standing refers to this period as one of "limited decommodification of labour" (Standing 2002: 70).

While those employed under the "standard employment relationship" made economic gains and acquired some protection from economic insecurity in the 1950s and 1960s, these gains came at a price. In exchange for some protection from economic insecurity and some rights against unfair dismissal from a job once acquired, workers were forced to accept management's right to organize work and structure jobs to maximize profit (Standing 2002: 12). There was increased managerial control over how labour was converted into effort. The division of labour was carried out to an extreme and effort norms increased, a process brilliantly captured in the classic work of Harry Braverman (1974). Privileged workers were well paid and had a degree of security, but were increasingly alienated from their jobs. For many, this was an era of repetitive and routinized work. One result was that efforts to improve occupational health and safety increasingly focused on the work performed rather than on the employment relationship itself. Consequently, most efforts were directed at reducing exposure to toxins and hazardous conditions and, more recently, to "job strain."

It is important not to exaggerate the gains workers made in this period. Outside of core labour markets in developed economies there were relatively few, and insecurity remained the norm for most workers. Even in developed economies, the minority who benefited from the "standard employment relationship" remained vulnerable to job loss through reorganization, technical change, and economic downturns. As Standing points out, "Not even in high industrialised countries was there ever a period in which most workers had strong employment security, in which they had strong protection against dismissal or sudden loss of employment for some other reason" (Standing 2002: 45). However, there were real gains under the "standard employment relationship" compared to the individualized markets of the late nineteenth century. Workers had acquired significant rights to further employment once employed and to negotiate changes in the terms and conditions of employment, in a context where employers' and workers' long-term commitments supported each others' interests. These gains were extended to a broader population through the formation of households with at least one member in a "standard employment relationship." These changes had also been somewhat successful in re-constructing community at work, at home, and in civil society. However, the protections and support these communities offered workers were still incomplete.

THE NEO-CONSERVATIVE REVOLUTION AND THE RETURN OF WORKING WITHOUT COMMITMENTS

As early as the 1970s, clouds were on the horizon for the minority of workers and families who were benefiting from the "standard employment relationship." Manufacturers from established economies found cost havens with low wages and weak labour-market regulations in newly industrialized countries. In the more developed economies, the oil crisis created "stagflation," a combination of high levels of unemployment and high rates of inflation, putting a squeeze on corporate profits. In North America and Europe, states tried to control wages directly, while unions fought to protect the hard-won gains of the previous two decades. Companies increasingly resisted high wage/high benefit strategies and, the more they faced competition from low wage/low benefit jurisdictions, the more they questioned the post-war consensus that employers should maintain a longer term commitment to their workers.

Around the same time, there was a shift in economic power to the financial community, and to share-holders with their focus on speculation and short-run profits. Aided by new information technology that allowed more effective surveillance of external suppliers, manufacturers responded to these pressures by contracting out work to low-cost jurisdictions. Market forces became more of a factor in corporate decisions, which in turn created pressures to transform employment relationships (Cappelli 1999: 5). The focus on short-term paper profits often came at the expense of strategies aimed at long-term growth in productivity: strategies such as the "standard employment relationship." Working *with* commitments, regardless of its long-term benefits, was seen as an unbearable short-term cost for employers. And of course, in some sectors workers themselves began questioning the wisdom of tying their future to a single company.

How to buy labour cheaply, how to extract the maximum effort from workers in the short run, and how to minimize tax burdens all took on a new urgency for employers who showed a renewed interest in less permanent employment relationships and a reduced concern for the negative effects of economic insecurity. Temporary employment agencies became important suppliers of labour and contracted out human resource managers. This was facilitated by re-interpretations of earlier ILO conventions that had severely limited the scope of their activity based on the view that "labour was not a commodity." Under the new interpretations, private employment agencies were allowed to trade in labour and to charge fees for the service, as long as they were regulated. In countries like Canada and the United States, the degree of regulation was minimal. In the mid-1950s, the temporary help industry in the United States provided employment for barely 20,000 workers. By the mid-1990s, estimates for the sector range between one and three million workers (Vosko 2000: 127).

Policy-makers faced growing resistance from employers, who opposed the use of the public purse to fund programs that insulated workers against labour market insecurity. There were increasing complaints that labour market regulations were preventing companies from competing in an increasingly global economy. For most organized workers in "standard employment relationships" in Europe and North America, wage bargaining shifted from maximizing gains to minimizing concessions. Evidence of this can be found in the stagnation of earnings in many economies. For instance, in Canada, the real median wage remained virtually unchanged between 1980 and 2005 and for men it actually *declined* by over ten percent (Statistics Canada 2008; Lowe 2007). At the workplace, lean organization became the new mantra with the goal of squeezing "waste" out of the system. Promoted as working "smarter," the reality seemed to be more a case of working harder (Garrahan and Stewart 1992; Graham 1995; Lewchuk and Robertson 1996 and 1997). The crisis for labour was compounded by the changing nature of globalization, including the rise of very large, multi-national corporations and the increased mobility of capital facilitated by trade deals and the growing reach of GATT.[5]

Equally significant, the 1980s witnessed the emergence of a renewed intellectual attack, particularly in the United States, on the social benefit of shielding workers from economic insecurity. In the process, Douglas Brown's demand at the start of the century that policy-makers find a way of insuring workers against economic risk was replaced by a new social philosophy that individuals needed to insure themselves. Using the concept of "moral hazard," influential economists such as Martin Feldstein (who would go on to head up the White House's Council of Economic Advisors under Ronald Reagan) provided a justification for abandoning the existing network of public and private benefits schemes that were central to the "standard employment relationship." They argued that insurance against unemployment actually made it more likely that someone would be unemployed, because the sting of being unemployed was minimized by the insurance plan and hence the incentive to minimize unemployment was reduced. In these early stages of neo-liberalism, it was a short step from suggesting that public insurance

---

5 The General Agreement on Tariffs and Trade was established in 1947 to regulate international trade. Its authority was increased in the 1980s to deal with the expanding range of goods and services exchanged between countries.

created moral hazards and thereby more of the very ill one was insuring against, to insisting that public insurance was inefficient, and hence needed to be scaled back. During this "Personal Responsibility Crusade" (Hacker 2006a: 46–53), the insights of early corporate reformers regarding the benefits of stable employment relationships were forgotten, as was John Maynard Keynes's warning that unregulated market systems are inherently unstable. The government in the United States moved to eliminate or to privatize many of its insurance and support programs, on the grounds of reducing moral hazard and making workers better off. Governments in Britain, Australia, and Canada followed the American lead. Employers shifted economic risks onto workers by moving to less permanent forms of employment, replacing defined benefit pension plans with defined contribution pension plans, and introducing personal savings-account benefit plans to cover the costs of health and education (Hacker 2006a: 54). The economic, intellectual, and political context that had facilitated the spread of the "standard employment relationship" was being undermined.

As was the case in the 1930s, when state policies such as Roosevelt's New Deal created a space for the "standard employment relationship" to spread, the policies implicit in Reaganism and Thatcherism hastened its collapse. In Europe, it was argued that loosening labour market regulations and facilitating flexible forms of employment would lead to more rapid economic growth. Schomann describe the trends as follows: "Non-standard forms of employment were discovered as instruments to combat unemployment in Europe. New policies were adopted under the general heading of 'flexibilization' and 'deregulation' of the labour market. Employment protection was declared to be a 'burden on business' and labour law in general came under attack for neglecting business interests. Governments embarked on policies which aimed at 'liberalizing' labour law and 'flexibilizing' labour markets" (Schomann et al. 1998: 8–9).

In Britain, the abolition of wage councils, the weakening of unfair dismissal protection, the undermining of trade unions, and the push to privatize work in the public sector all fuelled the spread of less permanent employment relationships (Allen and Henry 1996: 68). In Canada, the 1970s witnessed a growing government focus on inflation and deficits as problems. This was in direct conflict with the earlier focus on full-employment that had supported the rise of the "standard employment relationship." Lowered labour costs through wage controls, a harsher environment for organized labour, and a reformed unemployment insurance program became part of the new arsenal against inflation. These changes weakened organized labour's ability to insulate its members from market forces and, for the growing component of the workforce that lacked unions, increased their exposure to the risks associated with economic instability (Vosko 2000: 119–24).

The "standard employment relationship" and the sharing of labour market insecurity was always an implicit contract that was easily broken when employers felt it was no longer in their interest. Nonetheless, it did imply that workers made a long-term commitment to employers who, in turn, provided decent wages and benefits, access to continued employment, and a commitment to the development of individuals as they climbed internal career ladders. While employers got a stable and productive workforce, workers got security and a rising standard of living. The interests of both buyers of labour time and sellers of labour time were bound together in this dance of mutual interest that Hacker defined as "shared fate" wherein labour and their employers "rose and fell together" (Hacker 2006a: 65). As we move into the 1980s, the employment relationship was converted to one of "individual gain," wherein workers and employers remained together only as it suited the interests of each individual party. With the shift to "spot" labour markets characteristic of employment relationships in the early phase of capitalism, workers were free to grab higher paying alternatives as they came along, while employers were able to shift risks associated with changing technology and economic fluctuations onto workers (Hacker 2006a: 66). Increasingly, workers were asked to act entrepreneurially, and to accept individual responsibility for their welfare. The commitments between employer and worker were eroding. At the same time, there was a renewed interest in self-employment, which had been declining as a share of employment since the turn of the century (Arum and Müller 2004), the increased use of arms-length employment relationships through third parties such as temporary employment agencies, and an increase in layoffs by profitable companies seeking greater profits (Osterman 1999: 39; Cappelli 1999: 118). These changes in employment philosophy were nowhere more evident than in the ranks of white-collar workers who, by the end of the twentieth century, were exposed to the kind of employment insecurity that had typified many nineteenth-century employment relationships (Fraser 2001).

The impact of eroding commitments between workers and employers has been reported in à number of studies. Hacker's analysis of the United States paints a portrait of increased variance in earnings that an individual receives over a career and a decreased capacity to provide in old age. In the decade after 1973, an employed individual could expect that the ratio between his or her highest and lowest earnings years would be just over two to one. Two decades later, the ratio was over four to one (Hacker 2006a: 23), reflecting the increased insecurity in earnings. In 1992–93 in the United States, about fifteen percent of those laid off could expect a recall, down from the forty percent level in earlier periods (Cappelli 1999: 121). Between 1980 and 2005, there was a ten-fold increase in personal bankruptcies, and between 1970 and 2005 – even before the sub-prime crisis of 2008 – there was a five-fold increase in mortgage foreclosure rates. Only about one-third of medium and large companies now offer defined benefit pension plans, down from a peak of over eighty percent. This has contributed to the decline in the percentage of families able to replace at least half of their pre-retirement income upon retirement (Hacker 2006a: 14).

In Canada, there is evidence that new entrants into labour markets are currently employed in much more precarious relationships than their counterparts of two decades ago, even though the proportion of high-paying and low-paying jobs has not changed. Between 1981 and 2004, the median wage of newly hired workers fell thirteen percent, and between 1989 and 2004, the percentage of new hires employed in temporary positions increased from eleven to twenty-one percent. New hires were also experiencing a more dramatic fall in union density, with only nineteen percent of new hires being unionized in 2004 compared to thirty-eight percent in 1981 (Morissette 2005). The growing precariousness of new hires was occurring at the same time that the percentage of Canadians covered by registered employer pension plans was falling. In 1981, forty-seven percent of all working Canadians and fifty-four percent of all working men were members of a registered pension plan. By 2000, these figures had fallen to forty-one percent of all Canadians and forty-two percent of all working men (Morissette 2005).

Weakening commitments between employers and workers are placing new demands on workers to make themselves more employable. Rather than employers making investments in human capital, workers are increasingly on their own. According to Wallulis (1998), "employability" has become a more important determinant of success than "employment." He argues: "The struggle for employability functions as perhaps the largest source of individual insecurity in a destandardized world ... The long-term temporal frameworks of the career ladders which were offered many will be envied by those caught up in the struggle for preserving employability. Adaptability to the present now means for them the continual coming to terms with uncertainty in their lives" (Wallulis 1998: 165–7).

By the mid-1990s, IBM's model of a lifetime employment relationship with generous benefits was replaced by a leaner and harsher regime. Failure to respond to the emerging new technology of personal computers and to low wage labour in places like India resulted in a downsizing of the company and the erosion of lifetime employment security. IBM began shedding core workers in 1992, and announced its first layoff ever in 1994. Over the decade, its core workforce was cut in half as it began to rely on temporary employment agencies for clerical support and vendors for more complex functions (Cappelli 1999:73). The golf courses were closed, and highly skilled engineers were let go and then re-employed as consultants. In 2000, IBM began the transition from defined benefit pension plans to defined contribution plans as part of a new strategy aimed at recruiting younger, less expensive workers and the shift to shorter term relationships. The era when employment at IBM was for life was over for most workers (Lazonick 2009: 16). Studies of this period of IBM's history suggest stress at work increased and corporate loyalty was undermined (Sennett 1998: 123–5). According to Lazonick, the change at IBM was symbolic of a fundamental change in corporate policy in the US from employment security to employment insecurity (Lazonick 2009: 23).

While employment at IBM was the symbol of the "standard employment relationship", its competitor Apple captured the spirit of this new era with its "Apple Deal," a written contract between the company and its full-time workers initiated in the 1980s. "Here's the deal Apple will give you; here's what we want from you. We're going to give you a really neat trip while you are here. We're going to teach you stuff you couldn't learn anywhere else. In return ... we expect you to work like hell, buy the vision as long as you're here ... We're not interested in employing you for a lifetime ... It's a good opportunity for both of us that is probably finite" (quoted in Cappelli 1999: 26).

A number of authors argue that we are witnessing a return to the employment norms characteristic of the nineteenth century, a time when workers were exposed to high levels of employment-related economic insecurity. Hacker concludes, "The contingent workforce represents ... the culmination of the notion that workers are on their own, bearing all the risks and making all the investments necessary for economic success" (Hacker 2006a: 83). Beck argues that, "For a majority of people, even in the apparently prosperous middle layers, their basic existence and life world will be marked by endemic insecurity. More and more individuals are encouraged to perform as a 'Me and Co.', selling themselves on the marketplace" (Beck 2000: 3). Cappelli suggests the new employment relationships "outline a new set of obligations that employees must now bear, such as managing their own careers and developing their own skills. They make it clear that the company will keep them in jobs only as long as the relationship works for the company. No matter how these new deals are sliced, they make the employee feel like an independent contractor who has a very contingent relationship with his current employer" (Cappelli 1999: 28).

In summarizing their multi-sector study of enterprize organization and employment, Marchington and his colleagues concluded that "The paternalist idea that employers have a social responsibility towards their employees has been widely supplanted by the entrepreneurial doctrine that nobody is owed a living and that future employment depends upon more flexible and fragmented arrangements ... An increasing number of workers are required to accept part-time, temporary and insecure forms of employment, take greater responsibility for their future employment, and recognize that training is a recurrent obligation" (Marchington et al. 2005: 263). This shift to short-term relationships is having a profound impact on the nature of commitment between employers and workers. As Bauman points out, flexible labour markets neither offer nor permit commitment to a job. This is in contrast to more permanent relationships, which by their very nature generate social bonds even when the job itself is alienating. According to Bauman, "Even the most routine, uninspired and uninspiring, dull and often demeaning work favours the growth of stable, solidly rooted and durable human bonds only if (and because!) it is expected to last a long time to come – in practice infinitely. The feeling that 'we are all in the same boat' and in all likelihood will remain in the same boat whatever happens ... propels and fosters the search for the most satisfying or the least oppressive mode of cohabitation. Why bother, though, if one is pretty certain that with each successive clock-in one is likely to find oneself in different company?" (Bauman 2005: 65–6).

The financial crisis that began in late 2008 appears to be accelerating these trends. In both Canada and the United States, the unions representing auto workers, once the bastion of the "standard employment relationship," have been forced to accept drastic changes to labour agreements. Total hourly compensation was cut by over twenty-five percent, wages and pensions frozen, and long standing benefits such as tuition refunds that allowed workers to take courses paid for by their employer were axed. Many also lost their jobs, and research in Canada suggests that these displaced workers are finding new jobs in the service sector, in non-union companies, at low wages, and with few benefits. These new jobs are not secure; nor are they remunerative enough to allow workers to support a household (Vrankulj 2010). The pattern of job losses also suggests that they have fallen disproportionately on male workers who are more likely to be employed in "standard employment relationships." According to Hennessy and Yalnizyan (2009), eighty percent of the jobs losses in the United States and seventy-one percent of those in Canada have been jobs held by men.

CONCLUSION

This chapter has identified major changes in the characteristics of employment relationships in the last quarter of the twentieth century. It examined the rise of the "standard employment relationship" and then its fall in the last few decades with the corresponding spread of less permanent forms of employment in which the long-term commitments between employers and workers are eroding. Those interviewed as part of this study lend support to this thesis. Devon, who lost a full-time job in 2002, found it difficult to find work except through a temp agency.

> It seems like some companies don't want to offer full-time jobs anymore. When I got laid off and couldn't find another job, I started doing temp work right away, I registered with those agencies because they offer both full-time and temp work. I was hoping to be able to get another full-time job, but that has proved difficult (Devon #5051).

Mala offered additional insight into the situation.

> Most of the companies are not hiring on a full-time basis because they do not want to give any benefits and they also do not want to pay the salary that the full-time employees ask for. They would prefer to go the route of the short-term and then, when the work has slowed down, you know, cut off the work, and then call somebody back again when they feel like it. It's all a matter of finances and economics (Mala #5435).

To date, much of the analysis of this transition has focused on its impact on workers' relative bargaining power and on changes in the terms and conditions of employment. We contend that the changing nature of the employment relationship is *also* likely to have profound implications for the health of workers and the well-being of households and communities. Central to our argument is that the shift to short-term relationships, and the corresponding erosion of commitment between employers and workers, exposes workers to new types of employment stress. The next chapter will begin to explore this question using the Employment Strain Model introduced in chapter 1.

3

Working Without Commitments and the Characteristics of the Employment Relationship

I just want to feel secure; I want to contribute (Nabila #5494).

The situation is when a person has to live in conditions of uncertainty it's the human nature that you're going to live in fear, because uncertainty for people means fear. Fear because there are certain things that you have to have to be able to survive (Valdez #5542).

These comments from Nabila and Valdez help us understand the insecurity and frustration that many in less permanent employment relationships expressed during our interviews. In chapter 1 we made the case that the proportion of such workers is growing in industrialized economies, including Canada's. In chapter 2 we described how changes in the characteristics of employment relationships over the last several decades had weakened long-term commitments between employers and workers. This chapter will describe the characteristics of contemporary employment relationships, and explore what it means to be in a less permanent employment relationship. What are the indicators of commitment – or its lack – between employers and workers? What types of employment uncertainty do workers face? Here we will begin to introduce responses from participants in our study to the questions we asked. Our respondents were workers in all types of employment relationships. Those reporting that they were full-time students were excluded. They lived in the Greater Toronto region and had all been employed in the month before the survey was taken. Interviews took place with a sample of survey participants in different age groups who were in less precarious employment, and with participants in permanent employment who reported high levels of *employment relationship strain*.[1]

PREVALENCE OF DIFFERENT FORMS OF
THE EMPLOYMENT RELATIONSHIP

What is the distribution of working Canadians across different forms of the employment relationship? We stated in chapter 1 that employment form is not a measure that is sufficient to predict workers' health and the presence of commitments. However, it does provide a useful tool for describing broad conditions in contemporary labour markets, and therefore is a good way to begin this analysis.

The following forms of employment provide a rough measure of the level of insecurity in the labour market, although this study shows that not everyone in a less permanent relationship views their situation as insecure and, alternatively, not everyone in a permanent relationship views their situation as secure. Survey participants were asked to identify the relationship that best described their employment in the previous month. Their choices included four less permanent forms of the employment relationship and three that represented permanent relationships.

LESS PERMANENT FORMS OF THE EMPLOYMENT
RELATIONSHIP

• Temporary employment agency: workers in this category obtained at least half of their paid employment from an agency in the last month. Just over one-third of respondents in this category worked less than thirty hours a week. (n=172)
• Short-term contracts: workers are direct employees of a company, but are employed on fixed-term contracts of less than one year in

---

1 Most participants interviewed were in less permanent employment relationships, but a small number reported being in a permanent full-time relationship despite scoring high on the employment relationship uncertainty index.

duration. Just over one-third of respondents in this category worked less than thirty hours a week. (n=144)

- Own-account self-employed: workers describe themselves as self-employed working on their own account and without employees. Just over one-third of respondents in this category worked less than thirty hours a week. (n=167)[2]
- Fixed-term contracts lasting one year or more: workers are direct employees of a company and working on fixed-term contracts lasting one year or more. (n=112)

PERMANENT FORMS OF THE EMPLOYMENT RELATIONSHIP

- Permanent Part-time: workers working less than thirty hours a week on a permanent basis. (n=148)
- Permanent Full-time (Variable hours): workers report they have permanent full-time positions, but also report their hours vary and could sometimes be less than thirty hours a week. (n=112)
- Permanent Full-time: workers report having permanent positions and working thirty or more hours a week. (n=1,259)

Among the workers we surveyed, permanent full-time employment of at least thirty hours a week was the most common form of the employment relationship. Chart 3.1 shows that just over one-quarter of the sample reported being employed in one of the four less permanent forms of the employment relationship. These numbers are consistent with those reported by Vosko (2006 and 2009) based on data from the Canadian Labour Force Survey (See also chapter 1).

The distribution of men and women across the seven employment relationship types was relatively similar, and is an important indicator that a significant change is taking place in men's employment. For instance, 29.3 percent of men and 27.1 percent of women reported working in one of the four less permanent forms of the employment relationship. Women were more likely to report working on short-term contracts and were over twice as likely to work

---

2 The fourteen individuals who self-identified as employers in the survey were dropped from the analysis.

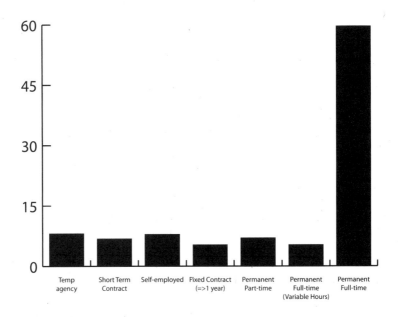

Chart 3.1: Prevalence of different forms of the employment relationship (%)

in a permanent part-time relationship.[3] Men were more likely to report finding employment through a temporary employment agency. Nor were there major differences in the prevalence of different employment relationships by race: 27.9 percent of white workers and 28.6 percent of the racialized workers reported working under one of the four less permanent forms of the employment relationship. These results suggest that, at least when measured by the form of the employment relationship, men and women and workers from all groups have similar labour market experiences. However, it should not be implied that male and female workers, or white workers and those from racialized groups, have jobs with similar relationship characteristics. This is an issue that will be explored in more detail in the next chapter.

Immigration was strongly associated with the form of the employment relationship – less permanent employment continues

---

3 19.3 percent of women in the sample worked fewer than thirty hours in the last month, compared with 14.4 percent of men.

to be the experience of recent immigrants, particularly women, as they break into the Canadian labour market. Nearly forty-five percent of immigrants who had lived in Canada for two years or less were working in less permanent employment relationships, compared with just under thirty percent of Canadian-born respondents. Recent female immigrants were more likely to be working in less permanent positions than recent male immigrants, and were slower to move out of less permanent employment. Even after two years, nearly one in three immigrant women were in less permanent positions. Recent immigrants were the most likely to be employed through a temporary employment agency or on a short-term contract.

However, immigrants who had lived more than two years in Canada were distributed across forms of the employment relationship similarly to Canadian-born respondents. Our participants echoed this statistical finding. Valdez, who was employed by a multi-national employment placement agency and worked at a multi-national energy firm, observed:

> Lately I have seen many, many Canadians, born in Canada, like me, in the same situation, so I think there is a switch in the way employment goes in Canada. I think that there is a trend to completely eliminate full-time employment, in my opinion, and to just have people like me working for contracts, because it is very beneficial for the companies. Like they are not responsible for anything happens to me, like if I am sick, they don't pay me, it's my responsibility. If they don't want me anymore, they just tell me we don't need you anymore, once the contract is over. So the shorter term the contract, the better it is for them because the more flexibility they have (Valdez #5542).

In a separate question, survey participants were asked if, in the last month, they were in an employment relationship that was permanent, full-time (thirty or more hours a week), working for one employer, with benefits and the expectation that they would be employed by the same employer one year from now. We consider individuals who responded "yes" to this question to have a "standard employment relationship." Just under sixty percent of the sample self-identified as being in a "standard employment relationship."

Women were marginally less likely to report they were in a "standard employment relationship" (56.3 percentage) than men (61.7 percentage). While this difference was statistically significant, it is surprising that the difference was so small. Recent immigrants were the least likely to report being in a "standard employment relationship." Just over forty percent of immigrants who had lived in Canada for two years or less reported having a "standard employment relationship." About sixty percent of immigrants who had resided in Canada for more than two years and Canadian-born respondents reported having a "standard employment relationship." Recent female immigrants were less likely to report being in a "standard employment relationship" compared to recent male immigrants, a difference that persisted for five years. Race also had some effect on the prevalence of the "standard employment relationship" amongst immigrants. Recent immigrants from racialized groups were more likely to be in a "standard employment relationship" than white immigrants, a difference that narrowed but did not completely disappear with their length of stay in Canada. This apparent anomaly can be explained by the much higher prevalence of self-employment and fixed-term employment of recent white immigrants (more than one in four) relative to those from racialized groups.

Chart 3.2 demonstrates the deteriorating expectations that workers have for security in a "permanent" employment relationship. It shows that respondents who reported being in a "standard employment relationship" were in a range of employment types, based on their responses to more detailed questions about forms of the employment relationship. Nearly one in six respondents in a permanent full-time relationship did *not* view it as a "standard employment relationship," while about the same proportion of those employed through a temporary employment agency *did* view themselves to be in a "standard employment relationship." At first, the weak correlation between responses to the "standard employment relationship" and the more detailed employment type questions was puzzling. One would expect those who reported having a permanent full-time job to also report being in a "standard employment relationship" as defined on the survey. As will be shown in the next section, this lack of correlation reflects variance in the employment relationship characteristics of individuals reporting the same

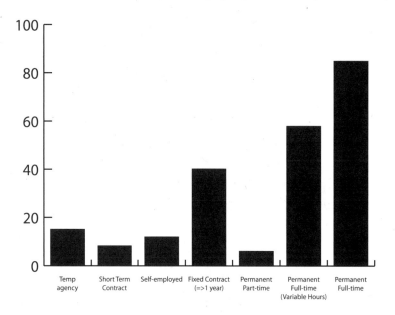

Chart 3.2: Distribution of respondents reporting being in a standard employment relationship across reported forms of the employment relationship (%)

form of the employment relationship.[4] Findings reported in other chapters of this study suggest that what some individuals view as a "permanent" job, may not, in fact, be very permanent at all.

Our study provided a snap-shot of where those in less permanent employment are employed. Chart 3.3 indicates that less permanent employment is relatively evenly distributed across occupational types and sectors with the exception of construction, where it is twice as prevalent as other sectors.[5] It is somewhat surprising that it is equally prevalent in retail and manufacturing, as these sectors are commonly believed to have been at opposite extremes of permanency during the 1960s and 1970s. This convergence likely reflects structural changes underway in manufacturing in the Canadian economy. Our study suggests, however, that an important difference remains between the retail and the manufacturing sectors.

---

4 A similar point is made by Tompa et al. 2007.
5 Own-account self-employment represented fourteen percent of those employed in construction, double the rate of the sample as a whole.

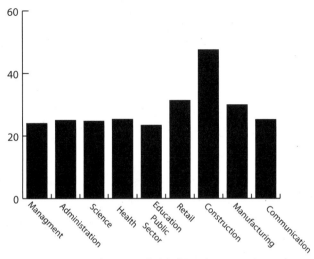

Chart 3.3: Less permanent employment relationships* by occupation and sector (%)

*Less permanent employment relationships includes employment through a temporary
employment agency, employment on short-term contracts, the self-employed, and those
on fixed term contracts.

Direct employment through short-term contracts was the most
common form of less permanent employment in retail while in
manufacturing it was working through a temporary employment
agency. This suggests that while employers in both sectors employ
a similar percentage of workers in less permanent relationships,
employers in retail prefer to have more direct control over hiring.
The relatively high percentage of respondents from the management and administrative occupations in less permanent employment relationship speaks to how much these types of employment
have been affected by recent labour market changes.

Where are those in "standard employment relationships" employed? Our findings show that the prevalence of the "standard
employment relationship" in retail is significantly lower than the
other sectors. This reflects the much higher prevalence of permanent part-time work in this sector. The prevalence is also lower in
construction, but higher in the management and science categories.

Study participants provided insight into the trend to less permanent employment in a wide range of sectors. This is the case in the

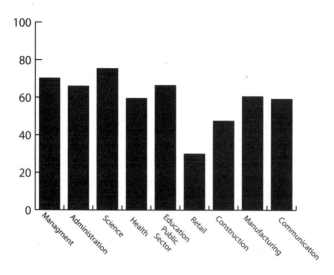

Chart 3.4: Standard employment relationships by occupation and sector (%)

education sector, particularly at colleges and universities, where contract work has become increasingly prevalent. A college instructor described her sector thus:

> The trend in colleges, not just my college, is to go to part-time workers who don't receive benefits, who are only paid for in-class hours, so the college sees it as a money-saving thing. But it is not a good for the students, and it doesn't offer me job security. I don't know from one semester to another if I'll even get a contract ... I'm just saying that isn't good enough (Stella #5093).

Less permanent forms of employment have also become more prevalent in the print and television media sectors, an issue that was at the centre of a prolonged strike by Canada's national broadcaster in 2005. Two respondents had been permanent full-time employees in the entertainment industry but had been let go as part of a restructuring. Both were working with the same company again, though on a contract basis, at the time of our interview. Phil liked the new flexibility, and the respect he received as an acknowledged expert in this field. He had more work than he could manage, but also noted his tendency to take contracts irrespective of how busy he was, given his uncertainty over what the future might hold and his concern that saying no might have negative consequences. He was able to work in this way, in part, because he had a small pension from his former permanent job which provided basic benefits, something that was not part of his current compensation package (Phil #5271).

Shawn, a worker in the arts sector, told a similar story. Until about five or six years ago he worked in permanent full-time positions, directing and producing theatre and television, but was now freelancing, writing stories and plays and producing music. At one level, he liked the freedom to work alone and to get full credit for his accomplishments. But he acknowledged that "It's a trade-off." He felt more socially isolated and insecure, without any real safety net. He expended significant effort networking and attending conferences to "stay in touch," and spent, on average, nearly an hour each day looking for work. He had more trouble sleeping and experienced what he described as "psychological" stress.

This first section of the chapter has provided us with several general observations about the labour market and three important insights emerge from examining the distribution of different forms of the employment relationship between men and women, and workers from different racialized groups. First, men and women were equally likely to report working in a less permanent relationship, although women were marginally more likely to report working on short-term contracts and marginally less likely to be working through a temporary employment agency. Regardless of gender, just over one-quarter of the sample reported being employed in a less permanent employment relationship and slightly more than half reported having a "standard employment relationship."

Second, there was a weak correlation between the form of the employment relationship and whether individuals viewed themselves to be in a "standard employment relationship." About one in six respondents who described themselves having a less permanent employment relationship also reported being in a "standard employment relationship." About the same percentage of those in permanent full-time employment answered "no" to being in a "standard employment relationship." This suggests that having an employment relationship that at one level appears to be less permanent does not necessarily imply precarity. Likewise, it may suggest that those in less permanent relationships have diminished expectations of the labour market and assume that ongoing, renewable, temporary contracts constitute "permanent" employment.

Finally, those interviewed painted a picture of a labour market in transition towards a higher prevalence of less permanent employment. This was not limited to low skilled or clerical positions. Respondents in lower level management positions, in the arts, in the media, and in education all argued that the labour market was changing, and that contract work and short-term relationships were becoming the norm.

DESCRIBING COMMITMENT:
DETAILED CHARACTERISTICS
OF EMPLOYMENT RELATIONSHIPS

To this point, we have used the form of the employment relationship to examine the prevalence of less permanent employment relationships. This tells us about the general profile of the workers themselves but reveals little about the level of commitments in each different type of employment. The second half of this chapter explores this question, and begins to provide a more detailed picture. This section groups the four less permanent forms of the employment relationship into one category and separates those in permanent employment into permanent part-time, and permanent full-time, relationships.

In chapter 1, three broad indicators were introduced to describe the core characteristics of an employment relationship: *employment relationship uncertainty, employment relationship effort,* and *employment relationship support.*[6] Further analysis of the survey data suggested that each of these indicators could be broken down into ten independent dimensions of the employment relationships. These are presented in Diagram 3.1. Each of these dimensions represents a series of questions from the survey (See the appendix for the questions). Each dimension represents an important characteristic of an employment relationship and will be used to organize the

---

6 For economy of presentation in what follows, we will refer to these three core characteristics as *"uncertainty," "effort,"* and *"support."*

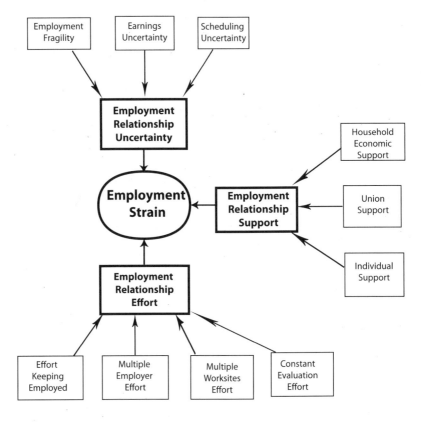

Diagram 3.1: The employment strain model

results from the survey questions. We argue that high levels of *uncertainty*, high levels of *effort*, and low levels of *support* are indicators of low levels of commitment between employers and workers within the employment relationship. Measuring the characteristics of the employment relationship as distinct from its form yields a number of interesting findings.

EMPLOYMENT RELATIONSHIPS
AND EMPLOYMENT RELATIONSHIP UNCERTAINTY

Employment Relationship Uncertainty is an important characteristic of "working without commitments." Since the 1980s, changes in Canadian labour policy have led to increased uncertainty in many employment relationships. In terms of *employment fragility*, existing gaps and weaknesses in labour laws, combined with exemption provisions that reduced the scope of legislative coverage and what Bakker (1996) refers to as "implicit deregulation," contributed to the steady rise of employment fragility for workers – especially those in less permanent employment relationships (Thomas 2009). One example of the limitations of labour legislation is that termination or non-renewal of temporary or fixed-term contracts is not considered a dismissal; thus labour legislation cannot provide any real protection to workers whose contracts are not permanent. Another is the narrow definition of an employment relationship that results in many self-employed workers not being covered by existing labour market regulations.

Public policy also affects levels of *earnings uncertainty*. Enforcement of provincial employment standards legislation has been weakened by the removal of inspectors from workplaces. The resulting complaints-based compliance system makes it easier for employers to default or haggle over even the most basic components of employment agreements without penalty. A number of workers in this study reported not being paid, not being paid what they expected, or not being paid on time. Employment benefits such as extended health care, pension plans, and maternity benefits are generally more generous for those in full-time, permanent employment. It is estimated that between two-thirds and three-quarters of Canadian workers in less permanent employment relationships do not receive financial compensation when they are sick (Lewchuk et al. 2000). Unemployment insurance benefits and other government-sponsored programs are also more easily accessed by workers in permanent jobs. In most provinces and territories, self-employed Canadians do not qualify for government benefits or insurance programs such as disability, maternity/parental leave, employment insurance, and pension programs.[7] *Earnings uncertainty* is exacerbated for workers not covered by collective bargaining arrangements. Union members in Canada are about three times more likely to be covered by an employer-sponsored pension plan than

---

7 As this volume went to press, the federal government had introduced changes that will provide partial unemployment benefits to some self-employed workers.

non-union workers, and twice as likely to be covered by a medical or dental plan (Jackson 2004: 6).

In 1996, the Unemployment Insurance Act was changed in many respects and renamed the Employment Insurance Program (EI); what happened then is instructive for understanding how existing regulations work against the interest of those in less permanent employment (Thomas 2009). From our perspective, the key change was the shift from a weeks-based to an hours-based system for calculating eligibility. This made it more difficult for anyone not in permanent full-time employment to qualify for benefits. Thus, while reforms *formally* extended coverage to more workers, the restrictive hours-based system took benefits out of the reach of many (Fudge, Tucker, and Vosko 2002: 31). The changes resulted in a dramatic drop in the proportion of unemployed workers – especially women – eligible for benefits (Pupo and Duffy 2003). It is estimated that only sixteen percent of temporary part-time and fourteen percent of permanent part-time workers who became unemployed were able to claim EI in 2001, compared with forty-one percent of permanent full-time workers (Kapsalis and Tourigny 2004: 7).

Recent changes in pension programs have also increased *earnings uncertainty*. Canadian workers continue to be reliant on workplace-based pension plans for the bulk of their retirement income. However, the number of workers covered by such plans has dropped since the early 1990s as a result of privatization, the weakening of collective bargaining, and the steady growth of self-employment, part-time, and contract work (NUPGE 2007b). Government policy that capped the size of pension plan surpluses in the 1990s, and also restricted employer contributions to pension plans, has also come back to haunt workers who now find that after the financial crisis of 2008, many of their plans are seriously underfunded. At the same time, there has been a parallel shift to more risky defined-contribution plans, where pension benefits reflect the performance of investment markets.[8] Therefore, as employment relationships become increasingly uncertain, so does retirement security. The reliance on

8 The lack of pension coverage for many workers has contributed to individuals and families saving for their own retirement through Registered Retirement Savings Plans (RRSPs) and other individual schemes. This too is risky. As the recent crash of the market demonstrated, individuals saving for retirement through RRSPs can have the value of their savings drop precipitously.

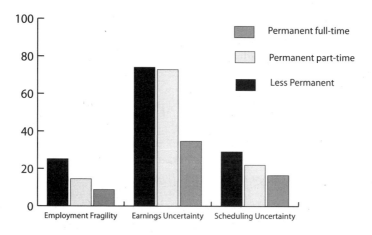

Chart 3.5: Employment relationship uncertainty by employment relationship

workplace-based pension plans makes it all but impossible for those on short-term contracts to amass sufficient entitlements to fund a reasonable retirement income. Our research underscores this problem. Apart from a few individuals who had benefits from previous jobs or whose partners had secure pension plans, most workers in less permanent employment relationships reported that they were not covered by workplace pensions and had been unable to save to fund their own retirement income.

Chart 3.5 reports average scores, by broad employment relationship type, for the three sub-indices that make up the *employment relationship uncertainty* index.[9] As predicted, respondents in less permanent employment relationships reported more uncertainty than those in permanent full-time relationships on all three sub-indices. They also reported more uncertainty than those in permanent part-time positions, but these differences were significantly narrower.

Looking at some of the individual questions that make up the indices reveals a number of key characteristics of "working without commitments."[10] Nearly half of all respondents in less permanent

---

9 Response to the individual questions that make up this and the other indices reported on in this chapter can be found in the appendix.

10 The tables at the end of this chapter report a summary of the responses to the individual questions by the three main employment relationship types that make up the indices.

relationships reported their average job lasted six months or less, compared to less than ten percent of those in permanent full-time relationships. Those in less permanent relationships were more likely to report an inability to anticipate their future income. Less than ten percent were members of a company pension plan and over seventy percent lost pay if they were absent from work. This compares with those in permanent full-time employment where over half were members of company pension plans and less than one-third lost pay if they were absent. Those in less permanent employment also reported a degree of informality in their employment relationship, as evidenced by frequently not receiving a record of pay, not being paid on time, and finding that their pay was different than expected. Nearly one in five respondents who were in a less permanent relationship reported regular errors in the pay they received. While these characteristics are more prevalent in less permanent forms of the employment relationship, they are not completely absent amongst those who report having a full-time permanent relationship. Another indicator of uncertainty and a lack of commitment in less permanent forms of the employment relationship is *scheduling uncertainty;* that is, the loss of control over when one works. About one-quarter of those in less permanent relationships reported not getting enough notice to accept work assignments or to plan household activities. Nearly one-third indicated that lack of notice about work schedules made it difficult to plan social activities.

Employment Relationship Uncertainty was a common theme amongst those interviewed. Those in on-call relationships appear to be particularly vulnerable, both economically and psychologically. A middle-aged man told us:

> Being on-call, this is difficult. My sleep is constantly disturbed. And it is difficult working on-call; you don't know why they don't call you sometimes. You are on-call, but there are other people also on-call. It is hard not to feel like if there is work, and they don't call me, then they don't like me. It is hard on my self-esteem ... We don't have benefits. This can be difficult. And the way I am treated sometimes, the part-timers aren't treated the same. We are not totally part of the loop. And the banks don't like part-timers, it is hard to go into the bank and get a

loan or whatever with having the proper status. What can you get if you are part-time? It seems like we are more vulnerable, there is just no power or authority. You are powerless as a part-timer ... They are arbitrary, this is the problem. You never know why you are called, or are not called into work. I'm having a problem with my supervisor now, I'm not getting called in for work I can do. They don't sit down with you and fill in an evaluation form or anything like that (Philip #5560).

Scheduling uncertainty was a concern for a number of those interviewed. Dalton had recently completed university and was working as an extra on a movie set and doing security work when he was interviewed.

It's basically, they'll call you and you go to work. You have no set schedule really. It's pretty hard to have a life when it's like that. They'll just call you whenever and harass you to go into work. I still get calls to go into work at some insane hour, like that day, and I don't return their calls because I'm like 'this is ridiculous,' you know? ... It's annoying, I mean, I like to know a minimum, at least a couple days before I'm going to do something, that ... I'm going to do something. And if that doesn't work out it really sort of messes with me. I'm not what you would call a planner but I like some notice if I'm going to do something, so it really, really makes me unhappy (Dalton #5449).

Dalton also reported a degree of informality in his employment relationship. As a result his pay often did not match what he expected.

There always seems to be problems with pay ... why am I five hours or eight hours short? It happens a lot ... I worked two hours of overtime and somehow I only got paid an hour of overtime ... I get my [pay] stub and I look at it and I'm like, okay, this is wrong. And then I spend an hour figuring out where it's wrong. And I'll call the people or I'll email HR and then they'll give me some story about why my thing is correct. I'm just like, you know what, I'm spending ten hours trying to figure out why my pay stub isn't right (Dalton #5449).

Other respondents reported similar concerns about *scheduling uncertainty*. Nabila, a contract interpreter, made these observations about the lack of notice.

You never know when you'll get called, and sometimes you don't get much notice. They might call in the morning and want you that same morning … This is very difficult because if my husband isn't home, then I need to get a babysitter for my one-and-a-half-year-old and this can be difficult without notice. Sometimes I have to refuse assignments because I can't get to it on time, then I don't make money. And I don't like refusing, I never know about the next assignment; maybe they'll call someone else. I don't know ever really know my schedule (Nabila #5494).

EMPLOYMENT RELATIONSHIPS AND EMPLOYMENT RELATIONSHIP EFFORT

Another indicator of "working without commitments" is the need to expend effort finding and keeping employment. As was the case with *employment relationship uncertainty*, policy changes since the 1980s have increased *employment relationship effort* for many workers. Like many other countries, Canada developed a system of labour market regulations in the post-World War II period that attempted to help workers through job creation programs, created coherence between unemployment and immigration programs, funded colleges and technology institutes to facilitate training and apprenticeship programs, and developed occupational standards and certification systems. Much of this capacity was dismantled in the 1980s, leaving the government with a significantly reduced ability to anticipate labour market trends or facilitate training. In response, the policy initiative of the 1980s was to establish tripartite boards (government, business, and union) to create coherence in industry or region-specific labour markets.

Training boards had some success in a handful of industries, notably steel and electronic products manufacturing, where extensive training and adjustment programs were jointly developed and delivered in the early 1990s with government financial support in the early 1990s (Anderson 1998). However, the success of these boards was short-lived because at the same time this new training regime was being developed and implemented, employers were adopting restructuring strategies aimed at reducing costs and increasing flexibility. They were moving towards a model of "working without commitments," and implementing and contributing to the costs of training was not part of this strategy. Indeed, not only did employers demonstrate their indifference or hostility to union-initiated sectoral training strategies and steadily withdraw from participating in tripartite boards, they became unwilling to contribute to the costs of training their own workers. At the same time, ideological and policy shifts in federal and provincial governments meant that the government cut off all but marginal funding to these training bodies, leading to the closure or commercialization of many (Anderson 1998; McBride 1998).

Subsequent changes to labour market training policy throughout the 1990s privatized the delivery of employment training, creating a proliferation of training institutions and certification systems that continues to bewilder workers and employers. At the same time, qualification for government employment-assistance programs was narrowed to include only those who qualified for employment insurance, which by definition marginalized workers in less permanent employment. The system also increasingly relied on private employment agencies to match workers with jobs (de Wolff 2006). These policies have themselves transferred the work of labour market analysis and training selection to job-seekers, and have effectively excluded most workers in less permanent employment from assistance with looking for work. As McBride has argued, while "earlier generations of job creation programs had emphasized community benefit, the new focus was consistent with the individualism which was an integral part of the government's neo-liberal ideology ... [the new focus] helped restructure the labour market by encouraging individual employees to 'retool' and adjust themselves to the type of economy being generated by increased international competition and technological change" (McBride 1998: 10).

Employment relationship effort is also shaped by legislation and policies that aim to protect workers from discrimination. In the post-World War II period, Canadian law-makers introduced a range of policies to protect workers from discrimination and promote equality in the workplace. For instance, employment statutes introduced in the 1950s and 1960s in most Canadian jurisdictions prohibited racial and religious discrimination, and increased pressure from the women's movement and from minority groups in the 1970s resulted in the adoption of new legislation to improve the employment situation of these groups. Important in this regard was the Canadian Human Rights Act passed in the mid-1970s, and provisions which deemed wage differentials between men and women performing "work of equal value" to be illegal discrimination.

While these legislative developments have been important, the main beneficiaries have been those workers in full-time permanent jobs in core sectors of the economy. The self-employed, and those in occupations dominated by less permanent employment, do not benefit from pay- or employment-equity legislation. The wage gap between self-employed men and women demonstrates the limits of equity legislation. In 2006, only seventeen percent of self-employed women made more than $30,000 a year, compared with forty-two percent of men (Statistics Canada 2006). Furthermore, workers in less permanent employment relationships have limited power to use existing regulations to challenge harassment and discrimination. Many of those we interviewed felt that they faced discrimination in getting or keeping work, but that they had no recourse because such discrimination is *invisible* in the constant selection and reassignment that takes place in less permanent employment. A human resource recruiter who was working on contract told us that she encountered discrimination when decisions were made about transferring workers into permanent positions.

I just felt that we only hired certain classes, certain minority groups, even women for the on-call contract positions. They were only good for on-call projects and we can put them on when we want, take them off – and you know I had to do a lot of coaching, [telling managers] like you know this guy is committed, he has worked for us for three ... years and worked every day, so I'm like, why can't we transfer these people to perm? Why can't we? (Chandra #2820).

Chart 3.6 reports average scores, by broad employment relationship type, for the four sub-indices that make up the *employment relationship effort* index. Compared to those in permanent full-time

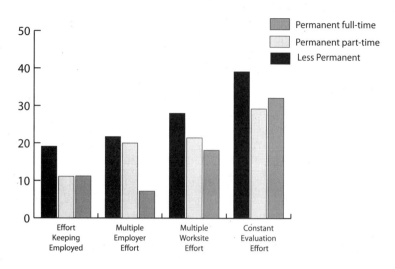

Chart 3.6: Employment relationship effort by employment relationship

employment, those in less permanent employment reported more *effort keeping employed*, more *multiple employer* and *multiple worksite effort*, and were more likely to report *constant evaluation effort*. Again, on all four measures, they reported more effort than those in permanent part-time employment

Workers in less permanent relationships expended more effort searching for work, with one in four looking for work at least every other day. About one in four reported having more than one employer in the last month, and most reported having more than one employer simultaneously; half reported working at multiple work sites. Working for more than one employer and working at multiple worksites created conflict for almost one-third of those in less permanent employment. Those in less permanent employment were more likely to report that constant evaluation of their performance affected the amount of work they were offered as well as their rate of pay. Discrimination was also a problem for many workers in our sample, regardless of the form of the employment relationship, but it was particularly prevalent for those in less permanent employment, where over half experienced it.

A number of those interviewed stressed what a burden it was finding and keeping work. Valdez reported constantly searching for new work, a task made more difficult because he was exhausted from his current job.

> Thinking about looking for a job, it's every single day, thinking to look for a job. Now how do you spend time on that, like when you come home you are tired, so you try to find something on the Internet, it's the only place where you can go because everything else is closed. And what you do is you send your resume by email or by fax. So on the one hand you have to think about your current duties; on the other hand there's not much time or energy left really to do full-time job search. So you do what you can, really (Valdez #5542).

Dalton was well aware of the extra burden associated with job search when not in a permanent position.

> I mean one day I am applying for something on one end of the spectrum and the next day, if there is a job on the other end, then I am applying for it ... All the time I am spending looking for work, I mean, I could be doing other things (Dalton #5449).

And Shawn, a freelance worker in the arts sector, indicated he was always networking, always staying in touch with professional organizations and going to professional conferences, writing, checking websites, and talking to recruiters. He estimated that he spent almost an hour every day in these sorts of activities (Shawn #5317).

Those "working without commitments" were also aware of the need to put in extra effort to increase their chances of getting more work. Many felt they were constantly being evaluated but that this was crucial to getting more work. Devon reported the need to work hard and be liked if a temp agency was to provide more work.

> If you work hard and if they are happy with your work performance you stand a better chance of getting more work from the company. It seems to all depend on whether they like your work (Devon #5051).

Being liked, of course, is often beyond the control of an individual, and the expectation that one should try to please higher-ups can lead to harassment and discrimination. Mala also worked hard at leaving a good impression to increase her chance of getting ore work.

> I always performed my duties as if I was a full-time employee. I took an interest in the job and got myself into it with the training and everything … I always put everything down, everything to the best of my ability. Like showing an interest like I'm going to be there for the rest of the time and when I left that desk, most of the time I left it in better shape than when I came in … They usually come back with a report card to the agency … I've never had, you know touch wood so far, a bad reputation in my workplace. It's always been my pride and joy to perform to the best of my ability (Mala #5435).

She went on to tell us that while she wanted to show solidarity with co-workers by accepting their pace of work, she felt trapped because she also needed to impress her supervisors by exceeding their norms in order to increase her own chances of getting more work. When asked if she worked hard because she was a temporary worker she replied,

> Yes. That can be also you know, it can be also a problem because then people think that you are trying to impress somebody. And I've been told off about that. So I said, I'm sorry, this is the way I work, and you don't have to worry because pretty soon I'll be gone (Mala #5435).

Regularly moving from workplace to workplace also can create added stress for those in less permanent relationships. Sachi, who worked through a temporary placement agency, noted the extra effort needed to adjust to new workplaces all the time.

> Yes because it would be very stressful … you have to learn the kind of stuff, say the system, or you know, how things are doing and decide, if they send you to just for one day for receptionist you have to remember all the names, you have to try and get to know all the names … If it is administrative assistant and you would be wondering, how would my boss be treating me,

how would my co-workers, how are they, are they nice, or not
or you know, all kinds of stuff that ... If I know it is like a
temp to perm job then I will try very much to impress but
sometimes it didn't work out so well, because if you are so ner-
vous and trying to impress your boss and then you know in the
end it might not be that smooth, right? (Sachi #5492).

EMPLOYMENT RELATIONSHIPS
AND EMPLOYMENT RELATIONSHIP SUPPORT

"Working without commitments" can also influence the levels of
support workers have from co-workers and even the community at
large. Recent reforms to unemployment insurance and cuts to social
assistance and social services in Canada have steadily reduced the
public support workers can access. It is not only individual workers that are affected by these cuts: these changes have a ripple effect
on families and households. Specific changes to benefits packages,
such as higher co-insurance and/or deductibles and the elimination
of coverage for family members, limit support for individuals in less
permanent employment relationships. In addition, declining union
membership and density since the 1980s[11] – not catastrophic, as in
the United States, but still significant – has made it increasingly difficult for unions to defend workers, especially those in less permanent employment relationships, who are less likely to be union
members. (Non-unionized workers in our study did connect their
sense of limited support at work to not having a union to turn to.)
    Alongside changing labour force conditions which have weak-
ened labour's bargaining power, working- and middle-class Canadians have been hard-hit by a shift in taxation to municipalities, the
steady withdrawal of the state from public and post-secondary education, and the delisting of numerous health services. Families, for
instance, have taken over a growing number of education-related

---

11 As Kumar notes, the decline has been most pronounced in the private sector, the source of employment for over three-quarters of Canadians. Union
density peaked in the 1980s at about thirty-eight per cent, and has been steadily falling since then, slipping below thirty per cent in 2007. The continuing
losses in the private sector and male unionization rates have been noteworthy
(Kumar 2008).

expenses such as music programs, and have been forced to fund-raise for core school needs through chocolate bar sales and various other activities. At the same time, the tax burden has shifted away from corporations and onto families through rising property taxes (Baragar and Seccareccia 2008). As researchers at the Canadian Centre for Policy Alternatives put it: "The federal government bailed out of its fiscal mess during the 90s by cutting expenditures far too quickly and downloading financial responsibilities for some programs to provincial and municipal governments ... Municipal governments are in a bind. They have been dealing with the impact of the federal and provincial underfunding of programs, but receive little direct financial benefit from the economic growth that has improved the financial position of other levels of government. Municipalities are dependent on increases in the market value of taxpayers' properties and transfers from other levels of government ... and some homeowners are faced with tax bills they just can't afford" (CCPA 2005: 1). Homeowners who cannot afford these bills include the growing number of households with at least one member working without commitments. Rising property taxes contribute to making home-ownership increasingly out of reach for those in less permanent employment relationships, thus limiting future security for their families.

Chart 3.7 reports average scores, by broad employment relationship type, for the three sub-indices that make up the *employment relationship support* index. "Working without commitments" had a relatively small impact on the individual support that workers received from their communities or on getting help at work. Two areas where this was not the case was having friends at work and family support, which were lower for those workers not in permanent employment. This suggests a degree of social isolation for those in less permanent employment. Those "working without commitments" were less likely to experience support from a union at work, although none of the employment types scored particularly high on this measure. They were also much less likely to have household economic support, and this was an important finding. Those "working without commitments" often came from low income and low employment-benefits households. Workers in less permanent relationships report household incomes twenty-five percent lower than those in permanent relationships and nearly half

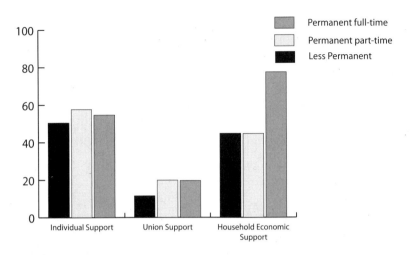

Chart 3.7: Employment relationship support by employment relationship

report having no entitlements to benefits even as a result of a part-ner's employment. By comparison, ninety percent of those in per-manent full-time work had at least *some* employment benefits, either from their own employment, or because of the employment another household member. The household norm of one secure earner with benefits and one less secure earner that might have been typical of the 1970s and 1980s does not appear to hold for many workers in this study.

Interviews with workers in less permanent relationships revealed a common sense of isolation at work and even the perception of hostility on the part of permanent co-workers. This appears to be especially true of workers placed through temporary employment agencies. Phil, a regular temporary employment agency worker indicated:

If they know you're from an agency they'll treat you like shit, because they think that you're only in that company to steal their (co-workers') jobs. Especially in a unionized spot, really bad ... I was with a construction company. It was all unionized construction and all that. We were just there supposed to be for outside cleanup. And they brought in a separate trailer for our lunch trailer because the union guys didn't want us to be there because they thought we were scabs because we were stealing their jobs. You get treated like a piece of poop from these unionized guys, because you're supposed to be in there stealing their jobs when it should be unionized. They think it should be unionized people doing it, not somebody else coming in to do it (Phil #5543).

Some workers in less permanent relationships also find it difficult to sustain friendships. In some cases this is related to their inability to schedule time with friends as a result of the uncertainty of their work schedules. For others, the lack of income makes socializing an expensive luxury. A sessional teacher lamented:

I have come to realize that they (former friends) have become invisible friends because I haven't had the time to maintain them. I saw a friend recently that I hadn't seen in seven years. Why haven't I been able to really maintain them? Well, my physical health, I was too exhausted, and then part of it was financial, I couldn't afford to go out, go to coffee shops, go out. That was part of it, and I didn't have a car. There were lots of excuses, but mostly it was because I was just so darn tired all the time (Stella #5093).

Socializing becomes a problem when individuals cannot confidently commit to social activities or lack money. A middle-age man without a permanent full-time job told us:

I feel financially and emotionally vulnerable. It wasn't always like this, but this is how it is now. It is hard to do things, social things; I sometimes lie about why I don't go out when friends invite me. I say I'm working, but really it is because of money … Sometimes friends won't include me in things because of the cost. They know I don't have much income right now, so it is hard. I don't know what work I'll get so I wonder whether I should say yes to a cottage invitation … Right now, I don't have money to fix up my apartment, so my apartment looks bad. My marriage fell apart quite some time ago. It is hard to date, I really can't socialize. How can I date when my apartment looks bad? You can't invite a date to come over when it is like this. When you're not full-time, you're not part of it (Philip #5560).

Survey participants were quick to identify the difference it made having union support or how having someone in the household with a secure income made "working without commitments" less stressful. A part-time teacher argued:

[Having a union made] all the difference in the world. Every bit. It might be shorter for me to say how it didn't make a difference ... I mean there's the collective agreement, there's rules they have to abide by, there's no principal who can force me to come back for a meeting at three-thirty when I'm with my children ... The collective agreement sets supervision time. So that means my supervision time is not to exceed X number of minutes for a week. What if that wasn't there? The principal would say you know what, you're half time, you've got more time, everyone else has a full time load; I want you to do recess every morning. Who would tell him no? Am I gonna call the board and tell them, claim that my principal not like me and have him evaluate me six months later? They've got you, don't they? So it says that it's X number for full-time, they've got half that for part-time, so he's got to stick to what the collective agreement is (June #5470).

CONCLUSION

The more detailed description of the characteristics of different forms of the employment relationship in the second section of this chapter provides a number of insights into the meaning of working without commitments. The first set of indicators of a lack of commitment between employer and employee was high levels of *employment relationship uncertainty*. Working in a less permanent employment relationship was strongly associated with higher levels of *employment fragility, earnings uncertainty, and scheduling uncertainty*. Those in less permanent employment relationships were more likely to be employed in short-term jobs where it was difficult to anticipate future income. There was an almost total absence of company pensions or sick leave plans, a higher frequency of not being paid on time or being paid incorrectly, and lack of sufficient notice of work to allow those in less permanent employment to accept new work or to accommodate their work schedule to their household and social demands.

A second set of indicators of a lack of commitment between employer and employee was high levels of *employment relationship effort*. Working in a less permanent employment relationship was strongly associated with higher levels of *effort keeping employed, multiple employer effort, multiple worksite effort*, and *constant evaluation effort*. The lack of commitment was indicated by workers expending significant effort looking for work, working for multiple employers and at multiple sites, and their sense that they were under constant evaluation. The latter played a role in determining if they would be offered further work and if so, at what rate of pay.

The third set of indicators of lack of commitments between employer and employee was low levels of *employment relationship support*. Those in less permanent employment relationships were about as likely to report receiving *individual support* as workers in permanent full-time jobs. They were somewhat less likely to report support outside of work, family support, or having friends at work. On the two other components of *employment relationship support, union support*, and *household support*, those in less permanent employment reported lower levels of support than those in permanent full-time employment and those in permanent part-time employment. Those in less permanent employment also tended to report living in lower income households and households where no-one had benefits such as a pension or a drug plan. The issue of household support is an important bridge to the next chapter, which looks in more detail at the experiences of men and women in the labour market and also at the experiences of different racialized groups. The next chapter will examine to what extent the traditional household pattern – a male in a permanent full-time job earning a family wage, supplemented by a female in precarious employment and having added household responsibilities – still holds.

RESPONSES TO INDIVIDUAL QUESTIONS
THAT MAKE-UP THE INDICES

Table 3.1
Employment relationship uncertainty by employment relationship (%)

	Less permanent[a] (n=595)	Permanent part-time (n=148)	Permanent full-time (n=1,371)	P
EMPLOYMENT FRAGILITY				
Average job lasts less than 6 months	45.8	21.8	9.2	***
Insufficient notice to accept work	21.4	15.8	14.4	**
On call at least half the time	30.5	30.5	16.9	***
Always receive record of pay	59.4	75.7	87.7	***
Not paid on time	12.1	4.7	3.5	***
Pay different than expected	19.2	16.2	8.0	***
EARNINGS UNCERTAINTY				
Unable to plan on the same income in 6 months	32.4	26.4	9.0	***
Lose pay if miss work	72.9	83.1	29.7	***
Covered by long-term disability	13.1	16.2	62.4	***
Company pension	9.8	15.5	53.2	***
SCHEDULING UNCERTAINTY				
Insufficient notice to plan work week	24.8	17.6	10.0	***
Insufficient notice to plan household responsibilities	28.0	21.6	12.5	***
Insufficient notice to plan social activities	32.4	32.4	21.0	***

[a]The less permanent category includes respondents who identified as self-employed or were employed through a temporary employment agency, as well as those on contract, whether short-term or fixed term. Those employed permanently were divided into a full-time category and a part-time category (those working fewer than 30 hours a week).
(* significant at the 10% level, ** significant at the 5% level , *** significant at the 1% level)

Table 3.2
Employment relationship effort by employment relationship (%)

	Less permanent[a] (n=595)	Permanent part-time (n=148)	Permanent full-time (n=1,371)	P
EFFORT KEEPING EMPLOYED				
Looking for work at least half the days	26.2	12.2	7.0	* * *
Discrimination barrier to getting work	51.1	29.7	35.9	* * *
Harassed at least some of the time by supervisors or co-workers	25.6	23.8	24.3	-
Harassment a factor in treatment at work	34.7	24.3	30.0	* *
Asked to do things unrelated to job	36.5	21.1	29.0	* * *
More than 50 hours of unpaid training	13.1	6.8	6.2	* * *
MULTIPLE EMPLOYER EFFORT				
More than one employer last month	24.7	23.7	7.3	* * *
Conflicting demands from multiple employers	30.4	26.4	10.9	* * *
More than one employer at the same time	22.2	21.6	6.6	* * *
MULTIPLE WORKSITES EFFORT				
Worked more than one location	44.0	36.5	25.8	* * *
Conflicting demands from multiple locations	28.9	21.6	13.2	* * *
Two or more hours of unpaid travel per day	27.3	25.0	24.4	-
Work in unfamiliar places most weeks	14.3	4.1	5.5	* * *
CONSTANT EVALUATION EFFORT				
Evaluation affects kind of work	56.1	51.4	49.4	* *
Evaluation affects amount of work	56.9	36.5	39.8	* * *
Evaluations affect pay	37.4	21.6	30.0	* *

[a] The less permanent category includes respondents who identified as self-employed or were employed through a temporary employment agency, as well as those on contract, whether short-term or fixed term. Those employed permanently were divided into a full-time category and a part-time category (those working fewer than 30 hours a week).
(* significant at the 10% level, ** significant at the 5% level, *** significant at the 1% level)

Table 3.3
Employment relationship support by employment relationship (%)

	Less permanent[a] (n=595)	Permanent part-time (n=148)	Permanent full-time (n=1,371)	P
INDIVIDUAL SUPPORT				
Support outside of work	68.6	76.4	75.5	**
Family support	72.8	82.4	79.3	**
Community support	52.0	61.2	54.1	-
Help with job	36.6	43.2	41.4	-
Some friends at work	41.7	50.0	49.5	**
UNION SUPPORT				
Union member	8.3	17.7	19.6	***
Union help with problems	16.9	26.7	23.7	**
HOUSEHOLD ECONOMIC SUPPORT				
Individual income ($)	25,438	16,369	42,945	
Household income ($)	43,397	40,714	53,917	
No employment benefits (own)	72.0	62.8	15.2	***
No employment benefits (house)	49.3	37.8	10.4	***

[a]The less permanent category includes respondents who identified as self-employed or were employed through a temporary employment agency, as well as those on contract, whether short-term or fixed term. Those employed permanently were divided into a full-time category and a part-time category (those working fewer than 30 hours a week).
(* significant at the 10% level, ** significant at the 5% level , *** significant at the 1% level)

4

Gender, Race, and the Characteristics of the Employment Relationship

My husband works in the private sector ... he could lose his job in the private sector with two weeks' notice ... unless I did something horrendous or illegal I wouldn't lose my job so in my mind I look at my job as a secure job ... I know I'll have financial security (June #5470).

I just felt that we only hired certain classes, certain minority groups, even women for the on-call contract positions (Chandra #2820).

Using the *employment strain* characteristics of the employment relationship, this chapter deepens our analysis of the gendered and racial patterns of working without commitments. The results presented so far suggest that there are only small differences between men and women, and between white workers and workers from different racialized groups,[1] in their distribution across different forms of the employment relationship. Does this mean that these groups face similar levels of employment insecurity, and experience

---

1 The question on race followed closely the standard categories employed by Statistics Canada. In this approach, individuals self-identify as white, or belonging to any of the other listed ethnic groups. In dividing our sample into a white and a racialized group, we follow the approach of Galabuzi (2004). The racialized group includes Blacks, Chinese, South Asian, Filipino, Aboriginal, Middle Eastern, Latin American, and other Asians. We differ from Galabuzi by including Aboriginals in this group.

working without commitments in similar ways? Employment inse-curity among men in our study was not significantly different than that of women, although these men earned more than women in similar employment relationships. We argue here that although there are still differences, the gap between men and women is nar-rowing and that the concrete expressions of labour market privi-lege are changing. Our analysis departs from other analyses of the gendered nature of precariousness in the Canadian labour market that contend that women remain concentrated in precarious employment and consequently the conditions of precarious employment are primarily of concern to women (Vosko 2009; Cranford, Vosko and Zukewich, 2003). Further, the study makes it clear that differences remain between white and racialized work-ers, and that race and length of residence in Canada continue to exacerbate precariousness.

White male workers can no longer assume that secure labour market positions are theirs, while new opportunities for hidden forms of both gender and racial privileging/discrimination have emerged in the less secure segments of the labour market, in the pay differences, constant scheduling, and rehiring/firing of tempo-rary and contract work. The experience of our study participants suggests that widespread changes in the labour market have sig-nificantly eroded the traditional household pattern of a male in a permanent full-time job earning a family wage supplemented by a female in less permanent employment. Indeed, the social and indi-vidual turmoil expressed by participants in our study suggests that this is a moment of profound change when the prevalence of dual precarious earner households is increasing, and when the work of social reproduction is often not adequately supported by two wages per household. These changes are creating strain on gender roles and identities forged during the relatively stable period of "standard employment relationships," perhaps to such an extent that we should begin to advance public policies that re-think social reproduction and the role of the household in *employment rela-tionship support*, rather than reasserting women's dual roles as less permanent workers and caregivers. While concrete options for pol-icy reform are explored in chapter 10, it is important to note that the insights regarding gender and race outlined in this chapter do expose the limited nature of much of the current debate surround-

ing the gendered nature of precariousness, and also appropriate
policy responses.

DEBATES ON GENDER, RACE AND PRECARIOUSNESS

A focal point of much North American discussion regarding recent
labour market changes has been the role of race and gender (Galabuzi 2004; Vosko 2006). This has led numerous authors to argue
that, for most of the twentieth century, the allocation of good jobs
and bad jobs, and of permanent and less permanent employment,
was shaped by discrimination and constrained opportunities (Gordon et al. 1982: 206–10). The "standard employment relationship"
has privileged the white male-dominated jobs in the labour market
that included managers, professionals, and workers in mass production sectors represented by strong unions. Women and workers
from racialized groups were more likely to end up in secondary
labour markets and employed in less permanent and less economically rewarding jobs (Luxton and Corman 2001). The increased
participation of women in the labour market after World War II,
and subsequent employment changes beginning in the 1970s, led to
the thesis that the labour market was being "feminized." For
authors such as Standing (2002) and Sassen (2001), the global feminization of employment was synonymous with an increase in the
number of women engaged in paid employment. According to
Standing, women's mass entry into the labour market was also
accompanied by two other key labour market changes: women
moving into jobs traditionally occupied by men, and the rapid
growth of jobs with the characteristics of women's work including
precarity, low wages and low status (Standing 2002: 34).

Feminist scholars have advanced slightly different analyses of
how labour markets are affecting the gender nature of employment,
and the allocation of good and bad jobs. In response to Standing's
claim about the "feminized" character of job types, Armstrong
(1996) argues that while there is more "women's work" in the
labour market, this work is not necessarily being done by women.
According to her, "This kind of feminization of the labour force
does not mean that the position of most women has improved.
Instead, it means that the position of some men has deteriorated,
becoming more like that of women. While some women and men

do have good labour-force jobs, many more women and men have bad jobs" (Armstrong 1996: 30). While she is not suggesting that widespread changes have taken place in the gender order in the labour market, she does argue that "the increased similarity between women and men can be explained in terms of a harmonizing down for some men and greater economic pressure on many women" (Armstrong 1996: 30). Vosko pursues this line of argument as well, suggesting not only that more women are doing "women's work," but that "women's work" has become the new employment norm. She says: "The feminization of employment means much more than women's mass entry into the labour market and even the creation of more 'women's work' in the labour market. It amounts to the rise and spread of feminized employment relationships ... The rise and spread of the TER [Temporary Employment Relationship] not only signals the extension of 'new' feminized employment relationships but the feminization of employment *norms*" (Vosko 2000: 197–8).

The observation that "women's work" is becoming the new norm in labour markets has led authors such as Beck to describe the coming era as one where "[the] ways of living will be more akin to those which women have known in the last few decades than to those which have been typical of men: that is, they will not involve careers, but rather combinations of part-time work, casual contracts, unpaid work and voluntary activity for the public good" (Beck 2000: 92).

Many of the findings in this chapter speak to this version of the feminization thesis. In general, our data indicates that men and women's employment experiences are becoming increasingly similar, due – at least in part – to the continued process of "harmonizing down." Hebson and Grugulis (2005) suggest that the shift to networked production has led to a re-gendering of work mainly associated with a downgrading of men's jobs. They note that, despite their pessimistic interpretation of the possibility for greater gender equality as a result of the shift to networked production, some opportunities have opened up for women to advance into middle level occupations that often serve as important bridges between companies in a supply chains. Other factors have also shaped the apparent convergence of men and women's labour experiences. Not the least of these has been the decades-long struggles by women inside and outside of the labour movement for greater economic equality that have created significant pressure on governments, employers, and unions to open up new opportunities for women.

Canadian legislative changes forcing employers to provide equal pay for work of equal value, and successful labour struggles conducted by government, health care, and education workers – sectors where women are represented in large numbers – have resulted in substantial changes. Canadian data shows that men continue to earn substantially more than women regardless of their employment relationship; however, the real median income of all male income-earners fell nearly ten percent between 1976 and 2007, while that of females rose by nearly forty percent. Restricting the comparison only to men and women working full-time does not change the trend. The real median income of men working full-time has not changed substantially over the thirty year period for which data is available (it fell just over one percent), while the real income of women who work full-time increased nearly twenty percent.[2] Despite three decades of economic growth and rising GNP per capita, the median male income earner was at best, no worse off in 2007 compared to 1976, while the median female wage earner was taking home significantly more in real terms.

CONVERGING LABOUR MARKET EXPERIENCES OF MEN AND WOMEN IN CANADA

When we interviewed Julianne and Darryl they were struggling with a change in Darryl's employment. Julianne is a health researcher who had been working in part-time and contract positions for at least fifteen years. Darryl had decided to leave a permanent full time position to become a self-employed construction contractor three years before our interviews. They started a family thirteen years before our interviews, and at that time felt that their situation was stable. When Darryl's situation changed, they both felt that the resulting stresses were going to be short term, but when we spoke they had continued longer than expected, and no end was in sight.

---

2 Source Statistics Canada, CANSIM Table 2020101.

When I started doing this my husband was in a salaried position with a company, so we were all completely cool about this
because my salary was just gravy so I could work ten hours a
week or I could work sixty hours a week and it was all bonus.
We were living on his salary so everything was fine. Well, but
then he decided to go into business for himself three years ago
and that changed everything. So I've been the sole breadwinner
up until very recently (Julianne #5703).

Julianne's work was flexible enough that she could create her own
maternity leaves between projects, and organize her schedule so that
she could be the primary after day care and school caregiver with
their two children. She was still supportive of Darryl's decision to "go
on his own," but it had created a tremendous strain on their relationship. Julianne had not been able to secure a permanent position
in her field, so she was dependent on projects and grants and could
not easily increase her earnings. Consequently, the conditions of her
employment did not change when Darryl became self-employed, but
the pressure on her increased tremendously. She told us:

For the last four years I've been trying to get it to be more full-
time work than part-time work but because it's grant-funded
and it's on contract I mean there are times when I'm not working at all ... I can accept peaks and valleys, but I did have a difficulty accepting like rock-bottom valley for like for three years
from him with no money. The way our relationship had worked
out was that he was the main breadwinner, I was the sub-bread-
winner which meant that if the kids were sick or needed to be
picked up from school it was my responsibility because he was
the main breadwinner and I could flex my time. And this was
an arrangement, you know, that worked out fine. I would take
the kids to school, I would pick them up after school, and it
worked. But when he stopped making money then I all of a
sudden sort of became the everything. Like, I still had to look
after the kids and have all that responsibility, but I was the only
person who was in a job where you work for an hour, you get
paid for that hour, you know, so on the one hand I was trying
to sort of maximize the number of billable hours because I was
"it."

I started then putting a lot of feelers saying hey I need work, hey I need work, hey I need work, and so I, things started to, for a short period of time, they were really insane because I was trying to maximize my billable hours because I was feeling a lot of pressure to really bring in as much money as possible. So that was very stressful for us because I actually kind of needed him to be a little bit supportive with the kids and the family and stuff and the home cause that's – I was working so much and he's like, wait a minute you're changing the rules! And I said well, you already changed them, and I'm like feeling stressed (Julianne #5703).

Darryl also described being stressed, but was not prepared to talk about their economic insecurity created by his lower earnings. He spoke about their tensions as being primarily about scheduling child care.

It's a source of stress like, my wife doesn't, like I don't really have an option to leave at three thirty so it's like, if she phones at three o'clock and says, look I need another hour, go get the kids, I don't have that option and that causes stress for her (Darryl #2704).

Julianne and Darryl's story, and the data collected for this study indicate that, apart from wages, the differences between men and women are surprisingly small with regard to most characteristics of the employment relationship (*employment relationship uncertainty, employment relationship effort,* and *employment relationship support*). These findings suggest that the converging labour market experiences of men and women is more complex than men moving into sectors of the economy long dominated by women, or more men being employed in less permanent employment. We think we are seeing fundamental changes in the nature of the employment relationship in *all* sectors of the economy, and that at least some men are losing the economic privileges, stability, and security they gained with the emergence of the standard employment relationship.

As Julianne and Darryl's story suggests, equity in employment insecurity has significant implications beyond the workplace. Reports published by Statistics Canada (Marshall 2009) reveal

important trends in the employment profile of Canadian households. Between 1976 and 2008, the proportion of single-male-earn-
er households fell from about half of all households to less than
one-quarter, while dual-earner households increased from forty percent of all households in 1976 to seventy percent in 2008. There has
also been a narrowing of the male/female contribution to household earnings as women's hours of work and their rate of pay have
steadily increased over the last two decades. In 2008, women contributed just over forty percent of total household earnings. Our
study suggests the changes may be more profound than simply
more women working more hours at better pay. The experience
reported by our study participants indicates that we are moving
away from the household norm of one permanent secure wage
earner (often a man) and one less permanent insecure wage earner
(often a woman) towards an economy/society of households com-
prised of two earners in less permanent employment.

The shift in household norms may be accelerating as a result of
the financial crisis that began in late 2008. Preliminary data on
post-economic crisis employment trends released by Statistics
Canada in September of 2009 indicate that self-employment and
part-time employment are becoming more prevalent, and full-time
employment less prevalent. Some commentators have gone as far as
to describe the transition as the "Death of Macho" (Stevenson and
Wolfers 2008; Salami 2009). This is, in our view, very premature,
but it does capture a sense of the insecurity, role confusion, displacement, and disentitlement that is being experienced by many
men. The displacement of men has not, however, shown up in dramatic redistribution of responsibilities for domestic labour, and
women's roles have not significantly changed: most women work
outside of their homes, and they continue to do most household
chores and have the majority of caring responsibilities. Recent studies show that men are slowly taking on more domestic responsibilities, although women are still largely responsible for looking after
their homes and families (Lindsay 2008).

PRODUCTION/SOCIAL REPRODUCTION
AND THE EMPLOYMENT RELATIONSHIP

There is a wide and rich body of feminist scholarship that explores
the ways in which gender is integral to the organization of paid and

unpaid work and the reproduction of inequality (see, for example, Rubery and Humphries 1984; Luxton 1990; Picchio, 1992; and Elson, 1995). Feminists have demonstrated that labour markets are gendered institutions operating at the intersection of the productive and reproductive economies (Elson, 1999), and have shown how organizations create jobs that incorporate and reinforce employers' assumptions about gender (Milkman 1987; Williams 1989, 1995; Acker 1990). Recent feminist scholarship has also examined the ways in which neoliberal policies and restructuring processes disproportionately affect women and visible minorities (Bakker 1994; Aronson and Neysmith 1997). In Canada and elsewhere, research has demonstrated that privatization and the erosion of social programs force health and child care back onto the family and the unpaid work of women (Brodie 1995: 54). Linked to this, research has argued that both women and visible minorities are disproportionately represented amongst unemployed workers, and the growing number of workers in low-income sectors and jobs, and in precarious employment (Vosko, 2000; Cranford, Vosko, and Zukewich 2003; Galabuzi 2004).

While our study generally supports arguments that restructuring processes are neither race nor gender neutral and certainly found evidence that women continue to bear the brunt of eroding social programs and other economic changes, our findings provide a different analysis that points to different consequences for social reproduction. Contrary to what we expected, women respondents did *not* report that their employment relationships were more insecure, or that they invested more effort in getting and keeping employment. In fact, on a number of individual indicators it was men, not women, who reported the most uncertainty, the greatest exposure to economic harassment at work, and were the most likely to report being asked to do tasks unrelated to their jobs that could influence whether they were offered more work. Our findings are indicative of a change taking place in both domains and suggest that we may be at the cusp of a third big shift in the interrelationship between production and social reproduction in the last century (Salami 2009).

A brief discussion of the relationship between the labour market and system of social reproduction helps to situate the current changes The last half of the nineteenth century marked a transition in much of Europe and North America from a pre-industrial society based on household family-based production to one where men and women engaged in paid employment outside the household (Tilly and Scott 1987). However, it is generally agreed that over time, as the household became a less important location of production, the roles of men and women in the economy shifted. Initially, wages paid to individuals in the external labour market rarely factored in the needs of households. For many, such wages were barely enough to sustain the individual worker. In this context, both men and women worked to support themselves, young children, injured or ill adults, and the elderly. The need to work to sustain life in the first half of the nineteenth century is reflected in the relatively high rate of female labour market participation. In Britain during the first decades of the Industrial Revolution and in industrializing states such as Massachusetts, women were almost as prevalent in paid employment as men (Lewchuk 1993). Gradually, men were relatively successful in laying claim to being the "real" workers and accordingly to paid employment that was considered "skilled" and had some potential to be rewarding in its own right. Women were increasingly viewed simply as "mothers" and, when in paid employment, were concentrated in work that was low paid and considered less skilled. For most women, employment was about earning enough for their families to eat; it offered limited pleasure or satisfaction in its own right and few opportunities to climb a career ladder. Rather than men and women being jointly and, to a degree, equally responsible for sustaining households, the ideology of "separate spheres" took hold, with men being seen as more suited to paid employment outside the household and women specializing in caring and nurturing and unpaid tasks in the household (Crompton 2006).

The emerging sense of working class respectability and, in particular, masculine and feminine respectability, further shaped the relationship between production and social reproduction and the characteristics of these two social spheres. Masculine respectability was increasingly measured by a man's ability to be the primary breadwinner of a household and his success in supporting his wife and children. Men, and at times women, often through their unions, forced employers to factor household needs into wage calculations and the characteristics of their employment relationships. They demanded more than an individual subsistence wage; they

demanded a family wage, employment benefits, and greater security. The idea gained ground within the middle class and amongst
policy-makers and religious leaders that, given the option, women
should opt out of paid work outside the home and take charge of
domestic tasks inside the home. For some women, this option was
made more attractive by the low paid and monotonous work available to them (Bradley 1989; Rose 1992). Less attractive working
conditions for women were perpetuated by the view – not always
consistent with reality – that women were only in the workforce
temporarily, and that they were never the primary wage-earners.
The view of Black, writing for the Women's Industrial Council in
Britain at the beginning of World War I, captures the sense of the
times. She wrote, "It is the general opinion and especially, perhaps,
among persons of the middle class, that the working for money of
married women is to be deplored" (Black 1915). Women got access
to a family wage by forming a household with a male partner. As
argued by others, while finding a soul partner remained a consideration in forming household partnerships, access to earnings from a
male's employment also became an important consideration (Newman and Chen 2007).

These forces led to an important shift in production/social reproduction structures at the beginning of the century, one characterized
by the emergence of the "standard employment relationship," the
single breadwinner model and the mother-centred home (Christie
2000). Many women, particularly those in households with children, were excluded from the paid labour market and made responsible for unpaid domestic and caring labour. Where women were
allowed to work, it was often in insecure jobs at low pay and with
few, if any, benefits. While reality is always more complex such gen-
eralizations imply, this view was exemplified by Henry Ford's "Five
Dollar Day" (Lewchuk 1993; Meyer 1981). Men were paid sufficient to support a household; women were responsible for the
household and for ensuring men were ready to work each day.
According to Martha May, "Ford's family wage implicitly recognized the contribution of women's domestic labor to a stable and
secure family life. In all likelihood, Ford believed that women's contribution was greatest in their emotional, nurturing, and motherly
roles. This emphasis on psychological rather than material comfort
parallels the arguments of many Progressive reformers, who saw

the female emotional, affective role as a necessary aspect of family life which should be supported by adequate wages" (May 1982: 416).

When the "Five Dollar Day" was first introduced, it was only available to men over the age of twenty-two. The reason given by management was that "[women] are not, as a rule, heads of families" (Myer 1981: 140). Criticism of this policy eventually led Ford to extend the program to women – but only if they could be shown to be heads of households, a form of discrimination that persisted into the 1970s. The combination of men's access to better-paying and more secure employment, the existing norm of a heterosexual household as optimal for raising a family, and the social construction of women as mothers, resulted in low rates of female participation in paid labour markets after World War I. In many jobs, married and pregnant women were legally barred from working. In 1921, barely two percent of married women participated in paid employment in Canada and as late as the early 1950s, fewer than ten percent of married women worked for pay (Luxton and Corman 2001: 46).

Over time, economic necessity, a thriving consumer culture, and the desire by women to have the broader social benefits of work outside the home, led to tension within the single-earner model. This led in turn to a second shift in production/social reproduction structures characterized by the large-scale entry of women into the workforce after World War II, and the growth of public services that provided some support to two wage-earner households with children. In Canada, the percentage of women aged fifteen to sixty-four involved in paid employment doubled between the start of the war and the early 1970s, and increased a further fifty percent by the end of the century. By 2002, seventy percent of women with children aged three to five were involved in paid employment (de Wolff 2006). Similar findings are reported in Britain where, by the late 1980s, two-thirds of women with children were working for pay and half of women returned to the workforce within nine months of giving birth (Purcell 2000: 116). However, men and women were not on an equal footing in this phase. The most recent norm in the household has been one earner, usually the male, in a relatively permanent and well paid "standard employment relationship" and one, more often than not the women, in a less permanent and less well paid "temporary employment relationship" (Vosko 2000). This was far from an ideal arrangement and led to a higher incidence of work-life stress, particularly for women who still bore primary responsibility for unpaid caring and housework (de Wolff 2006). For many women in Europe and North America, this stress became acute as state support for households eroded in the 1990s (Bezanson 2006). During this period, literature on the "double day," work/family life imbalance, and how women could gain access to "men's jobs" exploded (Ganage 1986; Sangster 1995; Hochschild 1997; Luxton and Corman 2001; Duxbury and Higgins 2001; Gornick and Meyers 2003).

The findings from this study suggest we may be in the early stages of a third shift in production/social reproduction structures characterised by the erosion of the male breadwinner model and the growth of two insecure incomes per household. At any moment of transition, there is a high degree of turmoil in relationships with many of the gendered roles of the early phase and old notions of masculinity and femininity are still shaping expectations and roles. It is a period of heightened stress, as both men and women are confronted with new realities that include the withdrawal of long-term employment commitments, the erosion of employment benefits, and the transference of state responsibilities (education, health care) to unpaid domestic caregivers (Wallulis 1998; Hacker 2006a). For men, employment insecurity makes it more difficult for them to fulfil the worker-provider role (Cherlin 2005). For women, the erosion of a stable income in the household can create more pressure to work for longer hours while at the same time performing unpaid tasks in a less supportive environment.

Julianne and Darryl were not the only workers we interviewed who came from households where both partners were employed in less permanent relationships. This was clearly a stressful situation. Nabila, an on-call translator, stressed that "the family can't function like this. Not having work, not having a permanent job, it impacts your own feelings, how you feel about yourself" (Nabila #5494). Kata worked part-time in a fitness centre. She liked the flexibility part-time work provided and that it enabled her to care for her children, but was concerned about her low pay and lack of benefits, particularly given the precarious nature of her partner's employment in manufacturing.

It doesn't feel like I really have a job. There is no mental satisfaction, no gratification that you get mentally when you work
and do a good job at work ... I feel stressed all the time. I don't
feel like I'm providing for my family; plus, my husband's job
isn't very secure so we worry. The insecurity is always there. We
did get an inheritance from my father, and this helped. But the
stress about money is always there (Kata #5214).

On the other hand, having at least one earner with a permanent
job lends stability to a household. A teacher suggested:

My husband works in the private sector ... he could lose his job
in the private sector with two weeks' notice. Now, as a teacher,
unless I did something horrendous or illegal, I wouldn't lose my
job. So in my mind I look at my job as a secure job ... I think
I'm the one who is more conservative in terms of wanting to
know there's a secure income coming in, and wanting to know
there's secure coverage for benefits ... I know I'll have financial
security (June #5470).

For some, the flexibility found in less permanent employment,
contributed positively to their households, allowing them to perform caring functions more easily. In Bette's case, it allowed her to
spend more time with aging parents.

There'd be no way that I could spend the time with my parents
the way I am doing currently as opposed to when I was working full-time and building a business part-time. It gave me the
greater flexibility to go over, like I could go over every day if I
wanted to. I'm sure they'd love that. I just wouldn't get as
much work done (Bette #5151).

The main story of what follows has less to do with changes in the
employment relationships of women, who historically have been
less likely than men to have experienced the benefits of the "standard employment relationship." As suggested above, women have
made some gains as a result of decades of struggle, and in some sectors work done largely by women has become somewhat more
secure. But it seems that the dominant change taking place is in the

employment experiences of men as they take on the characteristics that women have typically faced since their entrance into the labour market; characteristics which may, in part, explain some of the counter-intuitive findings of this study. Although limited research has been carried out on the gendered impact of the erosion of men's privileged position in labour markets, some studies have shown that men tend to report greater employment insecurity than women (Nelson and Burke 2002). While men still expect to earn more, have a reasonable level of employment security, and be the primary breadwinner for households, they face increasing challenges in fulfilling these expectations. This can lead to what some have described as a "crisis" in masculinity (Baron 1987) and others have called "gender strain" (Burke 2002; Golsch 2005). One of the young male participants who had moved in with his girlfriend but was employed in a precarious employment relationship expressed frustration at his inability to plan. He told us:

> In the greater scheme of things, planning for the future, like down the road, I mean you can't. I mean I don't know where the money will be coming from, if it's going to be there. Even from short-term, I mean planning's pretty hard. We're living day to day ... I didn't propose for a while because I didn't know. I said like listen, I don't know what the heck's going on. I told her flat out, I said, you know what, like honestly, now's not the time sort of thing. Eventually I sort of came around to, like we, we moved in together finally. I said, okay, I'll get engaged or whatever (Dalton #5449).

Another young man working full-time as a contract courier made it clear that given his situation, long-term planning was out of the question and that it would be impossible to "support a wife and mortgage payments and all that other stuff with just one courier income"(Ralph #5444).

Men's heightened sense of stress may also relate to existing social norms, and their reluctance to seek external support. Institutional structures and support networks that deal with insecurity appear to benefit women more than men, reflecting women's long-term exposure to employment uncertainty (Greenglass 2002). In what follows, we find it is men, not women, who most frequently report that scheduling uncertainty has an impact on their ability to carry out domestic responsibilities. Men in our study were more likely to report expending effort to find and keep employment, and concern that constant evaluation of their performance at work would influence how much work they were offered. Men were more likely to report discrimination, harassment, and being asked to do things at work that were unrelated to their jobs. In comparison to women, men also report less external support but no greater support from unions at work. Despite the reality that women still have primary responsibility for maintaining households and face significant insecurity in their own employment, men were more likely to report this tension, and state that insufficient notice of work made it more difficult for them to accommodate household responsibilities

Equally important, the withdrawal of commitments in the employment relationship is, by extension, a withdrawal of resources to households and to the future generations of workers. As a result, the spread of insecure employment relationships and confusion regarding the roles of men and women extends outside of the workplace to workers' personal lives and the realm of social reproduction. It introduces types of effort and strain that are not present in the "standard employment relationship" into the sphere of social reproduction. Household earnings are less secure, benefits are less likely to cover unexpected expenses, responsibility for health and education costs are increasingly borne by households, and control over time is eroding. Increased effort staying employed means that job searches, training, the social effort of networking, and scheduling disruptions are increasingly introduced into the activities of households. This is a shift with significant implications for social reproduction that has been structured for much of this century on the "male breadwinner and female domestic care" model. For example, in a recent study of American households, it was noted that household economic insecurity can result in tensions at home when children are left on their own and receive less support with school work, or when households are forced to rely on unqualified and poor quality daycare (Newman and Chen 2007).

The increased participation of women in paid employment since the 1960s has given rise to a lively debate over the implications this might have for households, motherhood, and social reproduction. A number of authors have explored how the spread of non-standard work hours is affecting social reproduction (Yeandle 1999; Presser 2003). However, much of the discussion of dual-earner households has assumed more or less stable forms of employment relationships. While men may no longer be the sole wage-earners, the security of their employment has not been questioned. This has led to a research focus on the changing distribution of caring labour between the sexes, and how to cope with the time pressures implicit in dual-earner households (Pfau-Effinger 1999; Crompton 1999; Luxton and Corman 2001; Marshall 2009). Our findings suggest that the concern should not be just about how to accommodate social reproduction with the stress associated with dual-earner households, but also how to manage the increased insecurity when *neither* earner has a permanent position. To sustain social reproduction in such a context will require far more than a rescheduling of men's and women's paid work hours or more childcare, whether supplied by the state or private sources (Ellingsæter 1999; Gornick and Meyers 2003). It may result in changes to households, gender roles, and how children are raised as profound as those associated with the rise of the family wage and the male breadwinner model. The future may look increasingly like the "Support Economy" of institutionalized personal and household support structures described by Zuboff and Maxmin (2002). It may result in an expansion in the numbers of workers who are paid to perform caring work in order to free others to participate in non-caring work (Yeandle 1999; Crompton 2006), or the spread of secure part-time work in place of full-time work (Crompton 1999). It might be tempting to propose that this transition provides an opportunity for greater gender equality since several of the men we interviewed did speak about liking flexibility in their work so they could be with their young children, but it is far from clear that this is the path society will take. It is more accurate to see this as a moment of turmoil – of not knowing *who* is able to provide for the economic needs or caring responsibilities of households. Our findings are indicative of such turmoil.

SEX AND THE CHARACTERISTICS OF EMPLOYMENT RELATIONSHIPS

Earlier in this chapter it was argued that men and women were almost equally likely to report being employed in a less permanent

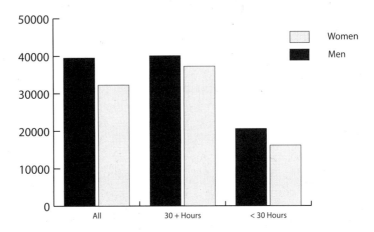

Chart 4.1: Annual income by sex and hours worked ($)

employment relationship. Does this mean men and women are also employed in relationships with similar characteristics? In this study and others, the answer related to earnings is a clear "no"; women consistently earned less than men. In our sample as a whole, women earned just under eighty-two percent of what men earned. Chart 4.1 shows that women working full-time hours (thirty or more hours a week) earned eighty-eight percent of what men working full-time earned. Chart 4.2 shows that women in less permanent employment relationships and working full-time hours earned just seventy-four percent of what men earn in similar situations. The only case where women earned more than men was women working in permanent part-time positions where they earned thirty-eight percent more than men.

However, on almost every other characteristic of the employment relationship measured in this study, the experiences of men and women in the labour market are surprisingly similar. Chart 4.3 reports average scores, by sex, for the three sub-indices that make up the *employment relationship uncertainty* index. There was very little difference between men and women in any of the sub-indices. Of the thirteen questions represented by these three sub-indices, there was only one question where the difference in the responses of men and women was statistically significant. Somewhat surprisingly, it was men, not women, who reported getting insufficient

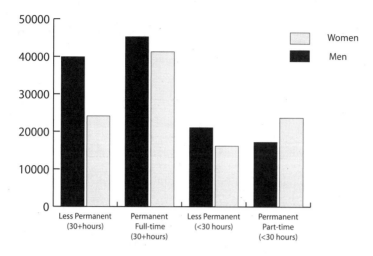

Chart 4.2: Annual income by sex, hours worked, and employment relationship ($)

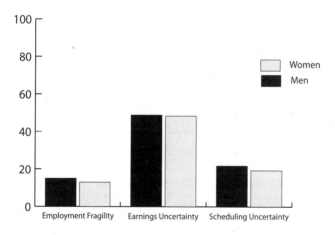

Chart 4.3: Employment relationship uncertainty by sex

notice of work schedules to plan household responsibilities. We think that this is a reflection of the turmoil associated with a period of transition and the difficulties some men are facing adapting to the decline of the "standard employment relationship." An equal number of men and women reported being in jobs that last less than six months, being unable to anticipate their income for the next six

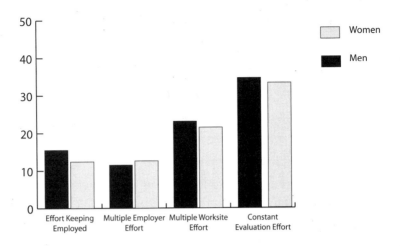

Chart 4.4: Employment relationship effort by sex

months, and having no access to sick pay, disability insurance, or a company pension.

A similar story is suggested for *employment relationship effort.* Chart 4.4 reports average scores, by sex, for the four sub-indices that make up the *employment relationship effort* index. Of the sixteen questions that make up this component, men and women reported statistically significant differences on only five questions and in each case it was men who were more likely to report characteristics associated with higher levels of *effort*. Men were as likely as women to be looking for work, engaging in unpaid training, and working for more than one employer. An equal percentage of men and women reported their continued employment and rate of pay was contingent on workplace evaluations. However, men were more likely to report being harassed by supervisors and co-workers, and being asked to do things unrelated to their job. Men were also more likely to work in more than one location, work in unfamiliar locations, and to report that the amount of work they obtained was affected by ongoing evaluations of their performance.

There was also little difference between men and women regarding *employment relationship support.* Women did report more support outside of work and more frequent family support, while

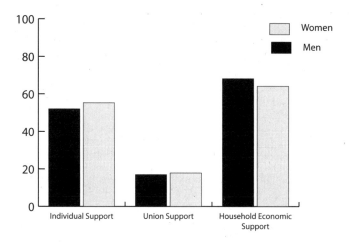

Chart 4.5: Employment relationship support by sex

men more frequently reported they were entitled to employment benefits as a result of their employment. However, the difference in this last indicator was relatively small and not what one might expect if men had greater access to permanent employment with benefits. Differences were present in men's and women's share of total household income. Men's earnings represented almost eighty percent of household earnings, while women's represented just over two-thirds. As such, this component of the male breadwinner model continues.

RACE AND THE CHARACTERISTICS OF EMPLOYMENT RELATIONSHIPS[3]

Earlier we reported that white workers and racialized workers in this study were fairly equally distributed across different forms of the employment relationship. Does this mean they are also

---

3 The study made an effort to include a broad representation of racialized and ethnic workers. The census area chosen for the survey was multi-cultural and the survey was advertised and available in the three most predominant languages in the greater Toronto area. See Methods Appendix.

employed in relationships with similar characteristics or that discrimination is not an issue in the Greater Toronto labour market? Certainly the recent immigrants and the racialized workers in less permanent employment that were interviewed had experienced significant discrimination. It is not unusual for a highly skilled immigrant to end up in insecure employment for a number of years after arriving in Canada. Hong, for instance, was a college teacher in China specializing in mining engineering who had lived in Canada for six years. His first job here was washing dishes in a restaurant. After a few years he began working in a nursing home as a smoking assistant, and later got a job as a personal support worker. Both these jobs were poorly paid and insecure. Unable to get teaching work in Canada, Hong added to his skills, hoping to find work as a pharmacy assistant. But the combination of long hours at low pay to make ends meet while learning new skills on his own left him exhausted.

I go home, the first thing I have to cook for my daughter, you know, do something. And after six o'clock I just lie down, sit down, relax. I can't do much more. Actually I want to, I am studying like pharmacy, pharmacy assistant, something like that, on weekends. But sometimes at six o'clock I cannot go. I feel tired, I am not doing very well in my studies (Hong #5293).

Kata immigrated to Canada about a decade ago. Her partner was a teacher before they immigrated, but neither of them was able to land any sort of permanent employment and she resorted to teaching Mandarin on a contract basis. Nabila had numerous qualifications and spoke multiple languages, but still only found temporary work as an interpreter.

I've been working this work for four years. I got a computer diploma from Seneca [College], but couldn't get work, so I went back to school ... took web design but couldn't get a job doing that when I finished. So now I'm doing work as an interpreter, this I've been doing for about four years ... I speak English, Arabic, and Turkish. I'm from Iraq, I was well educated there, but getting a job here has been very difficult (Nabila #5494).

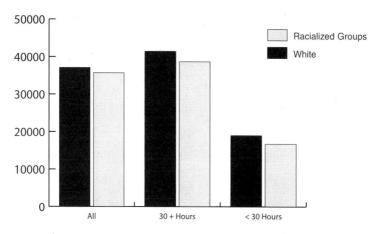

Chart 4.6: Annual income by race and hours worked ($)

Other racialized workers experienced discrimination and resentment from co-workers. Mala, who worked through temporary employment agencies for over a decade, was typical in this regard. She indicated that she put up with discrimination because as a temp worker she could not afford to complain. She felt it would be different if she had a permanent job. She told us:

Sometimes it's difficult, well you know with co-workers ... especially, and I'm saying this without any malice, is that if the person that's place I'm taking is white ... Causes a lot of resentment. So you know, you just sort of adjust to that ... I've very often gone up to them and said I'm sorry; I can't change the colour of my skin. This is me ... No matter how many times you tell me Canada is tolerant, it isn't. Believe me. I find the expression is hogwash (Mala #5435).

Data from the survey supports the perception that white workers and workers from racialized groups have different experiences. Racialized workers earned about ninety percent of white workers' earnings (Chart 4.6). This figure masks an important distinction between immigration and racialized workers. If one compares the earnings of white workers and racialized workers by length of residency in Canada, the findings are different. More recent immi-

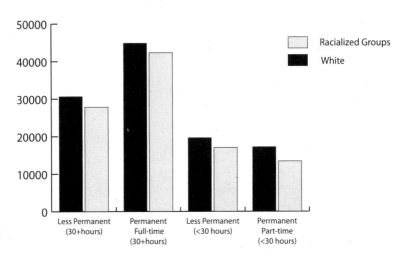

Chart 4.7: Annual income by race, and hours worked, and employment relationship ($)

grants from racialized groups were earning as much as seventeen percent less than recent white immigrants.

Racialized workers faced different employment conditions than white workers. Chart 4.8 reports average scores, by race, for the four sub-indices that make up the *employment relationship uncertainty* index. Workers from racialized groups report higher *employment fragility*, more *earnings uncertainty*, and more *scheduling uncertainty*. White workers were less likely to report insufficient notice to accept work, not receiving a record of their pay, or their pay being different from what they expected. They were less likely to lose pay when absent and more likely to be covered by a long-term disability benefit at work. They were also less likely to report that they received insufficient notice to plan social activities. There were also differences within the racialized group. When this group of respondents was broken down into three sub-categories (Chinese, South Asian, and Other[4]), the "Other" category most frequently reported characteristics associated with high *employment relationship uncertainty*, including insufficient notice to accept work, pay

---

4 The "Other" category includes Blacks, Filipinos, other Asians, Aboriginals, Middle Easterners, and Latin Americans.

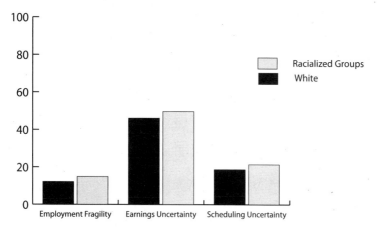

Chart 4.8: Employment relationship uncertainty by race

being different from what was expected, and losing pay if absent. All of this suggests that while the distribution of white workers and workers from racialized groups across the different forms of the employment relationship might have been similar, there is a significant difference in the level of working with commitments for the two groups of respondents. White workers were clearly at an advantage.

Chart 4.9 reports average scores, by race, for the four sub-indices that make up the *employment relationship effort* index. Workers from racialized groups consistently reported expending more *effort keeping employed* and were more likely to report *constant evaluation effort*. There were no statistically significant differences on *multiple employer effort* and white workers more frequently reported characteristics associated with *multiple worksite effort*. Of the three racialized workers sub-classifications, South Asians most frequently reported characteristics associated with high levels of *effort*. They most frequently reported discrimination and harassment, and *constant evaluation effort*. The more complex association between *employment relationship effort* and race was also apparent in responses to the individual questions that make up the indices. Workers from racialized groups were more likely to report looking for work, discrimination as a barrier to getting work, being

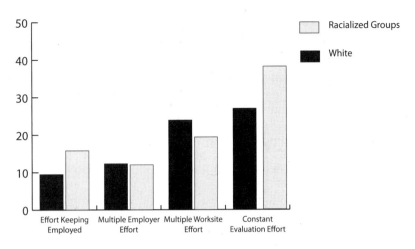

Chart 4.9: Employment relationship effort by race

harassed at work, and asked to do things unrelated to their job at work. They were also more likely to report that constant evaluation of their performance affected the kind and amount of work they did, as well as their rate of pay. However, white workers were more likely to report working in more than one location, conflicting demands as result of multiple locations, and traveling long distances to work.

Chart 4.10 reports average scores, by race, for the four subindices that make up the *employment relationship support* index. Workers from racialized groups earned less than white workers and lived in households with lower combined income. Of the three racialized sub-categories, South Asians were the least likely to report characteristics associated with *support*. They were the least likely to report having support outside of work, or support from family and friends. Their individual income was thirteen percent lower than white workers and their household income was twelve percent lower. White workers were more likely to report support outside of work, family support, and being a union member.

CONCLUSION

The findings reported in this chapter support the claim that changes in labour markets since the 1980s have resulted in a harmonization

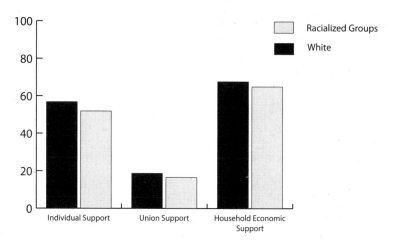

Chart 4.10: Employment relationship support by race

of male and female employment relationship experiences (Armstrong, 1996; Purcell 2000). This harmonization is evident in both the form of the employment relationship and the *uncertainty*, *effort*, and *support* characteristics of men's and women's employment relationships. This study cannot speak to the issue of trend, but it does suggest that on many dimensions, men and women are employed in relationships with similar characteristics. The findings seem to point to an erosion of the privileged male position in labour markets.

More detailed analysis of specific characteristics of the employment relationship revealed the extent of harmonization. On measures of *employment relationship uncertainty, effort,* and *support,* there were only a few statistically significant findings between men and women. The similarities between men's and women's experiences reveal that the type of uncertainty most commonly associated with women's employment has become more widespread for men. It appears that a key outcome of employment shifts over the last several decades, a combination of the erosion of the "standard employment relationship" and gains by women as a result of legislation and labour struggles, has meant that men are now just as likely as women to be employed with limited commitments.

While men's eroding position in the labour market suggests that gender is becoming less significant in shaping levels of employment insecurity, the same cannot be said about race. The more detailed analysis by race did reveal important differences. While race did not explain differences in the type of employment relationship, it remains an important factor in understanding how different groups experience employment. There was clear evidence that racialized workers experienced more *uncertainty* and expended more *effort* and were more likely to report discrimination at work. These results are consistent with research that indicates that race is an important factor shaping labour market experiences and that white workers continue to occupy a privileged position (Vosko 2000: 40; Vosko 2006: 58–61; Galabuzi 2004).

Precisely how these trends will impact social reproduction is an open question. It has been suggested that one reason the "standard employment relationship" was not resisted by employers early in the last century as vigorously as it might have been was the recognition that it was a compromise that facilitated both production and social reproduction (See Vosko 2000, for an extended discussion of this point). Beck described the relationship between industrial society, the nuclear family, and gender roles as one in which "Wage labor presupposes housework, production mediated through the market presumes the forms and ascribed roles of the nuclear family. In that respect, industrial society is dependent upon the unequal positions of men and women" (Beck 1992: 104). This simple picture of men in secure paid employment and women relegated to unpaid housework has been eroding for some time, as the male breadwinner model has been replaced by the two-earner household (Crompton 2006). Hacker (2006) argues that two incomes are now a necessity for maintaining a middle-class life, but that married couples with children have seen an increase in the instability of their incomes over the last two decades.

The finding that the levels of employment insecurity for men and women are converging throws into question the socially defined roles of men and women in society under the "standard employment relationship" and the "male breadwinner" model. Cappelli, in his study of shifting employment relationships, suggested that many aspects of contemporary American society could be affected by such a change: "Much of contemporary American society has been built on stable employment relationships characterized by predictable career advancement and steady growth in wages. Long-term individual investments such as home ownership and college educations for children, community ties and the stability they bring, and quality of life outside of work have all been enhanced by reducing risk and uncertainty on the job" (Cappelli 1999: 14).

In one of the few studies exploring the gendered implications of the spread of less permanent employment, Golsch reported that labour market insecurity was associated with decisions to move from cohabitation to marriage and from marriage to having children. Men in insecure employment delayed forming unions, while women in insecure employment formed unions earlier. However, both men and women delayed having children when faced with labour market insecurity (Golsch 2005: 201). A study of Spanish workers also found that men in fixed-term temporary contracts were less likely to have children when married, and more likely to remain single (Artazcoz et al. 2005). Wallulis suggests that the end of the "standard employment relationship" may also spell the end of the nuclear family and of "permanent" and "stable" marriages as the basis of social reproduction. It is argued that this shift in production relations may create "opportunities for a multitude of many individual recipes for sharing parenting, pooling economic resources, and achieving happiness" (Wallulis 1998: 125). Sidel argues that in the face of these changes, many young women view themselves as the "central characters" determining their future. They have come to realize that as a result of a number of factors, including men's increasing inability to earn a family wage, "they must be prepared to support themselves and anyone else for whom they feel responsible" (Sidel 1990: 27). The message of this chapter is that doing this might be as difficult for women in this century as it was for women at the beginning of the last century. However, the option of securing a secure source of household income by partnering with a man may also be more difficult.

In the introduction to this chapter, it was indicated that our findings suggested that a third major shift may be underway in production/social reproduction structures: a shift to a society with two insecure jobs per household. In this transition, the change in employment relationship has been most dramatic for men, but the impacts on the household are likely to be felt by both men and women. For men, the increasing challenge of satisfying their role as breadwinners is likely to lead to stress while for women, the continued responsibility for many of the unpaid household tasks in a less secure and supportive environment is certain to create stress. Our own data suggests that men and women are almost equally likely to be in the high *employment strain* category, while racialized workers are more likely than white workers to report high *employment strain*.[5] The health implications of this shift will be assessed in the next chapter and how households respond to these stresses will be a theme taken up in chapters 6 to 9.

---

5 Recall from chapter 1 that *high employment strain* is defined as the combination of high levels of *employment relationship uncertainty* and *employment relationship effort* that may or may not be buffered by high levels of *employment relationship support*.

RESPONSES TO INDIVIDUAL QUESTIONS
THAT MAKE-UP THE INDICES

Table 4.1
Employment relationship uncertainty by sex (%)

	Male n=1,003	Female n=1,108	P
EMPLOYMENT FRAGILITY			
Average job lasts less than 6 months	20. 2	20. 7	-
Insufficient notice to accept work	18. 5	14. 5	-
On call at least half the time	13. 7	12. 6	-
Always receive record of pay	78. 1	79. 7	-
Not paid on time	6. 9	5. 2	-
Pay different than expected	13. 0	10. 7	-
EARNINGS UNCERTAINTY			
Unable to plan on the same income in 6 months	15. 7	17. 7	-
Lose pay if miss work	46. 6	44. 7	-
Covered by long-term disability	44. 7	45. 9	-
Company pension	38. 3	38. 3	-
SCHEDULING UNCERTAINTY			
Insufficient notice to plan work week	15. 5	14. 0	-
Insufficient notice to plan household responsibilities	19. 1	16. 1	**
Insufficient notice to plan social activities	21. 1	19. 6	-

* significant at the 10% level, ** significant at the 5% level , *** significant at the 1% level

Table 4.2
Employment relationship effort by sex (%)

	Male n=1,003	Female n=1,108	P
EFFORT KEEPING EMPLOYED			
Looking for work half the days	13. 8	11. 9	-
Discrimination barrier to getting work	41. 9	37. 7	*
Harassed at least some of the time			
by supervisors or co-workers	26. 8	22. 7	**
Harassment a factor in treatment at work	31. 7	30. 2	-
Asked to do things unrelated to job	34. 0	27. 4	**
More than 50 hours of unpaid training	8. 6	7. 8	-
MULTIPLE EMPLOYER EFFORT			
More than one employer	12. 7	13. 8	-
Conflicting demands from multiple employers	17. 0	17. 9	-
More than one employer at the same time	10. 7	13. 2	*
MULTIPLE WORKSITES EFFORT			
Worked more than one location	35. 1	28. 4	**
Conflicting demands from multiple locations	19. 9	16. 6	*
Two or more hours of unpaid travel per day	26. 2	24. 5	-
Work in unfamiliar places most weeks	9. 3	6. 5	**
CONSTANT EVALUATION EFFORT			
Evaluation affects kind of work	52. 8	50. 3	-
Evaluation affects amount of work	46. 7	42. 3	**
Evaluations affect pay	35. 0	32. 0	-

* significant at the 10% level, ** significant at the 5% level , *** significant at the 1% level

Table 4.3
Employment relationship support by sex (%)

	Male n=1,003	Female n=1,108	P
INDIVIDUAL SUPPORT			
Support outside of work	69. 1	71. 6	**
Family support	73. 1	82. 0	**
Community support	53. 3	54. 7	-
Help with job	39. 5	40. 8	-
Some friends at work	49. 1	45. 9	-
UNION SUPPORT			
Union member	16. 8	15. 8	-
Union help with problems	20. 8	23. 1	-
HOUSEHOLD ECONOMIC SUPPORT			
Individual income	39,436	33,259	-
Household income	50,874	49,333	-
Employment benefits (own)	68. 7	62. 2	**
Employment benefits (household)	78. 1	75. 5	-

* significant at the 10% level, ** significant at the 5% level , *** significant at the
1% level

Table 4.4
Employment relationship uncertainty by race (%)

	White n=805	Racialized groups n=1,306	P
EMPLOYMENT FRAGILITY			
Average job last less than 6 months	19. 7	20. 9	-
Insufficient notice to accept work	12. 4	18. 9	***
On call at least half the time	13. 5	12. 9	-
Always receive record of pay	82. 5	76. 8	**
Not paid on time	5. 1	6. 6	-
Pay different than expected	8. 1	14. 0	***
EARNINGS UNCERTAINTY			
Unable to plan on the same income in 6 months	17. 7	16. 2	-
Lose pay if miss work	41. 8	47. 9	**
Covered by long-term disability	49. 6	42. 7	**
Company pension	39. 8	37. 4	-
SCHEDULING UNCERTAINTY			
Insufficient notice to plan work week	14. 7	14. 7	-
Insufficient notice to plan household responsibilities	16. 0	18. 5	-
Insufficient notice to plan social activities	16. 8	22. 5	**

* significant at the 10% level, ** significant at the 5% level , *** significant at the 1% level

Table 4.5
Employment relationship effort by race (%)

	White n=805	Racialized groups n=1,306	P
EFFORT KEEPING EMPLOYED			
Looking for work half the days	10. 4	14. 3	**
Discrimination barrier to getting work	23. 6	49. 6	***
Harassed at least some of the time by supervisors or co-workers	18. 9	28. 2	***
Harassment a factor in treatment at work	18. 1	38. 8	***
Asked to do things unrelated to job	25. 5	34. 2	***
More than 50 hours of unpaid training	7. 5	8. 6	-
MULTIPLE EMPLOYER EFFORT			
More than one employer	14. 4	12. 6	-
Conflicting demands from multiple employers	17. 5	17. 4	-
More than one employer at the same time	21. 2	11. 9	-
MULTIPLE WORKSITES EFFORT			
Worked more than one location	38. 4	27. 4	***
Conflicting demands from multiple locations	21. 8	15. 9	**
Two or more hours of unpaid travel per day	28. 2	23. 5	**
Work in unfamiliar places most weeks	7. 7	7. 9	-
CONSTANT EVALUATION EFFORT			
Evaluation affects kind of work	42. 9	56. 7	***
Evaluation affects amount of work	33. 9	50. 8	***
Evaluations affect pay	24. 0	39. 3	***

* significant at the 10% level, ** significant at the 5% level , significant at the 1% level

Table 4.6
Employment Relationship Support by Race (%)

	White n=805	Racialized groups n=1,306	P
INDIVIDUAL SUPPORT			
Support outside of work	81. 0	68. 1	***
Family support	83. 6	74. 2	***
Community support	55. 9	52. 9	-
Help with job	40. 9	39. 8	-
Some friends at work	53. 3	51. 2	-
UNION SUPPORT			
Union member	18. 4	14. 9	**
Union help with problems	22. 6	21. 6	-
HOUSEHOLD ECONOMIC SUPPORT			
Individual income	37,059	35,667	
Household income	51,683	49,076	
Employment benefits (own)	61. 7	67. 5	**
Employment benefits (house)	75. 7	77. 3	-

* significant at the 10% level, ** significant at the 5% level , significant at the 1% level

5

The Employment Strain Model and the Health Effects of Less Permanent Employment

Health-wise I'm just too stressed. I just don't know, I'm too tired, too stressed to do anything. I'll go out for a walk or something, still nothing, it helps relieve the tension a bit, the walk. But otherwise I don't have the energy. So I'm out there in limbo (Allan #2493).

I wouldn't sleep at night. It would affect my health ... Fortunately my eyes are pretty good for my age and my teeth are all my own, so I have no problem there. But I'm getting migraines and sometimes my pressure would go up, my blood pressure because I'm worried (Mala #5435).

Is working without commitments a health hazard for workers and their families? We introduced Kim and Pat in chapter 1, and discussed how their exposure to traditional workplace health and safety risks, including physical risks and the stress related to "job strain," were similar. They both had relatively boring desk jobs with little exposure to toxins or other physical risks. But their situations were very dissimilar in others ways. Kim's job was permanent in that she was confident her job would continue. Her relationship had many characteristics one associates with a career. Her terms of employment were being re-negotiated by her union and she could challenge her supervisor where she felt it was warranted. She got along with her co-workers and had a thriving household. In contrast, Pat was employed on a temporary contract and was not confident that his job would continue or that he had a career with his current employer. His employment relationship was short-term and either party could terminate it relatively easily. Consequently, Pat was looking for new work and taking some training on his own time. He faced uncertainty over the terms and conditions of his next contract as well as when and where he would work, and was reluctant to challenge his supervisor. He was isolated from his co-workers and his household was strained by the uncertainty. His was the life of someone working without commitments. This chapter will explore when and how these factors shape health outcomes.

WHAT IS KNOWN ABOUT
LESS PERMANENT EMPLOYMENT AND HEALTH?

The spread of less permanent forms of the employment relationship has led to a growing interest into the question of how they might impact health outcomes (Cummings 2008). In summarizing the findings of the World Health Organization's Commission on Social Determinants of Health, Marmot et al. (2008) reported, "Work is the origin of many important determinants of health. Work can provide financial security, social status, personal development, social relations, and self-esteem and protection from physical and psychosocial hazards. Employment conditions and the nature of work are both important to health. A flexible workforce is seen as good for economic competitiveness but brings with it effects on health. Mortality seems to be significantly higher in temporary workers than in permanent workers. Poor mental health outcomes are associated with precarious employment" (Marmot et al. 2008: 1663).

The main focus of research has been potential exposure to stress at work and hazardous physical working conditions under different forms of the employment relationship. A secondary focus has been the effectiveness of the labour market regulatory framework and, in particular, health and safety regulations. However, our understanding of both the positive and the negative health effects of the employment relationship remains incomplete. A limitation of the research has been the lack of a theoretical framework defining the characteristics that make employment relationships insecure or precarious, and hence a lack of understanding of the pathways from the employment relationship to health (Berhhard-Oettel et al. 2005;

Menéndez et al. 2007). Several papers have begun to address this limitation, but most ideas have yet to be tested empirically (Cooper 2002; Benach, Amable et al. 2002; Standing 2002; Scott 2004; Tompa et al. 2007; Benach and Muntaner 2007).

To date, most health studies of less permanent employment have used forms of the employment relationship such as temporary employment or permanent full-time employment as proxies for employment relationship characteristics. As reported in chapter 3, different forms of the employment relationship do tend to have different characteristics, but there is also a degree of heterogeneity within each form (Louie et al. 2006). As some have pointed out, having a "permanent full-time" position in the new economy can still be associated with high levels of insecurity (Tompa et al. 2007). Existing studies do suggest that less permanent relationships and, in particular, relationships that could be described as "precarious" are associated with poorer health. However, the findings remain far from conclusive. In an early review of this literature, Quinlan and colleagues found that over eighty percent of existing studies found less permanent employment to be associated with a "deterioration" in occupational health and safety conditions, caused by such factors as job churning, fractured management systems, and workplace disorganization (Quinlan, Mayhew, and Boyle 2001). A more recent review of twenty-seven studies comparing health outcomes of those in temporary employment relationships with those in permanent ones concluded that being in the former increased the likelihood of reporting stress-related illness (Virtanen M. et al. 2005). However, the results for poor physical and global health and for musculoskeletal disorders were less conclusive.

A study of Finnish public sector workers found that less permanent employment was associated with an increased risk of poorer health (Virtanen P. 2005). A similar finding was reported in a series of papers emerging from the Whitehall II study (Ferrie et al. 1998; Ferrie 2001; Ferrie et al. 2002; Ferrie et al. 2005). However, studies on the health effects of fixed-term contracts using British and German data found mixed results. Comparing workers in permanent full-time relationships with those on fixed-term contracts, the researchers found that German fixed-term workers reported poorer health but the British workers did not (Rodriguez 2002). Bardasi and Francesconi (2004) used the same British data and concluded that temporary and part-time employment were not associated with poorer health. Studies based on the Second and Third European Survey on Working Conditions also suggest that less permanent employment is associated with some indicators of poorer health, but not all. Less permanent employment was associated with greater job dissatisfaction, more fatigue, backache, and muscular pain, but less stress (Benavides and Benach 1999; Benavides et al. 2000; Benach and Gimeno et al. 2002; Daubas-Letourneux and Thebaud-Mony 2003; Benach and Gimeno et al. 2004).

Other studies have begun identifying the specific characteristics of employment relationships that might affect health outcomes. Studies using data from the Second European Survey of Working Conditions suggest that workers in temporary full-time relationships are exposed to more hazardous physical conditions than permanent full-time workers (Letourneux 1998: 34). However a later study, that included data from the Third European Survey on Working Conditions, found little evidence that workers in less permanent relationships were exposed to more hazardous working conditions (Goudswaard and Andries, 2002). A study of Spanish workers found those in fixed-term contracts were more likely to be injured at work (Guadalupe 2003). Benavides and colleagues found that while workers in temporary employment relationships had a higher probability of fatal and non-fatal work-related injuries, the findings became statistically insignificant once adjustments were made for factors such as gender, age, and length of employment. They concluded that less job experience in temporary employment may be a significant factor in the increased risk of work-related injury (Benavides et al. 2006). Seifert et al. (2007) argue that precarious employment can lead to intensification if workers only work peak hours, and if there is reduced co-operation between workers who are competing for a limited pool of hours. Workers in precarious employment relationships may also be forced to work irregular hours, which in itself can lead to increased stress (Bohle et al. 2004).

Other studies have considered issues such as control, workload, and the prevalence of "job strain." Goudswaard and Andries, (2002) reported that workers in less permanent relationships had less control over working time, less control over income, and less job control, but also fewer psycho-social job demands than permanent workers. Hence, on balance, they concluded that workers in less permanent relationships did not experience more "job strain." This is similar to findings by Parker et al. (2002), Pederson (2003), and Saloniemi et al. (2004).

More consistent results have been found in work that explores the implications of employment insecurity and health (Ferrie 2001). A review of numerous studies from various countries indicated that job insecurity was associated with poorer health and job attitudes, and a poorer relationship with the organization (Sverke et al. 2002). An Australian study found high job insecurity associated with a significant increase in poor self-rated health, depression and anxiety (D'Souza et al. 2003). Chirumbolo and Hellgren (2003) also found job insecurity was associated with less job satisfaction and more mental health complaints. There is also evidence that less permanent employment is associated with poorer knowledge of health and safety rights and more difficulty exercising these rights (Aronsson 1999; Quinlan and Mayhew 2000; Lewchuk, Clarke, and de Wolff 2009).

HEALTH OUTCOMES AND THE FORM
OF THE EMPLOYMENT RELATIONSHIP

Existing research indicates that less permanent employment is associated with poorer health outcomes, but the lack of a theoretical framework limits our understanding of why this is the case. The remainder of this chapter will offer a new approach to this question, and test it using data from our survey. We begin by examining the association between the different forms of the employment relationship and health outcomes. Our survey asked a series of questions about health that are described in more detail in the appendix.

Table 5.1 suggests that workers in different forms of the employment relationship *do* report different health profiles. Workers employed through temporary employment agencies reported health problems the most frequently, suggesting that the characteristics of this employment relationship are critical in understanding what makes an employment relationship toxic. However, it is not obvious which form of the employment relationship is associated with the fewest health problems. Workers in permanent full-time employment reported stress, tension, and work-related headaches relatively frequently, but poor-health, frustration at work, and sleep problems less frequently. Those who were self-employed reported frustration at work, as well as exhaustion, stress, and injury relatively infrequently, but poor health, poor mental health, and work-related headaches more frequently. The final row in Table 5.1 reports the average ranking amongst the six forms of the employment relationship on the ten health indicators. While the average ranking of those employed through a temporary employment agency stands out, there is really very little difference between the other five forms of the employment relationship. This finding is significant. Simply being in a less permanent form of the employment relationship does not appear to be a very robust predictor of health profiles. This raises two key questions: (1) what are the characteristics of the employment relationship that shape health outcomes? And (2), under what conditions will employment insecurity lead to health problems?

TOWARDS A THEORETICAL FRAMEWORK
TO EXPLAIN THE HEALTH EFFECTS
OF THE EMPLOYMENT RELATIONSHIP[1]

Research on the health effects of less permanent employment has provided clues regarding the characteristics that are likely to be the most significant in shaping health outcomes. As discussed above, research comparing exposure to physical hazards and "job strain" among workers in different employment relationships has produced mixed findings. Exposure appears to be shaped by a complex set of factors; for example, workers in less permanent relationships may be more vulnerable to hazardous conditions, but they may also have less to lose by refusing to accept such conditions, or even by quitting rather than enduring them, relative to permanent full-time workers. It would also appear that on balance, less permanent workers are no more prone to "job strain" than permanent full-time workers – they are likely to have less control over decisions at work, but at the same time fewer demands are made of them or are self-imposed upon them. However, research has indicated that workers in less permanent employment relationships face increased

---

1 An earlier version of some of this material was published in Lewchuk, Clarke, de Wolff (2008).

Table 5.1
Forms of the employment relationship and health outcomes (%)

	Less permanent employment relationships				Permanent employment relationships		
	Temp agency (n=172)	Short-term contract (n=144)	Self-employed (n=167)	Fixed-term contract (n=112)	Permanent part-time (n=148)	Permanent full-time (n=1,371)	P
Self-reported health fair to poor	16.9 (6)	13.p (4)	14.4 (5)	11.6 (1)	13.5 (3)	12.3 (2)	-
Self-reported mental health fair to poor	17.4 (3)	10.4 (4)	10.8 (5)	9.8 (2)	8.8 (1)	10.3 (3)	-
Pain at work at least half the time	30.2 (6)	21.5 (5)	15.6 (2)	14.3 (1)	16.2 (3)	16.9 (4)	**
Frustrated with work at least half the time	40.7 (6)	34.7 (5)	24.9 (1)	31.3 (3)	31.8 (4)	29.6 (2)	**
Exhausted after work most days	37.2 (6)	35.4 (5)	24.0 (1)	28.6 (2)	33.8 (3)	34.5 (4)	*
Tense at work at least half the time	44.2 (6)	29.9 (1)	30.1 (2)	31.3 (3)	36.5 (4)	41.6 (5)	**
Work stressful most days	43.6 (6)	25.7 (2)	25.2 (1)	28.6 (3)	30.4 (4)	37.6 (5)	***
Work leads to sleep problems at least half the time	27.3) (5)	20.8 (3)	22.2 (4)	28.6 (6)	12.2 (1)	19.6 (2)	**
Work leads to headaches at least half the time	26.7 (6)	14.6 (3)	17.5 (5)	14.3 (2)	12.2 (1)	16.9 (4)	**

Table 5.1 (*continued*)

	Less permanent employment relationships			Permanent employment relationships		
	Temp agency (*n=172*)	Short-term contract (*n=144*)	Self-employed (*n=167*)	Fixed-term contract (*n=112*)	Permanent part-time (*n=148*)	Permanent full-time (*n=1,371*)	P
Work-related injury or illness last year	16.9 (6)	13.2 (4)	12.6 (2)	10.7 (1)	16.2 (5)	12.8 (3)	-
Average rank	5.9	3.1	2.8	2.4	2.9	3.4	

Figures in brackets represent rank across the six forms of the employment relationship with a high number associated with more frequent health problems.
(* significant at 10%, ** significant at 5%, *** significant <1%)

insecurity (broadly defined to include uncertainty over future employment prospects, lack of control over working conditions, and income insecurity), and that this does have health implications. It also suggests that workers in less permanent relationships have fewer supports from unions and from co-workers, and are less protected by labour market regulations.

Findings from our study are consistent with the research described above. With a few exceptions, there was no clear pattern on measures of physical work risks or "job strain" between those in less permanent employment and those in permanent full-time relationships. There was evidence that workers employed through temporary employment agencies were, on average, exposed to more physical risks, including uncomfortable temperatures, poor air quality, excessive noise, and frequent use of toxic substances, compared to those in permanent full-time positions. However, the differences between those in other forms of less permanent employment and those in full-time permanent employment were generally much smaller, and statistically insignificant. The exception was the frequency that workers used toxic substances, which those on short-term contracts were the least likely to report. Questions that provide some insight into the combination of workload and control at work, the two elements that make up "job strain," also indicate that those in less permanent employment are not more frequently exposed to this form of workplace risk. Those employed through agencies were less likely to report influence over decisions at work compared to those in full-time permanent relationships, while the self-employed were the least likely to report that their work pace was too fast but the most likely to report having influence over decisions.

As understanding of how less permanent employment affects health has improved, researchers have begun calling for a shift in focus away from traditional workplace health and safety risks such as physical hazards and "job strain," towards considerations of issues like the social structure of employment, power relationships, and the changing social/psychological employment contract to explain health outcomes (Cooper, 2002; Benach et al., 2002a; Scott 2004; Benach and Muntaner 2007; Clarke, Lewchuk, and de Wolff 2007; Lewchuk, Clarke, and de Wolff 2008). While traditional occupational health and safety research has focused on exposures *inside* the workplace, this new approach suggests that health effects are embedded in the social structuring of labour markets, and therefore begin well before workers cross the factory gates, enter their offices, or begin their work tasks. Pederson (2003) argued that while temporary agency employees experience less stress at work than permanent employees do, a major stressor in their lives is their "job situation." The latter includes insecurity of job tenure, lack of control over work schedules, stress from being constantly on-call, insecurity regarding employment income, and the injustice associated with being treated differently than permanent employees doing exactly the same work. Malenfant (2007) examined the impact of insecurity on workers' well-being and demonstrated how intermittent employment and the need to constantly search for work negatively affected mental health. It was argued that the effects of intermittent work on well-being – specifically on workers' social recognition and self-esteem – can be as damaging to mental health as the stresses linked to unemployment.

Our research has indicated that less permanent employment relationships are associated with a different set of power relationships between worker and employers. This is the essence of "working without commitments." The insecurity that workers in less permanent employment relationships report is a reflection of a shift in power over who controls access to employment and its terms and conditions. In most cases, but not all, the shift to less permanent employment has enhanced employer control over who gets to work as well as the setting of the terms under which work is offered. In some cases, where the supply of workers is scarce, where the cost of losing a job is relatively low, or where the worker employed in a less permanent relationship occupies a critical node in an extended supply chain, the worker can be freed from internal job ladders and may actually be empowered by less permanent employment (Osterman 1999; Pink 2001; Marchington et al. 2005). But this is the exception rather than the norm. The shift in power over who gets to work leads to those in less permanent relationships adopting different strategies to maximise both their likelihood of employment and of negotiating terms that are attractive. It also leads to a different role for household and community support for these workers.

Our approach to understanding how less permanent employment relationships may affect health was shaped by Karasek's "job strain" model (Karasek 1979; Karasek and Theorell 1990). While the "job-strain" model does not factor in the insecurity associated with different forms of the employment relationship, it does provide a key insight into the pathways from work to health. The "job strain" model has shown that it is not control over how work is done or even workload on its own that affects health outcomes, but rather their interaction. "Job strain" is found when jobs provide low levels of control over how work is done while at the same time requiring high expenditures of psycho-social effort to complete assigned tasks. We developed a model that explores control over having employment and its terms and conditions, the effort expended finding and keeping employment, and the economic and social support at work and outside of work. A simple version of this model was introduced in chapter 1 and described in more detail in chapter 3.

Each component of the Employment Strain Model may affect health independently. Workers who spend large amounts of time looking for work or are constantly aware they are being evaluated at work may feel stress. The elements of the model may also interact and have an impact on health outcomes. We define *employment strain* as the interaction of *employment relationship uncertainty* and *employment relationship effort*. We define four categories of *employment strain* using the median values of *employment relationship uncertainty* and *employment relationship effort* as the cut-points (See Diagram 4.2). Workers are exposed to *high employment strain* when their score on both the *employment relationship uncertainty* index and the *employment relationship effort* index is above the median score of the sample as a whole.[2] Workers in this category are uncertain about future job prospects and they are expending considerable effort either to keep the jobs they have or to find new ones. We would predict that the majority of those working without commitments would fall into this category. The *low employment strain* category represents workers with scores below the sample median on both the *employment relationship uncertainty* index and the *employment relationship effort* index. Workers in this category have a degree of control over whether they will be employed, and over the terms and conditions of such employment, and therefore feel little need to expend effort to keep their current jobs or to find new ones. We would expect that the majority of workers working with commitments to fall into this category. Workers in the *high uncertainty* category score above the sample median on the *employment relationship uncertainty* index, but not on the *employment relationship effort* index. Despite the uncertainty associated with future job prospects, they spend relatively little effort maintaining employment. Those in the *high effort* category score above the sample median on the *employment relationship effort* index, but not on the *employment relationship uncertainty* index. They expend relatively high levels of effort maintaining employment despite reporting low levels of uncertainty regarding access to future employment or its terms and conditions. We hypothesize that workers exposed to *high employment strain* will report poorer health than workers in the *low employment strain* category. It is less clear what impact *high effort* or *high uncertainty* will have on health.

The third dimension of the Employment Strain Model is *employment relationship support*. We hypothesize that high levels of

---

2 Details of how the indices were constructed from the survey questions can be found in the appendix .

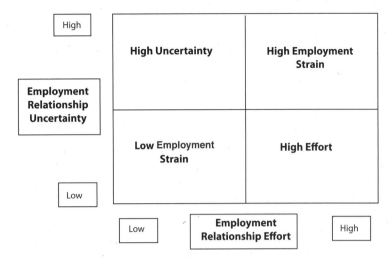

Note: Median values of the relevant indices were used as the cut points between the different categories of *employment strain.*

Diagram 5.1: Employment strain categories

employment relationship support could act as a buffer against the health effects of *employment strain.* We predict that individuals exposed to *high employment strain* and also reporting low levels of *employment relationship support* will be the most at risk of poor health. On the other hand, those exposed to *high employment strain* may be buffered from the stress associated with this situation if they have high *employment relationship support.* We tested separately for the association between *employment strain* and health outcomes, and between *employment strain* buffered by *employment relationship support* and health outcomes, and will discuss this later in the chapter.

CHARACTERISTICS OF THE EMPLOYMENT RELATIONSHIP
AND HEALTH OUTCOMES

Table 5.2 uses the employment relationship characteristics that define the different categories of *employment strain* to assess possible effects of the employment relationship on health. It is a significant advance over approaches that use the form of the employment relationship as a proxy for its characteristics. We tested the association of the three core constructs of the Employment Strain Model with each of the ten health indicators for which we have data. All associations were controlled for differences in age, sex, race, physical risks, and employment relationship type. The latter was included to control for unmeasurable differences in the characteristics of different forms of the employment relationship. One example would be differences in the effectiveness of the health and safety regulatory framework that is generally argued to be less effective for workers in less permanent employment relationships. We also constructed a detailed index of, and controlled for, physical risks in the workplace.[3] The findings reported in Table 5.2 suggest that, even after controlling for these confounders, there were a number of statistically significant associations between several of our health indicators and several characteristics of the employment relationship. For example, *Employment relationship effort* was consistently associated with poorer health and *employment relationship support* with better health. *Employment relationship uncertainty*, which reflects characteristics commonly associated in the literature with precariousness, was only associated with two measures of health and, in one case, increased *uncertainty* was actually associated with better health. This was an unexpected result, so we will explore its possible meaning in the next section of this chapter. The health indicators that showed the strongest association with employment relationship characteristics included frustration at work, tension and stress at work, work-related sleeping problems, and headaches.

We repeated the same analysis found in Table 5.2 using the sub-components of the Employment Strain Model as described in Diagram 3.1. We found a significant association across almost all of our health indicators and three particular sub-components of our model: *effort keeping employed, constant evaluation effort,* and *individual support. Scheduling uncertainty* was associated with exhaustion after work and stress at work. The other sub-components of the model were less consistently associated with health outcomes. Again, the weak association between *earnings fragility*

---

3 The physical risk index includes exposure to awkward working positions, time spent working in a standing position, exposure to poor air quality, uncomfortable temperatures, noisy work environments, and toxic materials.

Table 5.2
Impact of a ten-point increase in employment relationship indices on health indicators (odds ratios)

	Employment relationship uncertainty	Employment relationship effort	Employment relationship support	Physical risks	R^2
Self-reported health fair to poor	1.14(**)	0.94	0.86(**)	1.16(***)	.0680
Self-reported mental health fair to poor	0.99	1.20(**)	0.81(***)	1.16(***)	.0676
Pain at work at least half the time	1.09	1.21(***)	0.95	1.54(***)	.1799
Frustrated with work at least half the time	0.92(*)	1.42(***)	0.88(***)	1.36(***)	.1353
Exhausted after work most days	0.92(*)	1.23(***)	0.85(***)	1.34(***)	.1023
Tense at work at least half the time	0.94	1.35(***)	0.91(**)	1.30(***)	.1016
Work stressful most days	0.91(**)	1.32(***)	0.88(***)	1.14(**)	.0571
Work leads to sleep problems at least half the time	1.08	1.40(***)	0.95	1.33(***)	.1401
Work leads to headaches at least half the time	1.05	1.44(***)	0.96	1.44(**)	.1886
Work-related injury or illness last year	0.95	1.28(***)	1.02	1.43(***)	.1211

Health outcome=f (age, sex, race, physical risks, employment relationship type, employment relationship uncertainty, employment relationship effort, employment relationship support). Values greater than one represent more frequent poor health indicators.
(* significant at 10%, ** significant at 5%, *** significant at 1%)

and *earnings uncertainty* and our health indicators was somewhat surprizing.

EMPLOYMENT STRAIN AND HEALTH OUTCOMES

The weak association between *employment relationship uncertainty* and health indicators suggests that the health impact of precarious employment involves more than uncertainty. To examine this further, we explored how interactions between the different com-

Table 5.3
Distribution of employment relationship types across employment strain categories (%)

	Less permanent employment relationships				Permanent employment relationships	
	Temp agency (n=172)	Short-term contract (n=144)	Self-employed (n=167)	Fixed-term contract (n=112)	Permanent part-time (n=148)	Permanent full-time (n=1,371)
High employment strain	72.1	62.5	62.9	42.0	46.6	20.9
Low employment strain	5.2	2.8	6.0	17.0	18.2	41.9
High effort	2.9	2.8	5.4	17.0	4.1	23.5
High uncertainty	19.8	31.9	25.8	24.1	31.1	13.6

ponents of the Employment Strain Model were associated with health outcomes. In what follows, we report findings on the association between health outcomes and the different categories of *employment strain* as defined in Diagram 3.1. This is followed by findings on whether *employment relationship support* buffers the health effects of *employment strain*. Our data suggests there is a gradient of strain created by the interaction between *employment relationship uncertainty* and *employment relationship effort*: as *employment relationship effort* <u>and</u> *employment relationship uncertainty* increase, the poor health also increases. The data also suggests that *employment relationship support* acts as a buffer only for certain types of *employment strain*.

We first examine whether different forms of the employment relationship cluster within different *employment strain* categories as predicted above. The findings reported in Table 5.3 reveal clear tendencies. As predicted, workers in less permanent relationships were more likely to be located in the *high employment strain* quadrant and less likely to be in the *low employment strain* quadrant. The opposite was true for workers in permanent full-time positions who were more likely to be in the *low employment strain* quadrant and

Table 5.4
Employment strain and health (odds ratios relative to low employment strain)

	High employment strain	High effort	High uncertainty	Low employment strain	R^2
Self-reported health fair to poor	2.01 (**)	1.50 (*)	2.20 (***)	1.00	.0615
Self-reported mental health fair to poor	1.86 (***)	1.61 (**)	1.62 (**)	1.00	.0462
Pain at work at least half the time	2.05 (***)	1.35	1.15	1.00	.1695
Frustrated with work at least half the time	1.90 (***)	1.54 (**)	0.90	1.00	.1182
Exhausted after work most days	1.63 (**)	1.47 (**)	0.96	1.00	.0940
Tense at work at least half the time	1.54 (**)	1.52 (**)	0.81	1.00	.0903
Work stressful most days	1.81 (***)	1.66 (***)	0.88	1.00	.0484
Work leads to sleep problems at least half the time	2.51 (***)	1.72 (**)	1.07	1.00	.1197
Work leads to headaches at least half the time	2.02 (***)	1.64 (**)	1.01	1.00	.1660
Work-related injury or illness last year	1.44 (*)	1.36	0.67	1.00	.1192

Health outcome=f (age, sex, race, physical risks, employment relationship type, high employment strain, high uncertainty, high effort). Values greater than one represent more frequent poor health indicators. (* significant at 10%, ** significant at 5%, *** significant at 1%)

less likely to be in the *high employment strain* quadrant. However, employment relationship type did not perfectly predict *employment strain*. Between one-quarter and one-half of our respondents in less permanent employment relationships did not experience *high employment strain* while over one-fifth of those in permanent full-time employment did. A significant number of respondents in all forms of the employment relationship were found in neither the *high* nor *low employment strain* quadrants. (This helps to explain why using employment relationship type as a proxy for employment relationship characteristics does not yield a clear picture of the association between less permanent employment and health.)

Table 5.4 reports findings on the association between different categories of *employment strain* and health outcomes. The findings are relative to those in the *low employment strain* category. In general, workers in the *high employment strain* category were the most likely to report indicators associated with poor health. Those in the *high effort* category also reported poor health more often than those in the *low employment strain* category, but on fewer indicators and with smaller effects. Those in the *high uncertainty* category reported health profiles similar to those in the *low employment strain* category with the exception of general health status and mental health. This finding suggests that interactions between characteristics of the employment relationship are central to understanding how the employment relationship affects health. In particular, it suggests that working without commitments is only associated with poorer health indicators when workers also are expending effort with the goal of minimizing that uncertainty. In this context, the health effects of working without commitments can be significant.

Table 5.5 examines the extent to which *employment relationship support* serves as a buffer against the health effects of *employment strain*. Median index values were used to define high and low *employment relationship support*. The findings are relative to those exposed to *low employment strain* and reporting *high employment relationship support*. This is the category that we would argue best represents workers in relationships where there is a commitment between worker and employer that is more than short-term. These workers likely hold permanent full-time jobs with good benefits, live in households that offer them support, and have support at work from their unions. Three observations are worth noting. First, support provides a limited buffer for workers exposed to *high employment strain*. For the most part, workers exposed to *high employment strain* continue to report poor health indicators more frequently than the *low employment strain/high support* category regardless of the level of support. Second, support does provide some relief to those in the other two *employment strain* categories, the greatest effect being found amongst those in the *high effort* category. Finally, the combination of *high uncertainty* and *high support* is associated with a health profile statistically identical to the *low employment strain* and *high support* group. These findings suggest that workers in less permanent employment relationships do not all have the same experiences or face the same

Table 5.5
Employment strain, support, and health (odds ratios relative to low employment strain and high support)

	High Employment Strain		High Effort		High Uncertainty		Low Employment Strain		R^2
	Low Support	High Support	Low Support	High Support	Low Support	High Support	Low Support	High Support	
Self-reported health fair to poor	2.64(***)	1.84 (**)	2.23(**)	1.49	3.21(***)	1.26	1.68	1.00	.0695
Self report mental health fair to poor	2.46(***)	2.64(**)	3.51(***)	1.57	2.57(**)	1.26	2.54(**)	1.00	.0569
Pain at work at least half the time	2.10(**)	2.42(***)	1.99(**)	1.23	1.20	1.31	1.33	1.00	.1713
Frustrated with work at least half the time	2.23(***)	1.77(**)	2.59(***)	1.33	1.05	0.83	1.34	1.00	.1222
Exhausted after work most days	2.13(***)	1.40(*)	1.79(**)	1.57(**)	1.30	0.70	1.60(**)	1.00	.0994
Tense at work at least half the time	1.75(***)	1.41(*)	2.81(***)	1.23	0.88	0.82	1.20	1.00	.0953
Work stressful most days	2.11(***)	1.63(**)	2.66(***)	1.47(**)	0.90	1.05	1.33	1.00	.0524
Work leads to sleep problems at least half the time	2.88(***)	3.21(***)	3.30(***)	1.54(*)	1.41	0.90	1.83(**)	1.00	.1261
Work leads to headaches at least half the time	2.12(**)	2.21(**)	2.99(***)	1.28	1.07	1.06	1.24	1.00	.1701
Work-related injury or illness last year	1.25	1.48	1.43	1.18	0.58	0.72	0.66	1.00	.1207

Health outcome=f (age, sex, race, physical risks, employment relationship type, high employment strain and high support, high uncertainty and low support, high employment strain and low support, high effort and high support, high effort and low support, low employment strain and low support). Values greater than one represent more frequent poor health indicators. (* significant at 10%, ** significant at 5%, *** significant at 1%)

health risks. In particular, it indicates that a worker can be in a less permanent employment relationship but have a health profile that is similar to that of someone in a more permanent relationship. This is the case when workers in less permanent employment are not worried about their chances of future employment and have substantial support at work, at home, or in their community. This is an issue that will be explored in detail in chapters 6 through 9.

ARE UNHEALTHY WORKERS DIRECTED TOWARDS LESS PERMANENT EMPLOYMENT OR HIGH EMPLOYMENT STRAIN RELATIONSHIPS?

One possible explanation of our findings is that they reflect reverse causation and a sorting by the market of workers with health problems into less permanent forms of the employment relationship or into relationships that expose them to *high employment strain*. Such an interpretation assumes that employers can identify health problems at the point of hiring, and that discrimination in labour markets allows employers to reserve permanent full-time positions for those they perceive to be healthier. There are undoubtedly cases where employers, looking for "ideal" candidates for permanent full-time positions, do screen out those with health problems. (This may also be true for employers looking for temporary help.) It is also likely that some workers who suffer from health problems such as disabilities or chronic illness might themselves need a less permanent arrangement and therefore not even apply for permanent positions. However, there are other factors to consider, such as the possibility that some employers may find it more difficult to release permanent full-time employees whose health problems are not evident at the time of hiring or who became less healthy over the course of their careers. They might be blocked from such actions by written agreements, or by their desire to retain a valuable investment in human capital. They might also be restrained by the implicit contract between employer and worker that we have described as "working with commitments." On the other hand, employers will have more opportunity and ability to let temporary workers go when they become ill, since they enjoy fewer protections. In fact, if the health of such workers deteriorates significantly, they might be pushed completely out of employment and onto the welfare rolls.

Responses to questions in the survey suggest that the reverse causation argument is unlikely to be a major determinant of our findings. Respondents were asked if they suffered a physical or mental disability that limited either the kind of work they were able to do or the amount of work they were able to do. If reverse causation were an important factor, respondents in less permanent employment relationships or in the high employment strain category would be more likely to report such limitations. If, on the other hand, employers find it more difficult to release unhealthy workers in permanent full-time positions compared to those in less permanent positions, the opposite would be true. Respondents in permanent full-time positions were marginally more likely to report disabilities that limit the kind of work they could do (36.6 percent) compared to those employed through temporary employment agencies (32.0 percent) or those in short-term contracts (30.6 percent). Respondents in permanent full-time positions were also marginally more likely to report disabilities that limit the amount of work they could do (34.8 percent) compared to those employed through temporary employment agencies (29.2 percent) or those in short-term contracts (30.8 percent). In both cases, the differences were sufficiently small that none were statistically significant. Comparing the responses of those in the *high* and *low employment strain* categories yielded a similar result. Both groups were equally likely to report a physical or mental health issue that limited either the amount of work or the kind of work they could do.

There was no statistical difference between those in different employment relationships when they were asked if they had experienced bias as a result of a perceived physical or mental illness. About one-third of respondents felt employers did show such bias, but those in permanent full-time relationships were as likely to report this as were workers employed by temporary employment agencies or on short-term contracts. This suggests that such bias may have more of an impact on the type of job one obtains than the form of the employment relationship. One possibility is that individuals who are perceived to have a physical disability are prevented from getting full-time permanent employment that requires particular physical attributes, but not necessarily full-time permanent employment where such attributes are less critical. Comparing the responses of respondents in the *high and low employment strain* categories indicated that those in the *high employment strain* category were about twice as likely to report employer bias compared to respondents in the *low employment strain* category.

The final question in this series asked respondents if they had ever lost a job due to a work-related injury or illness. Here the results indicated that workers currently in less permanent employment relationships were much more likely to lose jobs for these reasons than those in permanent full-time employment. Over ten percent of those currently on short-term contracts, and over five percent of those employed through an agency, reported losing a job due to work-related health issues compared to less than three percent of those in full-time permanent employment. This difference supports the hypothesis that employers are less likely to shed full-time permanent employees with health problems than workers they employ on a short-term basis. A similar result was found with those in the *high employment strain* category, who were also more likely to report having lost a job than respondents in the *low employment strain* category.

The evidence does not support the hypothesis that reverse causation – or the sorting of less healthy individuals into less permanent employment relationships or into relationships with *high employment strain* – explains our findings. There was no clear pattern of health-related obstacles to the kind or amount of work individuals reported being capable of doing. Where there *was* a pattern was in job-loss due to health problems. Those in permanent full-time employment, or in employment characterized by *low employment strain*, were much less likely to report having lost a job due to health problems. This is consistent with the argument that those working with commitments have more protection from health related job-loss than those working without commitments.

There is evidence from our interviews that, in addition to the possibility that less healthy workers are sorted into less permanent employment, these workers experience a further decline in their health because of work-related issues. Two individuals reported their existing mental health issues had become aggravated because of working on a contractual or temporary basis. For instance, Gail, a self-employed artist doing various temporary jobs, reported that her mental health had deteriorated as a result of stress. According to her, "I now only sleep about five hours a night. I do feel stressed, I feel stressed all the time. I feel like I live in a constant state of panic" (Gail #5676). The result was that she had less ability and energy to look for work, or to do anything else to improve her employment situation.

Philip, a fifty-year-old, on-call disaster service worker on a fixed-term contract, and Mala, a sixty-four-year old temp worker, both reported deteriorating health. As a result of a workplace accident in 2000 (which was disputed, thus not compensated for), Philip suffered from neck pain leading to migraines. He reported that this pain and the resulting headaches had become much worse because of stress and his inability to properly address his growing health problems.

> I'm smoking much more, and I've lost weight. I get dizzy from the stress and I'm getting migraines more often again ... I can't afford the medicine though, so I end up in bed when I'm not feeling well (Philip #5560).

These workers' experiences underscore our argument that those who enter and remain in less permanent employment for extended periods of time are likely to experience diminished health. Our survey does not suggest that poor health is a factor determining who ends up in less permanent employment, but rather that once workers who start out less fit are in employment relationships with limited commitments, they are very likely to see a further decline in their health.

CONCLUSION

This chapter began with a review of what is known about the relationship between less permanent employment and health. Is working without commitments in insecure jobs bad for your health? In general, existing research suggests that it is. However, a significant problem with this literature is that there is little analysis of the specific characteristics of employment relationships that might affect health. As a result, researchers have used the form of the employment relationship as a proxy for these characteristics. This approach has produced mixed findings. For instance, the health of workers in less permanent employment was not significantly different from those in permanent employment in a number of studies while workers in less permanent employment reported better health in other studies. Our own data, reported in Table 5.1, yielded similar results to some of these studies. With the exception of survey respondents who acquired most of their work through temporary employment agencies, we did not find significant differences between the health indicators of those in less permanent employment and those in permanent employment.

The Employment Strain Model was used to understand better how the employment relationship shapes health outcomes. The analysis produced a number of significant findings. First, simply being employed in a relationship with high levels of *employment relationship uncertainty* was not consistently associated with poorer health. Second, *employment fragility* (not knowing whether you will have work in the near future) and *earnings uncertainty* were not good predictors of health outcomes on their own. This result was something of a surprise, as these are the characteristics of employment most often associated with precarious employment. Third, *employment relationship effort* and *employment relationship support* were more consistent predictors of health outcomes. In particular, the best predictors of health were: *effort keeping employed,* including constantly searching for work and engaging in unpaid training; *constant evaluation effort,* including a sense that your performance at work will affect the amount and kind of work you are offered; and *support* from family, friends and community.

We also tested how these core dimensions of the Employment Strain Model interacted in shaping health. We divided the sample into four categories: *high employment strain, high effort, high uncertainty,* and *low employment strain.* We found that respondents in less permanent forms of the employment relationship did cluster in the *high employment strain* category and that those in permanent employment did cluster in the *low employment strain* category. However, over one-quarter of those in less permanent forms of the employment relationship were not in the *high employment strain* category and over one-fifth of those in permanent full-time positions were in the *high employment strain* category. A significant number of respondents were in neither the *high* nor the *low employment strain* categories. It is obvious that the experience of workers in the same form of the employment relationship diverged substantially. Some workers in temporary employment relationships reported employment characteristics that looked more like workers in permanent relationships and vice versa.

We found that employment relationships with the characteristics represented by *high employment strain* (the combination of *high uncertainty* and *high employment relationship effort)* were the most consistently associated with poor health indicators. Employment relationships with the characteristics consistent with *high effort* were also associated with poor health, but in general, the size of the effect was smaller and the statistical significance of the associations was weaker than in the case of those exposed to *high employment strain*. Finally, workers in relationships with the characteristics consistent with *high uncertainty* reported health indicators that were statistically the same as those in relationships categorized as *low employment strain*.

We also examined the effect of *employment relationship support* and whether this acted as a buffer against the health effects of *employment strain*. Again, the findings provided further insights into how the employment relationship might shape health outcomes. High levels of *employment relationship support* did <u>not</u> buffer those exposed to *high employment strain*. The respondents exposed to *high employment strain* and reporting low levels of *employment relationship support* were the most likely to report poor health indicators. However, those exposed to *high employment strain* and reporting high levels of *employment relationship support* were only marginally less likely to report poor health indicators. This suggests that support was not much of a buffer for respondents in this category. For workers in the *high effort* category, *employment relationship support* did provide a buffer. Those in the *high effort* category and reporting low levels of *employment relationship support* reported poor health indicators as frequently as respondents exposed to *high employment strain*. However, those in the *high effort* category who reported high levels of *employment relationship support* had health profiles similar to the healthiest group in the study, that is workers in the *low employment strain* and high levels of *employment relationship support* category.

The Employment Strain Model has helped us identify the characteristics of employment relationships associated with poorer health. Workers in relationships that are characterized by high levels of *uncertainty*, high levels of *effort* and low levels of *support*, were two to three times as likely to report poor health as workers in relationships with low levels of *uncertainty*, low levels of *effort* and high levels of *support*. Workers in permanent full-time employment were more likely to report low levels of *uncertainty*, low levels of *effort* and high levels of *support* than workers in less permanent employment relationships. However, less permanent employment was not consistently associated with *high employment strain* nor was permanent employment perfectly associated with *low employment strain*.

The remaining chapters of this book explore further the association between employment and health using a series of interviews with seventy-two workers in less permanent employment and nine permanent workers who also reported employment characteristics consistent with *high employment strain*. Details on how individuals were selected for interviews can be found in the Methods Appendix. Analysis of this data suggested four distinct categories of working without commitments. Nine interviewees reported having a permanent full-time relationship but still reported *high employment strain*. They were placed in a *full-time* category and their stories are the basis for chapter 6, exploring why many of the survey respondents in permanent full-time positions still reported *high employment strain*. The seventy-two workers in less permanent relationships were divided into three different categories: *sustainable less permanent employment* (n=13), *on a path* to more permanent employment (n=25), and *unsustainable less permanent employment* (n=34). Chapters 7 through 9 explore the employment experiences of each of these categories of workers. Each had different employment characteristics, different expectations of whether less permanent employment was in their best interest, and different support contexts. We argue that there are important differences in the health implications for each of these three categories. Those in the *sustainable* cluster are less likely to be exposed to *high employment strain*, have considerable support, and experience health benefits from not having a permanent employment relationship. For this cluster, working without commitments is a positive experience (for a similar finding see Origo and Pagani 2008). Those in the *on a path* cluster may experience some short-term health effects, but they see this as a temporary trade-off until they obtain more permanent employment. The third and largest cluster of interviewees was the *unsustainable* cluster. Most of these workers reported feeling trapped, with little chance of finding more permanent work and with few resources to buffer their insecurity. This cluster also reported the worst health outcomes and were the most likely to be exposed to *high employment strain*.

Approximately one year after the initial interviews, repeat interviews were held with twelve workers in the *unsustainable* cluster, and follow-up telephone interviews were held with eighteen workers in the *on a path* cluster to assess any changes in their employment relationship. We also made use of several focus groups conducted during the pilot phase of the project. These focus groups involved home-care workers employed in a number of different forms of the employment relationship. They proved particularly useful in understanding the experiences of workers in nominally permanent full-time employment who had no guarantee of the number of hours they would work from week to week.

By dividing workers in less permanent employment relationships into three distinct categories we also shed some light on the issue of what it means to be in a precarious employment relationship. Of the three categories of less permanent relationships, only two, the *on a path* and the *unsustainable* clusters, can really be described as having "precarious" employment. Our research strongly suggests that workers in *sustainable less permanent employment* have succeeded in re-creating the commitments of the "standard employment relationship," or have found alternative sources of support that buffer them from the insecurity associated with less permanent employment. This more nuanced understanding of the implications of less permanent employment also has some relevance to our understanding of what it means to be in a permanent employment. We argue throughout the book that a sizeable percentage of those in permanent relationships have many of the employment characteristics of workers in precarious employment relationships. This observation points to the instability that is being built into a growing number of permanent jobs: such employment may have the form of a permanent relationship, but the practice is very different.

The interviews and focus groups provide the raw data for a more detailed study of how employment relationships shape health outcomes. This more detailed analysis confirms what has been suggested in this chapter: interactions between the *uncertainty, effort,* and *support* characteristics of the employment relationship are critical to understanding how working without commitments shapes health outcomes. This more detailed analysis will also point us towards policy recommendations that might improve health outcomes for workers in a period of changing employment relationships.

6

The Blurred Lines between Precariousness and Permanence

Well, the first time the doctor put me on medication for the heartbeat, to stabilize the heartbeat I guess, for two or three weeks. But he didn't find anything wrong with my heart and it happened again two months ago and he put me on medication again and this time suggested I go and see a cardiologist. He said it was just related to stress. So two years ago the stresses were the amount of work we had; this time it's probably the fact that I'm gonna lose my job (Denis, software engineer #216).

A new approach was developed in the preceding chapter to explore the health implications of working without commitments. *Employment strain* – the combination of high levels of *employment relationship uncertainty* and high levels of *employment relationship effort* – was shown to be strongly associated with poorer health outcomes. However, a critical finding was that less permanent employment was not always associated with high levels of *employment strain*, nor was being in a permanent employment always associated with low levels of *employment strain*. This chapter continues our investigation of the characteristics of the employment relationships that are associated with poorer health outcomes by focusing on a cluster of workers in "permanent" employment relationships who nevertheless reported having high levels of *employment strain*.

In general, permanent employment provides the kind of security that contributes to better health and well-being (see chapter 5). However, we found considerable evidence that not all employees in permanent employment relationships are working with commitments. We found that employers do not make the same commitments to all workers in the core jobs in our economy, that levels of commitments between employers and permanent employees in some workplaces are declining, and that the distinctions between permanent and less permanent employment relationships are blurred for many workers. Many of the full-time permanent workers who responded to our survey experienced surprising levels of *employment uncertainty*, and one in five experienced *high employment strain*. Less than half experienced the kind of employment stability that would be expected with permanent full-time employment and that is associated with *low employment strain*. The Employment Strain Model is useful in understanding and explaining this uncertainty and the impact it has on workers. In particular, it helps us see beyond job titles and exposes the extent to which some workers in permanent relationships have limited ability to anticipate their future income and therefore plan their lives.

Our interviews further the analysis by highlighting four kinds of permanent job situations that create high levels of *effort* and *uncertainty*. First, the ubiquitous restructuring and layoffs in North American institutions necessitate new kinds of effort for workers, accompanied by the general stress of not knowing what work will come next. Whether the threat of layoffs is real, or whether it is informed by rumors, the resulting *uncertainty* and *effort* for many workers is similar. Second, some "permanent" work does not guarantee hours or income. Several of our interviewees were living with a constant level of concern about scheduling and whether they could pay their bills. Third, some full-time permanent jobs do not pay enough for workers to sustain themselves or their households, which means that workers have to invest effort looking for better paid work, or take on second jobs and experience the strain of having multiple employers. And finally, "permanence" is only relative for some workers. While their employment may be permanent in theory, they do not have the benefits, protection, and security more commonly associated with full-time, permanent employment relationships. And while these situations are common, they are by no means the only potential uncertainties in "permanent" jobs.

The analysis that follows draws on the survey responses from over one thousand workers who reported having a permanent full-time job plus interviews with nine of these workers who reported *high employment strain*. It also draws on interviews and focus group discussions conducted in 2002–03 with home-care workers during the pilot phase of the study. Before we examine the blurring of the distinctions between "permanent" and "precarious" employment in more detail, we want to introduce Denis. He told us about his experience of learning how to work without commitments while still having a full-time job.

DENIS: LEARNING TO WORK WITHOUT COMMITMENTS[1]

Denis learned that his department was going to be closed several months before our first interview. He was employed by an international information service that brought him to Toronto from Europe because of his particular expertise as a software engineer. He had worked for them for eight years. Consequently, he thought that the company was committed to him, that they valued him, and that his employment was secure. The job paid well and offered him both benefits and an unusual five weeks of vacation each year that made it more like a European job than a Canadian one. He settled in the Toronto area, married, bought a house, and had two young children. However, after he had spent eight years with the company, management decided to discontinue the program he worked with, to focus most of their resources on sales, and to outsource any future software development to companies in India. The company was having financial difficulties and had, in effect, off-loaded the business cycle risks of software development to other companies and to their employees. There were no jobs in any of the company's North American offices for Denis or any of the other workers in his department. Employees were promised a minimal severance package as long as they continued to work until the department was shut down. Denis expected that the closure would be about six months from our first conversation.

When we spoke to Denis a second time, almost a year and half after the initial closure announcement, he was still in the same job. The company had extended the closing deadline three times, and he

---

1 Denis #216.

expected to work for at least another six months. He and his colleagues were still considered permanent employees despite the looming layoffs. Consequently, their relationship with their employer and with each other had changed, as they learned to live with their uncertainty. Denis described the stress he experienced thus:

> Falling asleep is sometimes not as easy as usual because I'm thinking about it. I've had strange dreams about this, not too often, but it has happened. It has happened. I've had dreams where I was out of a job and couldn't find a job or didn't know, went to interview and didn't know how to program anymore, would have like this skill-test questionnaire and wouldn't know how to answer any of it. Just went blank, like those kind of nightmares, the kind that you had back in school, before an exam (Denis #216).

Denis's stress the first couple of months after the company gave him notice was typical of those experiencing job loss. His nightmare that he was back in school was particularly apt – the new uncertainty threw him into an intense learning process. When he felt his employer was committed to him, he didn't need to figure out what other companies he would like to work for, who was hiring, how his household would survive if he wasn't employed, who would pay for the constant training he needed, whether to plan a vacation, and how to deal with a myriad of other problems associated with uncertain employment. This all changed when he was given his layoff notice. Prior to the notice, most of his employment-related learning and effort was technical and, to some extent, project management. During the second interview, Denis talked about how he learned to network with others in the same field, and to check out appropriate possibilities without setting off his nightmares. He also told us that because he was only servicing the program rather than building and re-building it, his work did not keep him on top of new programming languages. He and his colleagues had tried to get the company to send them to training as part of their separation agreement, since so many were spending their own time and money preparing to get back into the labour market, but they were unsuccessful.

Denis and his wife also had to go through a longer-term learning process at home to adjust to the uncertainty. He talked about how the new things he had to do to manage his employment situation affected their relationship. Before the layoff notice, his long working hours most affected their relationship. Because he worked so hard, they planned that she would not work outside of their home before their two young children were in school, but his immanent layoff had jeopardized this strategy. In the year after the first layoff notice, his wife enrolled in courses that "helped her handle her anxiety." They recognized that they could not manage financially for longer than a couple of months if Denis was not earning, so she was planning to go back to work. They had shifted their expectations for their children, and were learning about what kind of childcare they thought was appropriate, its costs, and its availability.

Denis hoped that the period he was going through was a transition from one permanent job to another. In the process however, he and his wife were learning to cope with stress and insecurity. This new situation echoes our understanding of the effort involved in *employment strain* that we introduced in the previous chapter, particularly the effort associated with looking for work and training for work. Denis's worry about income loss made him look for work, and increase his effort to stay current in the labour market. He was taking on some of the costs previously carried by his employer (training in particular), and was preparing to take new risks. The possible loss of income also transferred risks and costs to his wife, leading her to look for employment and thereby disrupting their long-standing household arrangements. Other issues he had to deal with included his disillusionment with his employer, changed relations with clients and co-workers, and changed expectations of the pace of his daily work. His story provides an excellent example of how the steady withdrawal of commitments between employers and employees impacts workers and their families. Individuals and their families are required to adopt new strategies to deal with rising levels of uncertainty, and the stress associated with this uncertainty. Workers in "permanent" employment relationships with low or declining levels of commitments therefore face similar challenges to individuals in less permanent employment relationships with *high employment strain*.

EMPLOYMENT RELATIONSHIP UNCERTAINTY

Denis was one of 1,371 full-time permanent workers who completed surveys in our study.[2] One fifth of these "permanent" workers reported *employment strain* and its associated poorer health. One fifth had high levels of *employment uncertainty*, and slightly more than one in six were investing effort getting and keeping work that put them in danger of experiencing poorer health. Although we expected most "permanent" workers to have *low employment strain*, we found that only forty-five percent were in that category.

Why would workers in permanent full-time employment relationships experience *employment strain*? The socio-economic characteristics of the full-time workers with *high employment strain* only begin to tell the story. Male and female "permanent" workers were equally likely to report *high employment strain*. Permanent *high employment strain* workers were more likely to have jobs in health care, retail, construction, manufacturing, and commerce than their less strained counterparts. On average they were three years younger than the whole group of permanent full-time workers, and they were more likely to be from racialized groups. About two-thirds had completed some university education, marginally less than the permanent group as a whole and about the same as those in less permanent employment.

The relatively high proportion of workers from racialized groups suggests that they were having difficulty breaking into those full-time jobs that come with more security and benefits. Chandra was a black woman in her mid-thirties who worked as a human resource manager for an employment recruiting company. She was well positioned to reflect on the barriers racialized groups face in finding and retaining full-time, permanent employment. Not only did she face discrimination in the workplace herself but she witnessed how the company she worked for treated others, and the barriers non-white workers often faced when applying for permanent employment. She told us that:

---

2 The discussion in this chapter is limited to the conditions of full-time "permanent" work and does not include part-time "permanent" work.

I found it [the racism] overt at times. I mean who got transferred into permanent jobs ... I have managers saying, you
know, their last name doesn't look English or how's their communication skills. So if the last name is Chan, they completely
assume that it's ... an immigrant who has poor communication
skills. I had to advise them that we cannot discriminate against
them, I cannot ask those kinds of questions ... I believe that
before I got there the company was very much an Anglo-Saxon
boy's club. But I was able to say, see beyond, not what people
think, well this is what a corporate manager looks like. Well,
it's not somebody who is fifty-something, with a [gray head] of
hair and talks very distinguished. It could be a woman, who is
Asian, at thirty-five (Chandra #2820).

Employment Fragility

A more complete story about why workers in permanent employment relationships experience *employment strain* emerges when we
look at the *employment strain* indicators among "permanent"
workers. Nearly one in ten full-time "permanent" workers was in
a job lasting less than six months on average; they were unable to
anticipate their income six months from now. Five percent of all
permanent workers were on-call workers without any guarantee of
hours, and eight percent said they did not always receive the pay
that they expected. One-third lost pay if they were sick and barely
half were members of company pension plans. This suggests that
for many workers – and employers – the concept of permanence has
been eroded and that any job that is not a temporary short-term
assignment is considered a "permanent" job. As a result, a significant number of permanent full-time workers reported levels of
employment relationship uncertainty comparable to that reported
by workers in less permanent relationships.

A feature of the current labour market that affects many workers
is workplace restructuring. It leaves many workers, like Denis, in a
permanent full-time position with the characteristics of short-term
employment. Whether such restructuring is intended to facilitate
"just-in-time" production and services, to downsize core operations, to contract out operations, to decentralize to project centers,
to merge with another company, or – in the public sector – to sat-

isfy demands for reduced government spending, workplace restructuring has introduced a pervasive sense of job insecurity throughout the workforce. Significant proportions of people have lost jobs
because of restructuring or are in "survivor" positions with heavier
workloads and with higher levels of uncertainty. One study estimates that one in four Canadians who lost their jobs in the mid-
1990s did so because of restructuring (Wilson 1998). This trend is
not unique to Canada. In the early 1970s in the United States, most
layoffs were the result of economic difficulties facing companies.
Less than one-third of all layoffs were carried out by profitable
firms looking to enhance earnings. By the mid-1990s, over half of
all layoffs were carried out by profitable firms looking to enhance
earnings rather than a response to economic distress (Osterman
1999: 39). Our study is not alone in making the observation that
the stress associated with restructuring can be harmful to workers'
health. A substantial body of research has found that restructuring
or downsizing and the resultant threat of job loss can create chronic stress, which in turn leads to a range of health problems (Kivimaki 2001; Quinlan 2001; Ferrie 2002; Sverke 2002; Bartley 2005;
Ferries 2007).

Other workers we interviewed revealed a trend towards a
reduced expectation of "permanency." Phil was a driver and general labourer in his late thirties. Over the previous fifteen years,
whenever he wasn't working in his wife's business he found work
through a temporary agency. The first thing Phil said during the
interview was that he'd just got a full-time permanent job. Four
months earlier he had been placed by the temporary agency for thir-
ty-four hours a week with a bottling company. Three weeks before
we talked, the bottling company approached him and asked if he
wanted a permanent job with them operating a forklift. He was
pleased because it meant "five dollars extra an hour and less
headaches of going to the [temporary employment agency] office
every morning to get my time card and have to bring it back every
Thursday and all that, now it's like, forget about you guys" (Phil
#5543).

However, Phil's recent experience in this labour market made him
cautious. He had agreed to work a regular fifty-two-hour week,
which suggested to us that while the possibility was open to him, he
intended to get all the work he could at the higher rate of pay, plus

regular overtime. He was clear about the company's motivation for hiring him directly:

It saves them money. It saves them money because they, instead of paying [the agency] like twenty-two dollars an hour or nineteen teen dollars an hour, they're paying you directly thirteen dollars an hour or fourteen dollars an hour, and they don't have to worry about paying so much to [the agency] (Phil #5543).

However, when we talked about whether he would get benefits, he said that would happen only after the three-month probation period. He recognized this as a potential barrier. He had not got past the probation period in at least five other companies and he knew this happened with other workers. In his words: "As soon as you get to this three-month period, it's like, oops, sorry. Here's your pink slip, laid off" (Phil #5543). When we asked whether that could happen at this company, he said: "I don't know, there's been three guys there from [the agency] and two of them already made it through the probationary time, so hoping. Keep my fingers crossed" (Phil #5543).

Others we interviewed had had very low expectations about the permanency of their jobs, or weren't even sure if their full-time job really was a permanent position or not! For instance, Kent, a computer call-center worker, responded to our question about whether his employment was permanent in this way: "I'm not really sure. I know that I am hired full-time" (Kent #691). He went on to suggest that the question doesn't really arise because the working conditions are very poor and the wages are low, so very few workers want to stay. Consequently, the company doesn't have to worry about their status, or even define it.

In contrast to Phil's and Kent's expectations that permanence was short-lived, we met several other workers who had the sense that permanence was close to impossible. These workers were working at full-time hours or more, had been in the same position for a number of years, and were generally treated as "permanent" workers. However, they were classified as casual or part-time, and struggled with their employers' almost impossibly high criteria for who got on their permanent payroll. Viv had worked forty hours a week for the same cafeteria owner for five years, but was still considered part-time. When we asked her who was considered full-time, she said that only the supervisor was in that category. Cole had worked full-time for over a year for a large unionized retailer. After working hard and applying for a permanent position, he began to understand that his employer classified most of the workforce – apart from supervisors – as "casual workers." Deepa was an administrative worker in a non-profit organization whose full-time work was paid from two separate funding sources. Because each funding source paid for a part-time position without benefits, her employer did not put her on the full payroll and did not provide her with benefits. Each of these workers could see that they were doing the same work as permanent employees and that they were putting in the same number of hours; they were frustrated that their employers would not make the extra commitment to them to provide them with security as well.

Chandra, the human resources recruiter we introduced earlier, underlined our interviewees' sense that employers are resistant to making commitments to workers who are initially hired as casual workers. She said:

> [T]he on-call projects have to be there to an extent, but when you have somebody working for twelve dollars an hour, for three years, on contract, and you have them working every day, then they should be full-time, they should have benefits. I can give you an example: this gentleman, he worked for three years, no benefits, in an on-call contract. I would say he was maybe forty or forty-something. He was a technician ... for one of our government clients. This gentleman worked for three years and no benefits, no nothing whatever. He had a heart attack. He had to go on Employment Insurance to get any benefits and I said, is there nothing that we can do in regards to his medical bills or anything, and this guy's committed for three years? And he had to reapply for the job six months later at the same rate. And I thought that was utterly disgusting (Chandra #2820).

Earnings Uncertainty

Despite being employed in full-time permanent positions, many workers still reported having high levels of *earnings uncertainty*.

Unstable and uncertain pay and benefits contribute to the blurred lines between permanent and precarious employment. For instance, while "permanent" workers were far more likely to know their income and to be able to plan accordingly than less permanent workers, there were still nine percent who did not know what their earnings might be in six months time. One in ten said that they had no guarantee that they would work (and be paid for) at least thirty hours each week. A significant proportion of "permanent" workers did not have protection for sickness or for injuries that might disrupt their work lives. Almost thirty percent were not paid if they were sick, a third had no long-term disability insurance, and only just over half had the kind of long-term security that comes with a company pension.

A situation that contributes to *earnings uncertainty* among many "permanent" workers is low wages. One in five of our full-time survey respondents were paid $24,000 a year or less. In 2008, Statistics Canada pegged the low income cut-off "marker" in large Canadian cities at $22,361 for a household of two, and $34,738 for a household of four (Statistics Canada 2008). The proportion of low-earners in our study is similar to that reported in a recent study of the Canadian workforce: one in six full-time workers earn less than ten dollars an hour, or $20,800 a year (Saunders 2006). For workers in Canadian cities, this is hardly adequate. In Victoria, where costs are comparable to those in other Canadian cities, a coalition of business people and social planners has agreed that a wage of anything less than fifteen dollars an hour is difficult to live on, particularly if workers have caring responsibilities for others (Challenge 2007). Low wages can create uncertainty on their own, and they also compound the stress experienced by workers in uncertain and insecure employment. For instance, low wages can make the possibility of layoffs, illness, or family crises very difficult to manage when workers do not have access to paid sick leave, family leave, or long-term disability benefits.

Tanisha lived with low wages and uncertain future employment related to her full-time job. For a young woman in her early twenties, it appeared that she was doing fairly well – on the surface. She was a full-time medical administrative assistant and lab technician in a doctor's office. She had trained at college for both occupations and had been in the same job for three years. However, while she thought that she had been hired into a permanent job, she did not feel like her position was secure; nor was she provided with the type of benefits, time-off, or control over her hours of work and workload as other permanent workers in the same office. In fact, while she had been there longer than some of the other employees, she was paid at the lowest rate in the office, had no benefits, and was not paid for sick days. Her employer required that she work long hours, often into the evening. She had tried living on her own but it was too expensive, so she was renting a basement apartment with her boyfriend. Her expenses were higher than she could manage on this salary because she was paying off a significant student loan, so she worked at a second job as a clerk at a vehicle rental office for an additional twenty-four hours a week. Unfortunately, this position also did not pay well: despite working six days a week at two jobs, she was just beginning to earn $25,000 a year. Tanisha had kept up this schedule for several years, but it was starting to frighten her:

And everything is just overwhelming; it gets like that, maybe twice a month, where everything just gets overwhelming. I cry, I shake, oh my gosh, I can't eat anything. It's treacherous (Tanisha #3064).

Tanisha experienced employment-related stress on a number of fronts. The medical office job had a heavy workload, with expanded evening clinic hours, but she generally felt good about her ability to do the work and felt ready to be the only one in charge of the office administration. However, she had not been promoted since she started working at the clinic; nor had she been given any significant salary increases. Further, she had been sexually harassed in both work locations. Neither situation had been dealt with formally – she did not feel either job was secure enough to make a complaint – so she worked with some anxiety, because the harassment could easily recur. Along with working more than sixty hours a week in two locations, she was also constantly looking for a better job. She rarely saw ads for full-time lab technicians and was beginning to think that most jobs in this field were temporary or part-time. This added to her sense that her future was very insecure.

Kent, the full-time computer call center worker, had a second job that offered him an additional eight hours each week in retail. He told us that he needed both jobs because his expenses and responsibilities were remarkably high for a young man in his early twenties:

I'm currently starting on probation pay which is only eleven dollars an hour. I'm finding because of my unique financial situation where I have huge [student loan] payments to make, and also because where I live it's government subsidized ... Based on how much I make, a portion of it, a quarter or a half of it has to go towards the rent of the apartment where my family is living. I keep the other job to help make my financial ends meet. That's why I'm keeping two jobs (Kent #691).

He lived with two younger brothers and his mother, who was paid a small amount by her siblings to care for his grandmother. His new job had quickly become their primary source of income. His life was very constrained and stressed.

Working two jobs is a bit tough, I guess. In the meantime, I'm trying to balance a lot of things. Trying to have a bit of a social life and also trying to look for other employment. I don't feel that the [call center] job fully utilizes my education because it is technical stuff over the phone, compared to what I studied. I also attend church. My weeks are pretty packed (Kent #691).

Scheduling Uncertainty

One in ten "permanent" workers did not have sufficient notice of their work assignment or shifts to adequately plan their workweek. This is a much smaller proportion than those in less permanent relationships, but it is still a considerable disruption for these workers. One in eight "permanent" workers reported that the notice they received of their work schedules significantly disrupted their ability to balance their home and work lives because it was difficult to plan their child care arrangements and other household responsibilities. A similar proportion said that short notice of schedules disrupted their ability to socialize.

One of Kent's biggest concerns about his new employer was scheduling. He found that not only was there not enough notice but that the schedule was inflexible, making it difficult to keep his commitment to his second job, and to do volunteer work.

They have too many unexpected shift changes. They don't consult us before they post shifts to their liking based on your availability. You can't normally say on your availability sheet that you want to work nine to five. I heard that will be rejected for lack of flexibility. I didn't really like that I needed only two Saturdays off to do my volunteer training but I unfortunately I couldn't get that, so it was pretty disappointing (Kent #691).

The unwillingness of some employers to provide scheduling certainty for their employees is linked to their unwillingness to pay for what they consider production "down time." For workers, however, the employer's "down time" is not necessarily time that they can use for their own purposes. The most invasive of this type of scheduling can be "on call" work. Of the full-time permanent workers who responded to our survey, 5.2 percent said that they were on call at least half the time, and one in ten of those who had *high employment strain* were on call all of the time.

We found a direct tie between *earnings* and *scheduling uncertainty* in "permanent" jobs when we interviewed homecare workers as part of a pilot study in 2002–2003. These workers were in unionized, reasonably stable relationships with their employers. Many worked part-time by choice, but the organization had recently agreed to a new arrangement whereby the company would try to provide full-time hours if a worker agreed to be available all the time. At the time of the interviews, those who agreed to this arrangement were getting more hours, but they were guaranteed only a minimum number of hours of work, and were paid only for the hours they worked: that is, they were "on call" all the time, but worked only when a client needed them. Compared to other full-time workers in the study, the *earnings uncertainty* of this group of "full-time" homecare workers was substantially higher; they did not receive paid sick days or other paid leaves, and they were not covered by health insurance or pension benefits (Lewchuk 2006a: 153). This same group of homecare workers also reported substantial *scheduling uncertainty*. Just over half knew their work schedule at least one week in advance. The other half had only a day's notice of how many hours they were expected to work.

EMPLOYMENT RELATIONSHIP EFFORT

One in five "permanent" workers in our study reported *employment relationship effort* greater than the median effort reported by workers in less permanent relationships. Much of their effort was related to keeping their jobs – doing extra tasks unrelated to the job description, dealing with harassment, and investing in unpaid training – the kind of issues that are often associated with workplace stress but rarely with the employment relationship itself. Seven percent reported that they were actively looking for work at least half the time. A surprising thirty-six percent said that they felt discrimination held them back from doing different work, either in their current workplace or in the labour market more generally.

It was very difficult for some of the workers we interviewed to look for better work. Tara, a full-time administrative assistant, was paid less than fourteen dollars an hour. She was not using her training in her current job and did not feel supported by her supervisor or colleagues. Moreover the pay was low, so over the previous year she had been looking for another job. Her husband had been a part-time and contract computer technician for a number of years and consequently it was her income that provided the household stability. They were raising two young children and she had responsibility for her adult brother who had a serious mental illness. Their financial situation was so tight that one unexpected incident could compromise their ability to cope, and ultimately that is what happened, several months before we spoke the second time. Tara had been in an accident in which her car was badly damaged. The insurance company wrote off the vehicle, but the settlement was not enough to replace it. Both she and her husband needed the car to get to work, and she did not have the finances to replace it, so the household was under extra strain. Her household responsibilities did not permit her to take an additional job (not that this is ever a great option), but even though it was always hard to find the time, she spent several hours each week looking for work by searching on-line for job ads. She knew that her job search was not as effective as it could be, but she did not have the time or the energy to do otherwise.

The homecare workers interviewed during the pilot phase of the project showed us that a range of extra *effort* associated with finding and keeping employment was required by some types of workers in permanent on-call relationships. This group worked in a large number of different locations and required constant learning and adaptation of a type that is not needed in most employment situations. They travelled an average of two or more hours each day without pay. They were constantly struggling to make their schedules more manageable. Michelle described the schedule she was working that month as follows:

[It] starts at seven in the morning and then the way the scheduling is set up makes the day very long for me because I start at seven and then I have a two-hour break and then I have an hour and then I travel. For me, I travel by bus and I walk, so I get to my client, I come back and I'm resting, but I'm not resting because I'm thinking 'OK, I have an hour now,' and it's not enough time for me to go home and you know, so I have to stay around until five, so I go get coffee or something. And on Mondays my day doesn't end until five thirty, so I am up at five o'clock in the morning and I get in the house at six (Focus Group, 1 December, 2003).

In addition to the strain caused by the irregular hours themselves, these homecare workers expended constant effort to stay in the good books of their clients, schedulers, and supervisors, so that they would be given more hours and the best possible assignments. Daily informal performance assessments by schedulers, supervisors, clients and their families affected where they would be sent next, the distance they had to travel, the unpaid time between appointments, and the type of clients they worked with. This type of effort is not required by most people who have a permanent commitment from an employer.

Denis, whose employment relationship was being restructured, exhibited another sort of effort related to working without commitments. When his employment status changed from permanent to a term-specific or a project-specific contract (that is, it became more fragile), he lost his ability to predict his income. The *effort* involved in maintaining his employment multiplied; while he continued to do a full-time job, he also had to take on a new set of tasks related to the immanent transition to a new job, including training, networking and job search. Denis and his partner went so far as to organize barbeques so that he could network with other people in his field. Work became harder because support amongst his colleagues dwindled as they left the company, and at home he and his wife had to renegotiate how they would support each other and their household.

Neelam was a fifty-year-old administrative worker who experienced a similar effort to keep employed. A year before our interview, the company for which she had worked for eighteen years closed the department she worked in. Because of the length of time she had been with the company, her employer made an effort to accommodate her, offering her a position in the shipping department. This new position paid less than her old one and had lower status within the company, in addition to which the new workspace was cold in the winter. Neelam took the position nevertheless because, as she said, "it's hard to get jobs when you're fifty" (Neelam #5760). The restructuring not only caused her distress, but because she really did not like her new position, it added to her employment *effort* the added task of regularly looking for a new job. She hadn't looked for work since her second child was born. She found searching the company's internal postings straightforward but not hopeful, but was quite challenged by the learning she needed to do in order to conduct an effective job search outside of her familiar context.

Several of the "permanent" workers we interviewed told us how they took on extra work to protect themselves from a very insecure work situation. Seven percent of our permanent full-time workers had more than one employer at the same time. Liana and Ye both took a second job as a "buffer," as did Kent, who we introduced earlier. Liana was an editor and web designer who had the unusual experience of being sought out and recruited into a full-time, permanent job during the summer of 2006. It was a break she had been looking for, and she was pleased. However, because she had seen enough uncertainty in her working life, she kept a part-time editing job for fourteen hours per week. The extra strain in her life over that period was that she worked fifty-five hours a week at two jobs. Her concern about the "permanence" of her new job proved to be well-founded. When we spoke the second time, she told us that seven months after she started, an American corporation bought her new employer and began a process of merging and lay-offs. Because she had just been hired, she was one of those laid off. Her part-time job provided her with a safety net.

Ye was a software engineer whose response to the uncertainty in his permanent job was to try to build his own safety net. He worked in a full-time position for the same company for six years, but over the year before we spoke, he had begun to build his own business as a consultant. He started with the company when it was an exciting, successful place to be, but it had been taken over by another company and doubled in size. Then it ran into difficulties.

> [T]he company itself isn't very stable. There are lots of companies in the same area that have gone under. Even senior people are now leaving voluntarily, including the company's CFO and some like manager level people slightly above me. Like, simultaneously, four of them gone just last month. So like there might be something going on, like restructuring or accounting scandal. Like, we had accounting investigation last year, but it turned out to be fine, but it caused a lot of worry too (Ye #2410).

When we talked about whether he was looking for another job, Ye told us that there were few permanent jobs in software engineering labour market, so he intended to become a self-employed contractor:

> But to get a similar job, full-time job, is not very easy, but not impossible either. Would probably take me two to three months if I look actively. However the same kind of job I'd get is also not very stable. I feel the only stable way to do it is to have your own business, that's why I have side projects going on, why I'm building my business (Ye #2410).

His strategy was to create another source of income that he had some control over, and he was spending an additional ten to twenty hours a week building a client base and working on their projects.

EMPLOYMENT RELATIONSHIP SUPPORT

The full-time permanent workers in the study were significantly more likely to have support at work and at home than most workers in more precarious positions. That said, almost one-quarter had no support outside of work, and one in five had no family support. Forty-two percent said they had help at work when they needed it, and almost half had friends at work. One in five was a member of a union, and even more (23.7 percent) were in workplaces where they had some access to the assistance of a union. Their incomes were much higher than those in more precarious positions, and they contributed the most to their household incomes.

Ye was concerned about the deterioration of support among his co-workers that developed as his employer began to run into difficulties and lay workers off.

I have fewer friends than I used to have, with co-workers. Like, in the first two, three years I felt a sense of belonging. Now, I don't really, it is less so now. We [used to] go for lunch together (Ye #2410).

There was also a sense of weakening commitment from management. Ye reflected;

They've become less and less committed ... At the beginning they would spend a lot of money to throw nice parties; now they are cheaper. They would spend money on wine and nice restaurants, and now they just give us pizza ... and the new HR person doesn't know us, it is becoming very mechanical (Ye #2410).

Denis made it clear that he too had lost critical support at work. His previously cohesive department began to break up, so he had fewer colleagues and dramatically less support in his workplace. His company was not assuring any of the employees on layoff notice that they would receive special training or a separation package at the time of the layoff, and he was feeling very alone there. Denis said it took everyone in the department two or three months to learn how to minimize the effect their employment uncertainty had on their ability to focus on the job. His colleagues were a tight group who socialized together, worked hard together, and negotiated as a group with management around issues related to their department. But the support they provided for each other had deteriorated; some had already left and the rest were preparing to say goodbye to each other and to their clients. Denis valued his relationships with his co-workers and did not want to work without them.

> I like the idea of making friends; you know building a relationship with people at work. And when you're a contractor you change jobs, it could be a six month contract, it could be a year, it could be nine months, three months ... So I don't really like that (Denis #216).

Denis's situation also illustrates how, as the employment relationship becomes more precarious, the management of employment, income, schedule, and other uncertainties becomes a regular feature of, and creates new stresses in, the dynamics between couples, their dependents, and their friends. Denis and his wife had difficult conversations about how they would manage the financial insecurity and disruption of their situation. Increasingly their home, rather than his workplace, was where he was having strategic conversations about what to do next. Together he and his wife were dealing with their joint anxiety and his sleep disruption. She agreed to re-think her unpaid contribution to their household and how they cared for their two children, and was preparing to re-enter the workforce. He was fortunate that she was supportive, although she was not able to provide them with financial support to ride through his insecurity.

HEALTH, EMPLOYMENT STRAIN AND PERMANENT EMPLOYMENT

As we noted earlier, one in five permanent full-time workers experienced both the effort and uncertainty that combine to create *high employment strain* which, in turn, is associated with negative health. This *high employment strain* group was particularly likely to feel the effects of working full-time while pursuing strategies to provide a safety net through a job search or a second job. The impact of this strain on workers' health and well-being was evident. Almost half were exhausted after work most days, and three in ten worked in pain at least half the time. Over sixty percent found that everything was an effort on most days, which is an indicator that workers were feeling discouraged and depressed. Proportionately more workers in this group reported poor mental health than those in other clusters of workers in less permanent relationships.

The workers we interviewed described the particular ways that their health was affected by the combination of the stresses in the full-time work itself, and the *uncertainty* and *effort* in the employment relationship. Denis's layoff notice negatively affected his heart arrhythmia and his sleep. Liana said that she was not getting enough sleep. Kent had gained weight because he wasn't able to exercise as much and was eating junk food. Towards the end of our interview he said, "I think it might be detrimental to my mental health to work at this job for too long" (Kent #691).

After at least a year of working long hours each week, which isolated her from friends and family, Tanisha experienced a serious deterioration in her social life and access to support. Just before our conversation, she also had a health crisis:

I had a panic attack last Sunday. I didn't want to go to work on Monday morning. I was bowling, I was looking around and saw that everyone was friends with each other and I turn around and see that the only person I'm really friends with there is my boyfriend and his friends, I don't really have friends of my own, and everyone else is there socializing and talking about going out later and I haven't even gone shopping in such a long time, I don't even know what the new styles, things like that, simple things (Tanisha #3064).

Her low income and need for support was also keeping her in a relationship that was not good for her – towards the end of our conversation, when she was feeling more comfortable, she told us that she wouldn't be living with that boyfriend if her work situation hadn't been so bad.

CONCLUSION

This chapter has shown that precariousness and uncertainty may exist in what are usually understood to be the core, "good" jobs in industrialized economies: permanent, full-time jobs. Our study shows that approximately one in five workers in permanent full-time employment relationships are unable to make plans based on their current income, are uncertain about their employment future, and are investing extra effort in order to get and/or keep work. Many in this group also experience both a withdrawal of support at work and in their households, and negative effects on their health

The experiences of workers in this study suggest that the uncertainties in their employment relationships result from several features of contemporary workplaces. Layoffs and restructuring have targeted the core of permanent jobs in many workplaces and the associated rumours have introduced a component of uncertainty into many "permanent" jobs. Employers have created tiers of flexibility to lower costs and protect themselves from business cycles; workers experience these tiers as gradients of uncertainty. Whether the uncertainty is created by threats of layoffs, or no guarantee of hours, or by low wages with few benefits, workers must maintain full-time jobs while worrying about their future income and therefore invest effort getting better jobs, or even take on additional jobs.

The stories of *employment uncertainty*, *effort getting and keeping work*, and dwindling *support* that are presented in this chapter will be echoed in the chapters that follow. Their importance here is that they are found among permanent full-time workers.

7

Sustainable, Less Permanent Employment

To a certain extent, where I start a week, where I end a week, there's flexibility there. I do my research, I do my writing. So they're long days, but *they're my day* ... For me it's freedom. I get to pick and choose. I don't get a call saying I have to go in and do someone else's class because it's in trouble. I can choose to say, yes I'll do it or no, I don't want to do it. I don't have to ask, can I do it? ... So it's the freedom, right? (Cayla #5442).

INTRODUCTION

Our study identified a cluster of workers able to benefit from the flexibility that can come from working outside a permanent, full-time employment arrangement. We termed the work in this cluster *sustainable, less permanent employment*. It represents the smallest of the three categories of less permanent employment discussed in this volume. The characteristics of this cluster are markedly differ-ent from the other two clusters, and are often more similar to those of permanent, full-time employment relationships. For example, although the workers we interviewed in *sustainable, less permanent employment* were not in permanent contractual relationships, they had been able to preserve or reconfigure employment commitments between themselves and their clients or employers. Fairly strong employment commitments combined with high levels of *employment relationship support* buffered these workers from the negative impact of *employment relationship uncertainty*. Consequently, the overall health and well-being of these workers was good – often even better than those in permanent, full-time employment.

Our findings seem to support claims made by some researchers regarding the positive consequences of employment shifts for both employers and workers (see, for example, Pink 2001) that less permanent forms of employment allow workers to have more fulfilling work, more freedom in both their work and personal lives, and more control over their working hours and career direction. But even though our study did identify some workers who were clearly benefiting from less permanent employment, our research findings lead us to a substantially different overall argument. We contend that workers who benefit from less permanent employment are in the minority, and the conditions that allow them to benefit from flexibility are not easily replicated. A particular set of factors, including high *employment relationship support*, seem to be necessary for less permanent employment to be sustainable, much less beneficial, for workers. Furthermore, many of these supports are slowly eroding, making it increasingly difficult for such employment to be a healthy and advantageous option.

Four overall claims are advanced in this chapter. First, not all workers in less permanent employment relationships are precarious. Some, albeit a small minority, are able to enjoy the benefits that come with working outside permanent, full-time employment relationships. Second, workers' ability to preserve or reconfigure employment commitments is key to the sustainability of their working arrangements. Third, a specific set of circumstances and forms of support make it possible for these workers to function, even thrive, in an employment environment of relatively *high uncertainty*. However, these conditions are not easy to replicate, especially in the current economic and policy context as permanent employment with benefits becomes less common and social safety nets are eroding. Therefore our fourth claim is that there are limits to the growth potential of *sustainable, less permanent employment relationships*.

WORKERS IN SUSTAINABLE, LESS PERMANENT EMPLOYMENT RELATIONSHIPS: A PROFILE

Workers in this cluster are a privileged group amongst those in less permanent employment relationships in that they are able to have the benefits of flexibility and often have better overall health and employment satisfaction than many workers in full-time, permanent employment relationships. This cluster makes up a small minority (seventeen percent) of those we interviewed. As one of the workers interviewed noted: "I guess I'm one of the lucky ones" (Cayla #5442).

Four key characteristics differentiate this cluster from the other two clusters of less permanent workers. First, workers had chosen this type of employment, were not looking for more permanent work, and planned to continue working in this manner for the long-term. Second, although workers generally reported high levels of *employment relationship uncertainty*, they put little effort into getting and keeping work, and were able to function well in this environment of relatively high uncertainty. Third, this cluster had relatively high levels of control over their workload, working time, and schedules. Finally, this cluster benefitted from high levels of *employment relationship support*; most frequently from *individual* or *household economic support*, although sometimes from work networks. *Employment relationship support* served to buffer these workers against the employment insecurity generally associated with less permanent employment. The overall result is that these workers benefitted from working in less permanent employment, and reported relatively good health and overall well-being for themselves and their families. Cayla, a fifty-year-old, self-employed, contract university lecturer, is representative of workers in this cluster.

PROFILING A SUSTAINABLE, LESS PERMANENT EMPLOYMENT RELATIONSHIP: CAYLA'S STORY[1]

Cayla lived with her partner – an individual with a full-time, permanent job – and their two teenagers. After almost a decade as a permanent, full-time, senior manager in a large company, Cayla decided she wanted a career change. She returned to university to complete a graduate degree and then chose to become a sessional lecturer – self-employed, working on contract – rather than pursue permanent, tenure-track positions. In contrast to the high stress, long hours, and frequent overtime of her previous job, she reported that her current

---

1 Cayla #5442.

employment situation offered her more control over her workload, her hours, and her schedule. She reported having more freedom and flexibility in her schedule, more time for her family and for leisure activities such as exercise, and significantly less stress in her work life. Cayla also told us that her health and work-life balance was good: in fact, much better than when she was in permanent employment.

Although her employment was not permanent, she had established good working relationships with several universities. As a result of the specialized courses she was teaching, as well as her level of seniority, she was regularly offered the same or similar courses each year, which gave her a degree of control over her schedule. Cayla reported having fairly strong commitments from her employers while also having the freedom and flexibility to pursue research and writing projects at her own pace. "Each term I know, at least with one institution, maybe with two institutions, that I'm guaranteed at least two courses a term." As a result, Cayla said that she rarely worried about future employment and spent little time looking for work. She explained the benefits of her employment thus:

> I chose not to go tenure track ... after having worked in senior management and in administration I didn't want to have to go back into spending most of my time on administration and less of what I wanted to do. Now, I can pick and choose what I want. I have flexibility in my days; flexibility in arranging the marking and the due date of assignments within weeks and days. I love it. I work hard, but I really enjoy it (Cayla #5442).

She did note that there are some challenges associated with less permanent employment. "The disadvantages? Well, I don't get a pay cheque every two weeks or monthly so I don't have that. Benefits can be a problem at times because I don't have steady benefits." While her husband's income covered the main household expenses, her teaching income was still necessary for paying bills and supporting their two teenage children.

> Sometimes I am concerned, I do like to know where my money's coming in the next term ... I guess that the flexibility I have as far as finances is that I know I don't have a mortgage payment to make this month and, if I don't get this course, I

don't have to worry. But I still have bills; there's still our household and recurring bills with two girls (Cayla #5442).

Nonetheless it was clear that high levels of *individual* and *household economic support* buffered Cayla from *employment relationship uncertainty* and allowed her to make choices and take risks surrounding her work. Her partner had a permanent, well-paid, full-time job that provided health benefits to her and her children. She also earned a higher salary than most contract lecturers. In addition, she entered this type of work after many years in permanent employment with benefits, and therefore had savings and investments that she could draw on if necessary. Further, Cayla had established work networks and research relationships with other academics that provided her with a sense of community and support. Given all these factors, Cayla's situation does not typify that of most contract lecturers. Nonetheless, like them, and like most workers in this cluster, Cayla successfully became a "free agent," maximizing her skills in a labour market that encourages "working without commitments."

Demographics and Occupational Categories

While there was an equal gender split, workers in this cluster were marginally older than in others, and several were in the latter stages of their careers. No one was under twenty-five and almost a quarter was fifty or older. A range of sectors and occupations were represented in this cluster, including an accountant, a geologist, a fork-lift operator, an engineer, a multi-level marketer, a sessional university instructor, a courier, a contract bank employee, a researcher, and a few contract part-time teachers. For the most part they were working in their chosen occupations, and in employment for which they had extensive skills and training. Those not working in their trained occupations were doing work that they had chosen; work that interested them or had previously been a hobby. Furthermore, many workers had acquired additional skills that allowed them to successfully navigate working independently, either on contract, or as a self-employed person.

   This issue of choice sharply differentiates this cluster from both the *unsustainable* and *on a path* cluster. Everyone in this cluster had chosen this type of employment relationship, and several workers had taken early retirement or had voluntarily left full-time, permanent employment in order to work more independently. Many found that working in less permanent employment provided less stress and allowed them more time for leisure activities. A few women in the cluster said that domestic responsibilities, child rearing in particular, had influenced their employment choice, and that contract work allowed them greater flexibility and more time for their families.

A twenty-nine-year-old self-employed computer programmer reflected the attitude of most workers in this cluster: "How long will I work like this? As long as I can; I have no plans to do anything else" (Brian #1686). Another individual had chosen to take early retirement (at age fifty) from his full-time, permanent job in order to turn a hobby collecting sports information into a new career as a self-employed contract researcher. He was in his fourth year doing this type of contract work when we interviewed him, and had no plans to do anything else. According to him, "I don't call it work actually; it is fun!" (Perry #5271). As will be discussed below, the issue of choice versus compulsion is important to workers' enjoyment of and control over their work, and therefore to their overall health and well-being.

Self-Employed or Disguised Employment Relationships?

A key difference between this cluster and the other two is the degree of employment commitment between workers and their clients / employers. In contrast to the other clusters, workers in the *sustainable* cluster were in relationships with fairly strong levels of commitment. In contrast to the large number of temporary workers in the *unsustainable* cluster, only one person in the *sustainable* cluster was employed through a temporary employment agency and many were self-employed. A number of self-employed and short term contract workers in the *sustainable* cluster received ongoing work from clients and were quite embedded in their clients' business operations. In most cases, workers were supervised or reported directly to someone in the company, received all or most of their work from one client, and were closely involved with the company's ongoing projects. In fact, the employment relationship between many self-employed workers in the *sustainable* cluster fits what the International Labour Organisation (ILO) refers to as "disguised employment relationships"

(International Labour Office (ILO) 2003; ILO 2007). According to the ILO, a "disguised employment relationship occurs when the employer treats an individual as other than an employee in a manner that hides his or her true legal status as an employee, and ... situations can arise where contractual arrangements have the effect of depriving workers of the protection they are due" (ILO 2007: 55). False self-employment and the false provision of services are listed as two examples of disguised employment. Attention focused on this issue by the ILO and member states stems from concerns that workers are increasingly falling outside regulatory protection.

The ILO's research as well as other studies suggests that disguised employment relationships are growing in Canada and may be found in various forms of less permanent employment. Our study supports these claims; we found workers in disguised employment relationships in all three clusters. However, most such workers were concentrated in the *unsustainable* and *sustainable* clusters. As will be discussed in chapter 9, and consistent with the ILO's research, those in *unsustainable, less permanent employment relationships* in our study were negatively impacted by the disguised nature of their employment relationships because it deprived them of rights, benefits, and protections. In general, workers' health and well-being suffered as a result of being constantly exposed to high levels of stress associated with less permanent employment, and being deprived of employment benefits. In contrast, being in disguised employment relationships did not negatively impact those in the *sustainable* cluster because these workers had alternative sources of support and access to employment benefits. In fact, the disguised nature of their relationship meant that they had quite high levels of commitment for ongoing and future work despite not having a formal or permanent employment relationship. As will be discussed in more detail throughout this chapter, the higher levels of commitment, combined with alternative sources of support, allowed these workers to actually *benefit* from less permanent employment arrangements.

A good example of a "disguised" employment relationship is that of Brian, a twenty-nine-year-old, self-employed computer programmer working on continuous, six-month contracts. Brian had been working with the same large financial institution for over five years; the client set his working hours, which were the same as those of the company's regular employees, and determined when Brian could take time off. Although he considered himself self-employed, Brian's situation fit the ILO's definition of a "disguised employment relationship" since he expected the institution to continue renewing his contracts, worked on their premises and under their supervision, and was not looking for work from anyone else.

From our perspective, the issue is not necessarily whether a relationship like Brian's is "disguised" or not, but if and how commitments are made in the absence of a standard employment contract. We are also interested in understanding how workers like Brian access support and protection in order to benefit from working in less permanent employment. Brian's experiences are indicative of many self-employed workers' experiences in this cluster. While not having a permanent contract, he was nonetheless in a relationship with fairly strong commitments. Not only was his work quite embedded in his client's core activities, but he had built up strong workplace networks, considered his client's employees to be his colleagues, and expected to have ongoing work from this client. He earned a good salary, and was able to save and invest most of it because he lived with his parents. Brian accessed workplace support from friends at the company and from informal networks of other self-employed computer programmers. In addition to provincial health care coverage, he also had private insurance. Brian said that he liked working in this way and had no desire to look for more permanent employment.

> The money is better ... I can write off my expenses and there are fewer deductions. It is good for me. I'm not looking for other work, no need to. I've been at this [institution] for over five years now; I can't see that the work will dry up, they need me, the work is ongoing, [they] always need this type of computer work (Brian #1686).

However, despite Brian's confidence that his employment relationship would continue, it is important to note that his client could terminate his employment by simply not renewing his contract. Our findings also support the argument made by Vosko and others that greater attention needs to be paid to variations within self-employment. Only a minority of the self-employed workers in our study benefited from this type of employment arrangement; mainly those who had fairly strong commitments of ongoing work from their clients. The particular set of circumstances and supports that allow workers in the *sustainable* cluster to benefit from this employment situation are discussed below.

SUSTAINABLE, LESS PERMANENT EMPLOYMENT: PRECARIOUS OR NOT?

Differences between this cluster and the *unsustainable* and *on a path* clusters leads to an important question: are these workers really precarious? Research on precarious employment has tended to describe all workers in non-permanent employment as precarious. At the same time, employment insecurity has been an essential aspect of scholars' analysis of precariousness (Rubery et al. 2002).

While researchers' understanding of employment insecurity has changed and expanded in recent years, Rogers' analysis has continued to inform research on insecurity and precariousness. According to Rogers, four key issues can be used to establish whether employment is precarious (Rogers 1989). These are: certainty of continued employment; control over the labour process and working conditions such as wages and work-pace; the degree of regulatory protection in terms of employment standards legislation, and / or coverage under collective bargaining law or other forms of union representation; and income levels (that is, whether the wage is sufficient to maintain the worker and any dependents) (Rogers 1989). Although workers in the *sustainable* cluster have some degree of income uncertainty, they are quite certain that they will have continued employment. They also exercise control over their workload and the conditions under which they work. Further, individual incomes – often combined with savings or benefits carried over from other sources – are sufficient to maintain them and their dependents.

Using these criteria, workers in the *sustainable* cluster should not be considered precarious. Their employment is not permanent, but it is not necessarily precarious. How and why less permanent employment becomes unsustainable and precarious for some workers, while other workers benefit from this type of employment relationship is a key issue in our study. Our model's focus on the characteristics of the employment relationship explores the ways in which commitments between employers and employees are changing and can be reconfigured in ways that prevent less permanent employment from becoming precarious. It is to these issues that we now turn.

EMPLOYMENT RELATIONSHIP UNCERTAINTY

Some indicators of the sustainability of this cluster's employment relationships are evident in issues related to *employment relationship uncertainty*. In general, those in the *sustainable* cluster reported having more certain future employment, and much more predictable incomes and schedules, than either of the other two clusters of workers in less permanent employment.

Employment Fragility

Workers in the *sustainable* cluster are far more likely to have longer employment contracts than the other two less permanent clusters. While sixty-seven percent of the *on a path* and fifty percent of the *unsustainable* cluster reported that their average job lasted less than six months, only twenty-three percent of the *sustainable* cluster reported having these short contracts. However, the duration of employment does not necessarily explain the overall confidence that most workers in the *sustainable* cluster appeared to have with regard to future employment. Interviews helped us understand the concrete ways in which these workers had created relationships with reasonably high levels of employment certainty. This certainty often came when these workers did work that required a local presence, or had specialized skills, and/or had developed close relationships with core clients.

In many cases, workers had strong networks, specialized training, and a level of expertise in high demand or well-suited to a niche market. For example, the geologist, the engineer, the university contract lecturer, and both contract researchers all felt certain about future employment due to their specialized skill sets. One of our respondents, Zevi, provides a good example of the employment security that can come from having specialized skills and a core group of clients. A forty-four-year-old, self-employed geological consultant, Zevi sold and installed mining and geophysical equipment, as well as instructing others about how to use it. He had been working in this capacity since 1989; global clients and networks supplied him with work on a regular basis. His specialized skill set, combined with his strong global networks, meant that he received continuous contracts with a core group of clients and felt confident about future employment.

Another person we interviewed, Perry, a fifty-four-year-old, self-employed media researcher, had similar confidence about future employment for precisely the same reasons. According to him:

> when you have the expertise in an area ... and you have other contract offers, you can pick and choose. And if something [the pay] is outrageous for you, you don't have to take it because invariably they will come back to you because they need you (Perry #5271).

Other workers we interviewed benefited from having a few core clients, and working in sectors or occupations that were relatively embedded in the local economy (thus being reasonably protected from competitive pressures from globalization). Often, workers had worked for the same client or groups of clients for many years in contracts that were constantly renewed. The other clusters of less permanent workers were exposed to highly competitive labour markets, but the *sustainable* cluster often relied on local clients and was made up of workers in occupations that required local residency. For example, Perry had a few core clients that regularly hired him on quite lengthy contracts (longer than six months), and his work tended to require locally based archival research. Julianne, a forty-year-old self-employed health researcher also worked on locally based health research projects in the city. Her skill set and clients' need for a locally based individual with experience and networks in the sector provided her quite a high degree of employment stability.

Ralph, a thirty-nine-year-old self-employed courier, provides another good example of a worker who developed ongoing relationships with fairly strong commitments with local clients. For the last twenty years, Ralph received work from two courier companies on an on-call basis, and all his income came from this work. Although technically he was not an employee of either company and therefore did not have formalized, permanent work, he had long-term relationships with people at the companies and saw his clients as his employers.

The dispatchers from different carrier companies, I know them for twenty years ... I know they are friends of mine ... So you can put yourself on-call for nights or weekends, whatever you want ... They will call you and say okay, go and get this one here (Ralph #5444).

Ralph was confident that his relationship with the companies would continue for as long as he chose, largely as a result of his ongoing relationship with both companies and the fact that courier companies need local drivers that they know and can trust.

Earnings Uncertainty

In contrast to the other two clusters of workers in less permanent relationships, workers in the *sustainable* cluster were able to predict earnings and plan for the future. This reveals the higher level of commitments in their employment relationships. Very few (only eight percent) in the cluster said that they were not paid on time, or were paid a different amount than what they expected. As with workers in permanent employment relationships, most (eighty-five percent) in *sustainable* employment said that they could anticipate that their income would be the same in six months. However, like other workers in less permanent relationships, few in the *sustainable* cluster were covered by company pensions or had paid sick benefits, but unlike the others the majority (seventy percent) was entitled to some benefits as a result of another household member's paid employment. On the whole, those in *sustainable* employment relationships reported an ability to plan their future income similar to those in more permanent employment relationships.

Interviews demonstrated that the more predictable earnings of workers in the *sustainable* cluster contributed to their positive experiences with less permanent employment. Several workers noted that they could make holiday plans quite far in advance because of their predictable incomes and schedules. Take Abby, a fifty-nine-year-old self-employed individual with regular ongoing administrative work from a single real estate agency. When we interviewed her, she had been working from home this way, on a variable schedule, for over five years. The agency contacted her on Monday mornings with her tasks for each week. While her hours varied during different times of the year, she could generally predict when she would be busy and what income she would make from month to month. This certainty helped her plan family vacations ahead of time.

> Because I still have family overseas and we like to plan our holidays in advance, we try to book off the time, my husband books off the time from work ... I usually try to plan my time off when he [the realtor] is away or when the work is slow, this is no problem (Abby #5078).

Similar predictability was what allowed Brian, the self-employed computer programmer, to save enough money for a down payment on a house and get ready to move out of his parents' home. Since the bank gave him a mortgage, they must have been confident that his employment would continue despite his not having a permanent contract. As he put it:

> I've saved a lot, but yeah, sure, it is a little scary moving out and taking on a mortgage when I'm a contractor. It isn't the same as having a regular job. ... but I'm fine, things are good (Brian #1686).

Julianne, a researcher on grant-funded research for several health organizations, benefitted from having a few core, multi-year projects, including one in which she was the research coordinator. When we interviewed her, she was working on a large, multi-year contract and feeling confident about her income for the next several years. Like most workers in this cluster, she felt that having ongoing contracts gave her income certainty, and that this certainty allows her to plan for her future.

Scheduling Uncertainty

Low levels of *scheduling uncertainty* also differentiated this cluster from the others. Although workers reported to being on-call almost as frequently as other workers in less permanent employment relationships, they were able to exert far more control over their schedules and had fewer problems planning their domestic responsibilities around their work. In fact, the *sustainable* cluster reported to less *uncertainty* on these indicators than did the full-time, perma-nent cluster. For instance, survey data shows that very few (only eight percent) in the *sustainable* cluster reported that they received insufficient notice to plan their workweek and to plan household responsibilities. However, as with the other "less permanent" clus-ters, almost a quarter of this cluster reported that they received insufficient notice to plan social activities. Interview material sug-gests that this *scheduling uncertainty* stems from spontaneous demands from clients that require workers to work on the week-ends or during unplanned times during the week.

Several interviewees reflected that they could predict and often control their work schedule and workload due to their long-term relationships with key clients. For example, the English as a second language (ESL) teacher, having taught the same language classes on Saturday for several years, was able to predict exactly how many classroom hours she would have and how long it would take her to prepare for them. Most others in this cluster noted that they could generally predict and control their hours. Brian, the computer pro-grammer, told us that, "unless there is something urgent that I need to finish, I usually work just the regular days, you know, regular nine to five hours" (Brian #1686). Abby's ongoing work relationship with a real estate agency also resulted in her having predictable hours.

I generally know what work I need to do, he will contact me at the beginning of the work week or in the morning and let me know if there is anything in particular I need to be doing, other-wise I generally know what I need to do. So I'm working at home and I can balance my work with other things I need to do at home. I do enjoy this work (Abby #5078).

Not only were their schedules generally predictable, but workers in this cluster said they had control over their hours. Danny's experi-ences with both permanent and contract work led him to believe that he had more control and flexibility as a contractor than as a permanent employee.

As a permanent employee, you worked standard hours but you don't necessarily have a say in the number of hours you have to work and your pay, so as a part-timer doing contract work you can have more control in this area. And there is better compensation for more hours worked sometimes as a contractor. And between contracts you can spend time as you wish" (Danny #2005).

Perry, the self-employed researcher, and many other workers in this cluster, shared Danny's experiences.

Freedom. I almost always make my own hours, unless there is a meeting I have to go to. I don't have to get up early in the morning and stay there a certain time (Perry #5271).

Of course these workers were not immune to times when their workloads were heavy or unpredictable. Some noted that they did have times when they took on too many contracts or a client's expectations changed. However, most reported that they were able to regain control over their schedules or had support they could draw on during these busy patches. Julianne, one of the contract researchers, cut back her hours to get her work-life balance back.

In 2000, I got myself in a bit of a pickle where I was invoicing sixty hours a week and I only had part-time day care for my kids. That was completely insane. And after going through that I swore, I promised myself, that I would never take on so many projects at once ... I was making great money but I was bitchy, you know, like I was strung out and it just wasn't worth it ... Now that I'm working a shorter work day with my three-year contract ... that's all good, so I can be home after school and I'm not so run around (Julianne #5703).

Several workers who had previously had full-time, permanent employment noted that their quality of life improved when they shifted to less permanent employment. Cayla told us that she had much more control over her time as a contract lecturer – and hence more leisure time – than she did in her previous career as a full-time, permanent worker. Danny, a thirty-nine-year-old software design consultant, had worked in both permanent and contract positions. He said that when employed in permanent positions he had to demonstrate his commitment by working long hours, and by being available for emergency calls. In contrast, as a consultant, he did not feel obligated to work such long hours, or to be on call to problem-solve. He offered these insights:

There is a trade-off; permanent full-timers get the short end of the stick in some ways. In turn for them having the certainty of a full-time position, they wind up paying for more encroachment in their personal life, such as having to carry pagers and doing extra work (Danny #2005).

EMPLOYMENT RELATIONSHIP EFFORT

A key characteristic of this cluster's employment relationship is their low *employment effort*. On most *effort* indicators, the *sustainable* cluster scores better than the other clusters, including the permanent, full-time cluster. Survey and interview material revealed that this cluster spent relatively little time and effort finding and keeping work. Perry, a self-employed researcher, spent virtually no time looking for work. Because he was so closely connected to several clients and to a larger network of people in his field of work, he said the work usually came to him. "If you see something that you like, you let them know you are around so that is searching I suppose, but not searching by saying 'I need work, what do you have for me?'" (Perry #5271).

However, other workers in this cluster did take actions that they felt would contribute to keeping employed, such as maintaining networks and engaging in unpaid training. In contrast to the other clusters, those in *sustainable* employment said that these activities did not add stress to their workload and were not decisive in securing future employment. Further, in comparison to the *on a path* cluster, workers in the *sustainable* cluster saw training as one way of remaining competitive, but not as a requirement for ensuring future or more permanent employment. For instance, Cayla noted that she continuously improved her skills to stay up-to-date and also to position herself for future teaching contracts. She said: "I'm upgraded, I need to have the little edge that maybe someone else doesn't have" (Cayla #5442). Brian, the contract computer programmer, told us that his unpaid training is just part of what he needed to do and that he enjoyed it. "I do about fifteen hours a month; read books, read stuff on the internet; talk to friends and other people in the industry, just stuff like that" (Brian #1686).

Workers in this cluster also reported low levels of harassment and discrimination in their working relationships. According to the survey data, none of the workers in this cluster faced harassment by supervisors or co-workers, and only a few reported that discrimination was a barrier to getting work. Interviews confirmed that harassment and discrimination were rarely an issue for these workers; their ability to easily secure other contracts and relatively high levels of control over their working conditions and environment meant that they simply would not accept contracts from clients that treated them poorly. In general, this cluster also experienced lower levels of effort with regard to demands from multiple employers and multiple worksites.

Overall, lower levels of *employment relationship effort* are linked to higher overall employment certainty. Limited effort is required to secure future contracts because workers have ongoing work from a few key clients, because they have specialized skills, or because they are more embedded in the local labour market. In general, *sustainable* workers have built commitments into their employment relationships, yet are able to maintain a degree of independence that places them outside the ongoing evaluation process often associated with less permanent employment relationships. Brian's lack of concern regarding future employment sum up the feelings of most workers in this cluster.

I have a lot of experience now at the company, and it's cheaper for them to have so many of us on contract. And, there are other systems we need to work on ... I'm not really concerned; my work is good, I'm never late with my projects and I get along with the managers (Brian #1686).

EMPLOYMENT RELATIONSHIP SUPPORT

Support is central to the sustainability of less permanent employment. Survey data shows that the *sustainable* cluster reported the highest average levels of support, and higher levels of *union* and *household economic support* than the other two clusters. For instance, these workers were almost three times more likely to have *family support* than the *unsustainable* cluster. They were also more likely to have support at work, and access to employment benefits. Perhaps most significantly, workers in the *sustainable* cluster had much higher individual incomes themselves, and came from households with the highest average earnings. That workers in *sustainable* relationships earn a significant proportion of their households' income challenges the assumption that workers in less permanent relationships are always the secondary earners in their families. And of course, high household incomes and greater access to employment benefits greatly contributes to the sustainability of this cluster.

Interviews revealed that the sustainability of less permanent employment for this cluster was shaped by the nature, form, and sustainability of support – not just by the level and degree of support. In contrast to the other two clusters, those in *sustainable* employment benefited from three key forms of support: (1) secure and ongoing support from friends, family, or household members; (2) support from formal and informal work networks; and (3) support in the form of benefit entitlements associated with a previous periods of permanent employment or provided as a result of another household member's permanent employment. For most workers in the *sustainable* cluster, these three sources of support buffered them from negative aspects of less permanent employment and allowed them to make choices and take risks in their lives.

First, workers had support from friends and family. Some were living at home and had ongoing emotional and financial support from their family. For instance, Brian lived at home for the first five years of working as a self-employed computer programmer. He said that he wanted to stay there while he established himself in the industry, and so he could save money to buy a new condo. In addition, he also benefited from having friends doing similar work and drew on their knowledge and support when he needed it.

> My parents covered most of the bills, I had my own money for going out, but I was mostly saving to buy a place ... And support from friends? Yes, I have lots of friends, many work doing similar work, we talk about work sometimes, or just hang out – have some friends at work, and I get along well with my manager so can talk to him if I need to (Brian #1686).

Similarly, Ralph, the thirty-nine-year-old self-employed courier, lived with his parents in a house they co-owned without a mortgage. He acknowledged that his ability to remain self-employed for almost twenty years was largely due to having financial security and support from his family.

Others had strong and consistent sources of *individual support* that helped them establish themselves in the labour market. Julianne told us that although she had been the primary income-earner for her household for almost three years, her husband's support was critical to her establishing herself as a contract researcher.

> When I started doing this, my husband was in a salaried position with a company, so we were all completely cool about this because my salary was just gravy, so I could work ten hours a week or I could work sixty hours a week and it was all bonus. We were living on his salary, so everything was fine (Julianne #5703).

Similarly, Danny, the self-employed software designer, relied on his wife's income when he first began working on short-term contracts. "My wife said explicitly not to worry about not being without work 'cause we could wait it out on her salary, and we have money in the bank to provide a parachute" (Danny #2005).

Phil, a forklift operator who had been working through a temporary employment agency for almost fifteen years prior to our interview, also helped his wife with her business. Her income provided ongoing financial stability for their household, thus allowing him to accept only those temporary jobs he liked. Also, he could choose to work with his wife when she was busy or if the temp agency had not supplied him with work. This situation suited them as a couple, and buffered him, as an individual, from the negative aspects of working for a temporary agency. He told us:

> My wife, she owns a business and when things would quiet down with her, I'd go to the temporary agency to work. She's in her tenth year now ... She is always busy in the winter so I stay at home and work with her. I do deliveries and all that; help her out with everything and all that. And in the summertime when it quiets down, she might have like two or three weddings, which she mostly does on her own, then I'll go work. In many ways, [the temp agency] is really backup in case things slow down (Phil #5543).

Zevi, the self-employed geologist, had strong emotional support and some financial stability from his wife and could rely on financial assistance from friends.

> And there is always, if everything goes bad, there is always friends. And I did, yes, I've been in the situations where, sort of the cash flow crashed. Well as I said, it's good to have friends. With real friends you don't have to explain too much, they can guess from. I remember one of those situations where, it was quite a few years ago, and I called my buddy in, I don't know where he was at that time, New Zealand, I think. He said, oh nice to hear you, what's up. I said, oh not much I just wanted to say hi. He says, well, I can do five thousand, no more. And the next day I had the money in my bank account. I didn't have to say nothing (Zevi #1077).

In addition, several workers had built up support structures outside the traditional workplace, generally loose networks of people working in similar employment arrangements. Brian told us that many of his friends were working the way he did, so they regularly supported each other. For instance, they met to talk about projects or work issues. Perry said that he belonged to informal networks with other researchers working on similar projects. At the same time, his contracts were generally long enough that he could access some support at work without getting too drawn into what he called "typical office politics and admin tasks." Drawing on his twenty-nine years of experience in the public sector, he said that he preferred informal networks and temporary forms of work support:

> I worked full-time and I know what it's like there and I know the politics that can go on, and compare my work as a free-lancer; as a freelancer you are not there long enough to get involved (Perry #5271).

Other workers with long-standing relationships with key clients had more formal sources of support from their workplaces. Abby's five-year employment situation with the real estate agency meant she did not hesitate to call the office if she needed assistance. "If I have a question or something like that, I'll just phone the office, if he isn't there, then I can sometimes talk to someone else. I know most of the people in the office" (Abby #5078). Cayla also said that her ongoing relationship with some institutions meant that she could count on support.

> I've been there a while. I get a computer card and I get access to a few other things and they support me. They support me; they support my research and my educational needs within their means, within the department (Cayla #5442).

Finally, many workers in this cluster had employment benefits from another family member, usually their partner, or had benefits from previous permanent employment relationships. A number of workers had extended medical coverage for themselves and their children from their partner's full-time, permanent employment. Others had personal savings, investments, or other sources of financial security such as home ownership. Several others were collecting pensions or other benefits from their previous jobs. Two workers – one of whom had worked in the public sector for twenty-nine years – still had health coverage from their previous jobs; they had been able to retain these benefits when they took early retirement. This, according to them, was critical to their ability to keep working with limited commitments. One individual put it bluntly: "Sure, if I didn't have the benefits [from his previous permanent job] I would have to take a full-time job" (Perry #5271).

EMPLOYMENT STRAIN AND HEALTH

It is no surprise that workers in this cluster report having good overall health; much better than those in the other non-permanent clusters and often even better than those in full-time, permanent employment. The health outcomes of this cluster can be explained with reference to our Employment Strain Model. As previous chapters have argued, it is the characteristics of the employment relationship, rather than employment type, which shape health outcomes. Our study found that those who experience *employment strain* had poorer health, and that *employment strain* increases when *employment uncertainty* and *employment effort* are both high. As the discussion above outlines, despite some uncertainty about future employment prospects, those in the *sustainable* cluster spend relatively little effort maintaining employment. Few in this cluster were exposed to *high employment strain*. Further, those who were exposed to *high employment strain* were buffered from the stress associated with this situation because they benefited from high *employment relationship support*. Some survey data about stress-related health issues was especially instructive. For instance, few reported having work-related sleep problems or headaches, and no one responded that "most days at work were stressful."

Interviews confirmed that workers in this cluster generally had good overall health. No one said that they experienced anything more than occasional stress or anxiety about their employment situation or future employment, and most said that they enjoyed their work and were able to achieve a good work-life balance in non-permanent employment. Abby put it simply: "My health is very good, I don't have any problems" (Abby #5078). Brian had similar comments.

> My health? Excellent. No problems. I eat well and hang out with my friends on the weekends. I have enough time and money to enjoy myself. I don't have complaints. Yah, things are good (Brian #1686).

Bette, a forty-four-year-old self-employed sales person, when asked a question about whether her health changed when she shifted from permanent full-time employment, replied:

> Oh yeah, tremendous. Now? No stress. I'm primarily a healthy person. Headaches? Well, I don't really get them. I can't really remember the last time I had one (Bette #5151).

Danny had similar experiences. He had been a self-employed computer consultant for several years preceding our study and was working like this at the time he completed the survey. By the time we conducted a full interview a few months later, Danny had moved into a permanent job. He was not enjoying it and planned to go back into consulting. He told us that his health was better as a consultant:

> I am actually more stressed now. I think it is a result of politics at work that I must deal with, and the corporate culture at

work that is in need of improvement. It is harder to maintain the same health and fitness level that I had before when I had more flexibility and free time because I'm working more hours (Danny #2005).

In general, this cluster had better overall health as a result of having more control over their hours and the pace of their work; doing work that they enjoyed; having little stress at work or stress having to find and keep work; and having a good work-life balance that allowed them plenty of time for relaxing, leisure activities, and social time with family and friends.

CONCLUSION

Workers discussed in this chapter represent a privileged cluster: in less permanent employment by choice; doing work for which they have been trained or which they prefer to do; benefitting from strong and secure levels of support that help to buffer them from the risks and uncertainty linked to less permanent employment. For all these reasons, workers in this cluster enjoy the flexibility that can accompany employment that is not full-time or permanent.

In comparison to others, these workers have very good health and overall well-being. The health outcomes of the *sustainable* cluster are a stark contrast to the *unsustainable* cluster who, as will be discussed in chapter 9, experience chronic stress as a result of their uncertain employment. A particular set of circumstances and supports have made their less permanent employment relationship sustainable. One key factor is that they have high levels of certainty about future employment because of close and ongoing relationships with a core group of clients. In other cases, employment certainty comes from being embedded in the local economy or having established strong employment networks. In short, those in this cluster have replicated some of the commitments that are associated with full-time, permanent employment relationships. As a result, they put limited time and effort into finding additional or future work, and are neither impacted by constant evaluation nor anxious about future employment. A second key factor relates to support. Workers in this cluster have strong and consistent sources of support, particularly *household economic support*. In addition, strong work networks or close work arrangements with clients or businesses mean that they can access support from other colleagues and benefit from having some employment security built into their relationships.

Two important points need to be made. First, these workers were in the minority of those we interviewed. Second, although everyone felt their situation was sustainable for the long-term, a few did acknowledge that they could be negatively impacted by changes taking place around them. A few workers felt that their support structures were not as secure as they had once been, and others worried about the long-term consequences of eroding support. For example, a few workers in this cluster acknowledged their partners' employment was not as secure as it had been in the past. Others noted that more competitive labour markets were impacting the sustainability of their employment. For instance, Paul said that he had seen other people's benefit packages being cut back in the department where he'd been permanently employed for twenty-nine years, and acknowledged that this would make it difficult for others to take early retirement to start a different career the way he had done. Cayla acknowledged that the availability of fewer tenure-track jobs meant that competition for contract positions within the university was increasing while wages were not. She noted that her specialized skills and long relationship with the institutions where she taught made her feel confident about future work, but that nothing was guaranteed.

> There's a lot of intervening variables that can change for me that are outside of my control. So from that, I guess from that perspective I do have to be concerned. So that's why I'm constantly making sure that I'm current … Because once you lose a position it's very hard to get it back (Cayla #5442).

In short, not only are workers like these privileged, it seems that the circumstances that have allowed their employment to become beneficial to them are changing in ways that will make it more difficult for other workers to turn "precarious" employment into *sustainable, less permanent employment*. Some of the conditions and policy interventions that might be necessary to support more precarious workers into becoming "*sustainable*" will be discussed in chapter 10.

8

"On a Path" to Employment Security

Someday I'd like to have kids. And like, you know, doing the contract thing would obviously not help that out at all … So I mean obviously that's a big part of the reason I would like to have full-time work is to get in, be established, know I can do the maternity leave thing, come back and be secure (Liana, graphic artist #695).

INTRODUCTION

The second cluster of workers in less permanent employment relationships that we identified in our study viewed their employment situation as temporary; one that would eventually lead to a relationship with commitments. We termed this cluster *on a path* to employment security. Although these workers were in employment arrangements that were nearly as fragile as those of the most vulnerable workers (described in the next chapter), their employment situation was unique in two key ways. First, whether they had chosen to be in less permanent employment or not, they saw their employment situation as temporary and were investing considerable effort in securing permanent employment. Second, *on a path* workers generally experienced high levels of relationship support, albeit not necessarily secure or long-term. This support provided them with an important buffer – even if only temporary – from some of the negative consequences of working without commitments and allowed them to work long and hard hours to try to secure more permanent employment. Partly as a result of the ongoing effort they were investing in improving their situation, workers in this cluster expected that they would soon be working with commitments.

This chapter explores how these two key features of this cluster shape the health and well-being of workers who believe they are *on a path* to more permanent employment. The level and nature of effort (what our study refers to as *employment relationship effort*) is very specific to this cluster. While the other two clusters of workers in less permanent relationships did spend time searching for future work or additional work, those in the *on a path* group constantly expended high levels of effort trying to move into more secure and permanent employment. For this cluster of workers, *employment relationship effort* was often in the form of "self-marketing" outside work in order to establish their reputation and secure future employment, self-directed skills development initiatives, and looking and applying for additional and/or future work. For some workers, this meant completing specialized training (often unpaid), while for others it meant numerous hours writing grant applications or proposals to secure future contracts.

The level and nature of *employment relationship support* was also unique to this cluster of workers. Many workers in the *on a path* group were able to cope with – and sometimes even enjoy – their employment situation because they had individual and household economic support. Although comparable to the level of support reported by the *sustainable* group (see chapter 7), that available to the *on a path* cluster was far less secure. *Employment relationship support* available to the *on a path* cluster was generally temporary, and often required them to dip into their own savings, borrow against future earnings, or draw on short-term family support (e.g. housing or financial support from parents). Further, the temporary nature of this support resulted from the fact that those in this cluster (in contrast to those in *sustainable, less permanent employment relationships)* had not replicated the type of networks and support structures that are an inherent part of permanent relationships with commitments (e.g. professional associations, workplace social or career-focused groups).

Linked to these two key factors, workers in the *on a path* cluster faced a unique set of health issues and challenges. In general, they accepted this situation – including the low wages and *employ-*

ment relationship uncertainty – as a necessary phase of their careers, whether a transitional phase or a stage of apprenticeship. However, while they saw this phase as a necessary one, they were also aware that they were postponing taking care of themselves and were putting their personal lives "on hold" until they found more permanent employment. Most workers acknowledged that their employment situation was not manageable over the medium or longer term and were aware that they were putting enormous stress on their health and well-being. Indeed, despite high levels of support and a degree of confidence that their employment situation was temporary, the health of many in this cluster had already been impacted by their situation. Particularly telling is that eighty percent were in the *high employment strain* category and were particularly prone to exhaustion, stress, and tension.

This chapter explores these issues and advances two overall arguments. First, we contend that workers in this cluster are strongly motivated to accept high levels of *employment relationship uncertainty* and exert high levels of *employment relationship effort* because they believe their situation will lead to more permanent relationships with greater levels of commitments. Further, they are able to cope with this employment situation and expend time, energy, and effort engaging in unpaid training and other activities aimed at improving their employment situation because they have high levels of *employment relationship support*. However, our second claim is that because this support is generally unsustainable, workers in this cluster risk depleting their own resources and thus compromising their long-term health and well-being. Further, given recent developments in the Canadian labour market, there are indications that workers in this cluster may find it difficult to move into more secure employment relationships. Indeed, the actions of workers in this cluster reveal that although they had made commitments to their employer or clients, their employers did not reciprocate by making commitments to them. And, given current employment trends in the country (increasing self-employment and other forms of working without commitments), it is unlikely that the types of employment opportunities these workers expect to move into will be available to all of them. Thus, our overall concern is that many workers in the *on a path* cluster run the risk of slipping into the *unsustainable, less permanent employment relationship* cluster in the years to come.

"ON A PATH" WORKERS IN LESS PERMANENT
EMPLOYMENT RELATIONSHIPS: A PROFILE

Twenty-five of the people we interviewed fell into this cluster. In comparison with other workers in less permanent relationships, those we identified as being *on a path* were in the shortest contracts with their employers and were the least able to predict their incomes. Almost three-quarters wanted more permanent positions and were working hard to ensure they achieved them. Approximately sixty percent were in short-term contracts, twenty-one percent were self-employed, and seventeen percent were in part-time permanent jobs.

This was a highly educated cluster: forty percent had university degrees, and twenty percent had postgraduate degrees. Education appeared to contribute to their hopes for decent, fulfilling employment, and was an important component of what kept them working to their limits. Almost half of the workers in this cluster were either augmenting their professional education while they were working, or had completed a post-secondary program in the previous couple of years.[1] These extra investments, however, loaded on top of the strains of insecure work, created considerable pressure in their work and personal lives.

The individuals in this cluster were generally optimistic about their employment future, and were trying to make the flexibility of the labour market work for them. Most had a good understanding of the sectors in which they worked as well as of the labour market and the opportunities within it, and were driving themselves so that they would have the best possible chance at jobs they cared about that could provide them with security. Workers in this cluster recognized that contractual or temporary work was a good (and sometimes the only) way to get the necessary experience to "break in" to fields of their choice or into institutions offering secure jobs. In a study of the high tech industry, Smith (2001) observed exactly this kind of strategic thinking: workers regarded even temporary positions in a desirable workplace to be a potential advantage in a very

---

1 The focus of this study is on those who are full participants in the labour market. Watkins (2007) points out that the concerns of working students parallel those in our *on a path* cluster.

difficult labour market. In workplaces or occupations where a limited number of temporary placements offer a route into permanence, temporary workers are likely to stay in poor conditions for longer.

PROFILING A WORKER'S EMPLOYMENT STORY:
GABE: "ON A PATH" TO STABILITY?[2]

Gabe is a good example of workers in this cluster. Born elsewhere, he grew up in Canada and was now in his mid-thirties. He was a self-employed photographer and a teacher, with considerable experience in the film industry and overseas teaching. Gabe had been the contract photographer for a school for a number of years, and recently had been asked to teach a summer course there. He liked the work environment and the students, and had seen possibilities for more stable employment with them. A year or so before our first interview, Gabe presented the school with a proposal for a part-time position that he called "Artist in Residence." They negotiated this proposal for several months and eventually the school found the funds for a 2.5 day a week position for one semester. He continued photographing school events, and developed and taught new courses. When we asked him how many hours he was working, he, like a number of others in this cluster, replied: "Well, how many hours am I getting paid for and how many hours I'm working are two different things." This was because he worked more than the 2.5 days he was being paid for as a result of attending evening and weekend events in order to take photographs, and because he worked on his courses at home after school hours. At the same time, he continued working as a free-lance photographer, and took several university courses towards a Masters degree in Education. He was not being paid as much as the other teachers; however, he was prepared to accept this lower salary in the short-term because he thought he was working towards more permanent employment.

I'm falling a little short this year of what I probably should get. But I don't mind, I'm enjoying the work and I think within that

2 Gabe, #2625.

environment it's a way of showing you're willing to play ball and you're serious about what you do (Gabe #2625).

Towards the middle of that semester, he developed a proposal for a full-time teaching position. The school let him know they wanted to keep him, but only agreed to a continuation of the part-time position for the next full teaching year. Gabe was still in the same part-time position a year later when we interviewed him a second time, but was very hopeful that the school would find the funds to hire him full-time for the next school year. However, the uncertainty meant that he needed to take an extra job over the summer as a waiter as well as keep up his freelance photography.

In the short term, Gabe was able to draw on financial support for himself and their household from his wife's salary from her permanent full-time job. They had a two-year-old son, and hoped to be able to purchase a house in the near future. However, her salary as an early childhood educator was not particularly high; not high enough to ride the ups and downs of Gabe's employment over the long-term, or to take sole responsibility for a mortgage. Gabe found their inability to purchase a house particularly frustrating: "We both have university degrees, and we should be able to make this work. But it's not, not yet anyway."

DEMOGRAPHICS AND OCCUPATIONAL CATEGORIES

A slightly higher proportion of this cluster was female (sixty percent) compared to the *sustainable* and *full-time* clusters, and two-thirds were white. Workers in this cluster tended to be at the earlier stages of their careers. For instance, the average age of workers in this cluster was 32.8, with a fifth under twenty-four years of age and few over age fifty (twelve percent). Workers in this cluster represented a wide range of sectors and occupations: graphics and web designers, private school and ESL teachers, arts workers, administrative assistants, a mechanical engineer, a software designer, a trauma counsellor, an arts producer, a property manager, a retail warehouse worker, a construction manager, a real estate agent, an articling law student, an accountant, and a fraud analyst.

EMPLOYMENT RELATIONSHIP UNCERTAINTY

The workers in the *on a path* cluster all experienced significant *employment relationship uncertainty*. In a number of cases, reported levels of *employment fragility, earnings uncertainty,* and *scheduling uncertainty* were even higher than those in the *unsustainable* cluster. They were in jobs that were short-term, had a degree of informality, and often produced unpredictable schedules. However, what differentiates this cluster from the others is that these workers were willing to put up with uncertainty as the short-term cost of eventually getting a job with commitments.

Employment Fragility

Individuals in the *on a path* cluster were in less permanent employment relationships to a similar degree as those in our other clusters we have examined, but they were treated particularly poorly in a number of ways. They had shorter tenure in their positions than workers in other clusters, and they experienced a faster pace of turnover, with more unpredictability than workers in the other clusters. For instance, they were three times as likely as those who had *sustainable, less permanent employment* to have jobs or contracts that lasted less than six months. While their employment situation was better than those in the *unsustainable* cluster in some regards, at least one in five had unreliable employers, or their relationship was "informal"; twenty-eight percent did not always receive a record of their pay, sixteen percent were not paid on time, and twenty percent said that often their pay was different than they expected. We are tempted to speculate that these workers' eagerness to work made them particularly vulnerable to exploitation by employers.

The wide range of occupations held by workers in this cluster underlines the extent to which employer flexibility and the withdrawal of commitments is structural, and permeates all industrial sectors. Their experiences reveal some of the changes that have taken place in different sectors and occupations, and the corresponding increase in employment fragility. The three web designers, for instance, reported that two crucial developments have taken place in their field in recent years. First, although they finished their training fairly recently, the current technology is almost completely different than what they learned during their training. This makes it harder to secure employment, and means that they must engage in unpaid (re)training in order to stay competitive. Second, they have witnessed a steady shift in this sector towards contractual employment. According to them, not only is this work increasingly contractual, but the field is highly competitive, and contract times and prices are continuously being driven down. Similarly, several teachers who were looking for work outside of the public school system told us they were surprised to find that most of this work has become contractual. The articling law student, the mechanical engineer, and the accountant were each in occupations where the qualifying phase for their certification required short-term placements or contracts. Their perception was that each of these industries increasingly relies on professional trainees' lower paid, flexible work.

Service and retail workers in this study also described the extent to which these sectors rely on less permanent workers. These workers were hopeful that they would be able to find more permanent employment, and considered their current status to be the equivalent of a long rite of passage. Nonetheless they recognized the prevalence of a structure that made it possible for employers to avoid paying for benefits for a substantial part of their workforce. Cole provides a good example of this. A unionized retail worker in his late twenties who had worked hard for a year in a casual position, he was discovering that his effort would not easily earn him even a part-time permanent position with his employer.

> There's only a certain number of slots that they have to fill and I mean everyone from all over the [city] goes and applies for this and the manager has to recommend you for it and you have to go ... to Brampton and do like a four-hour interview and a meeting and so I mean, I don't know, I guess I mean there's lots of other people who have been at the store for years and years and they still haven't gotten permanent part-time, so I mean maybe they just, maybe they had too many people who had like three or four years under their belt and they only, and they only award so many slots (Cole #2698).

Hien, a unionized personal-support worker, encountered similar systemic "flexibility." He told us that he and many others worked full-time hours but were not considered full-time workers by their employer. It took him three years to move from a part-time position to a full-time position.

> Okay, if I work seventy-five hours per pay period, that's full-time hours. But it's not full-time position, part-time position working for full-time hours. I have no benefits, I just working the full-time hours (Hien #5293).

A surprising number of employers contributed to the *employment fragility* of this cluster at the most basic level by not paying when or what workers expected. This ranged from the nickel-and-diming of a temporary agency, to late payments, to complete breach of contract and non-payment. Maggie was an administrative assistant who had just been hired into a permanent position after several years of working through her employer's in-house pool of temporary workers. She described how as a temp worker, she was paid only for the full hours she worked, not for partial hours, and thus her pay varied. This level of detail was hard to keep track of, but she needed to stay on top of it in order to manage her very tight monthly budget.

> I notice now, you know if [a permanent employee], for whatever reason, they are running late in the morning and they come in it's not a really big deal. But if I was working temp and I was an hour late in the morning well that comes off of my time sheet at the end of the week. So even just, you know, little tiny things like that were stressful ... And in the summer, we get off at 3:30 on Friday ... but everyone else got paid until 4:30 [and the temps did not]. Now I'm one of the people that gets paid until 4:30 ... You count on every single penny, because you know where every single penny is going to go (Maggie #668).

Shawn was a mid-career artist and events producer who described what many in this cluster experienced – that employers were less prompt and reliable when it came to paying people who were not on their regular payroll.

> In my writing work I'm paid by established publishers, so the pay is unproblematic. It's smoother than with the [arts company] who sometimes take months (Shawn #5317).

Darryl told us that he had to learn about the more dramatic uncertainty of broken contracts and simply not being paid for work he had done. He was an engineer, a second generation Italian-Canadian in his mid-forties, who had started a construction management business three years before the interview. Because he was new to managing this kind of work, one of the bigger clients for whom he had finished a project had simply not paid him, and he could not afford to take him to court. He has since learned that such non-payment is not unusual and avoiding it requires experience in the field.

> Yeah, it's illegal what he's doing, but for me now to go prove it in court, I need $50 to $60,000, because the way the courts work, everybody starts from zero and you gotta prove your case ... The more you talk to people the more you hear that that's part of business, almost every contractor or sub-contractor that I've spoken to has encountered at least one of these (Darryl #5704).

Earnings Uncertainty

Many *on a path* workers reported high levels of short-run and long-run *earnings uncertainty*. For instance, over half – much more than the *sustainable* cluster and slightly higher than the *unsustainable* cluster – were not able to count on having the same level of income six months from when they responded to the survey. Four of every five lost pay if they did not work: that is if they were sick or took a vacation. Very few had long-term disability or pension coverage.

The classic insecurity of self-employment was described well by Mao. A counselor who took referrals through companies that offer Employee Assistance Plans, she was just learning to manage the workload and financial unpredictability of working on contracts.

> I would like to know that I'm guaranteed at least this amount of work per week. One of the hazards for me is that I don't know if I will get any, get enough work next week, and that's financial. This week I might overwork to compensate for next week. And then even if next week I get a lot I might overwork again, because maybe next month [there won't be any work]. So I'm still new to this part of the industry and I'm, you know,

it's only been a few months for me that I'm full-time, so to speak, independent. It will probably take me six months to kinda see exactly how, or even a year (Mao #5700).

Sarah had more experience with temporary and short-term contracts, and had come to realize that she needed other sources of income to provide stability. She was in her late twenties, and had worked and trained as a mechanical engineer. She had been on this path for over ten years, and was in a senior training phase, working in temporary positions to get enough paid hours for her professional qualification. Sarah felt certain that at some point she would earn a stable income, but was concerned because she felt she had spent too many years in lower paid positions and that her earnings across the whole of her working life had already suffered. Her concern took her into a completely different endeavour – she wrote and self-published an investment guide for people new to financial markets. When we conducted our follow-up interview, she was even clearer that she did not expect the engineering work to support her completely, and that she hoped it would be supplemented by a combination of book sales and her own investments.

Scheduling Uncertainty

Workers in this cluster had high levels of *scheduling uncertainty*, much higher than either the *sustainable* cluster or those in permanent, full-time employment. For instance, twenty-eight percent said they did not get sufficient notice to plan their workweek or their social activities, and twenty percent were unable to make arrangements for their household responsibilities.

While more individuals in this cluster reported *scheduling uncertainty*, their day-to-day experience of this kind of disruption was not necessarily different than that of individuals in other clusters. Hien, the personal support worker, had experience working on call for the nursing home. Both the anti-social timing of his shifts and the uncertainty of when he would be notified were disruptive for him.

Okay, evenings you are starting from three to eleven at night. So they only call me between eleven to one in the afternoon. Yes, for three o'clock shift. But sometimes they will call me like four o'clock, late call, maybe four-thirty in the afternoon so I have to go, like have to get there within an hour. So that's very, you know, very hard for me. I cannot do anything, just wait for the call, you know (Hien, #5293).

Rupert worked as a physiotherapist who filled in at several clinics, but found the lack of notice very difficult to handle.

The biggest problem was the hours, the fact that I wasn't on a set schedule, I didn't know where I was going to be the next day so I couldn't really plan for, like if I wanted to stay out a little later on the previous evening. They'd call me to go to like Scarborough at seven-thirty in the morning. Well I don't know that until six-thirty in the morning, you know (Rupert #5689).

Mao was a counselor who had just become self-employed. She described the uncertainties in her new arrangement.

It's probably more difficult now because at least before there was a schedule. Like I was given shifts whereas now because work is a day to day thing I never know if I have to cancel my doctor's appointment or my lunch with a friend, or whatever. Or even like I have to stop this interview and go off because there might be, my cell might go off (Mao #5700).

Scott, a self-employed real estate agent, was in the minority who experienced this uncertainty as beneficial: evidence of a flexibility over which he had some control. His experience was much more like that of those in the *sustainable* cluster. Scott had settled into a routine that relied on the flexibility of his schedule:

The biggest [advantage] is flexibility of scheduling. I work, I work hard when I work, but I've also got a lot of ability to schedule when I work. If a client calls me and says that they would like to go out and look at homes, I always have the ability to say that I can't … It gives me a chance to spend time with my kids during the day. It gives me a chance to, I'm usually involved in grocery shopping and preparing meals, dinners and stuff like that during the week, which takes a lot of the burden off of my wife (Scott #2317).

EMPLOYMENT RELATIONSHIP EFFORT

Workers in the *on a path* cluster invested considerable effort trying to secure more permanent employment, and in comparison with the other clusters, more were actively looking for work (twenty-eight percent). One in five was investing in training that was not paid for by an employer. Almost three in five experienced discrimination, which led to greater efforts on their part to establish their reputations, and to further job applications.

Effort Keeping Employed

Individuals in this cluster were as likely to look for work by creating networks, developing projects, and self-marketing, as they were to respond to job ads. Shawn was an events producer and an artist who emphasized this point. He said he was always thinking about the next project and who he needed to talk with. "It never stops. You can't go on cruise control" (Shawn #5317). Gabe, the private school teacher, developed work by writing and promoting proposals for the next year's courses. Several artists we interviewed worked with agents who would find them calls and auditions to attend. Scott also said that the need to stay open to the possibility of future contracts was constantly with him, and that this interfered with his ability to relax and enjoy social activities. He told us that:

> The way that I phrase it with friends is that, I'm always 'on.' It's difficult for me to just be my kid's dad, my wife's husband, my friend's friend … Like I was at a softball game last night. In between innings or as I'm waiting for my turn at bat, people are asking me questions because they know that I'm a real estate agent. I'm always available for people. And I try to be … But it is tough sometimes, I can't just sort of throw it all in, relax. Whereas a lot of people with the full-time jobs go to work, go home, the job gets to stay at the workplace (Scott #2317).

Sheila, a self-employed writer and editor, echoed this experience.

> I always seem to manage to find work, but looking for work takes up a lot of time, like more time than I expected, to try to get in touch with people and pitch them ideas so I spend a lot

of my time doing unpaid work before I get the project (Sheila #2678).

Others in this cluster regularly used online lists to look for work. One temporary employment agency worker, for instance, checked the job postings three times a week. Hien worked at a hospital as an assistant to patients who needed help smoking, and he was concerned about the health effects of the job. This employment was part-time when we first interviewed him, but became a permanent, full-time position in the year between our two interviews. The full-time salary was better, but it was still not sustaining him and his family. He had been in Canada for more than five years, but he continued to struggle to find a permanent job related to his training and interest. This constant effort over and above his regular work was a significant contributor to his *employment strain*. He told us that he still spent two to three hours a week looking for work:

I am still looking for another job. I do not like this job; it is bad for my health. I have to sit outside all the time even when it is very cold outside, and I have to breathe the smoke. I do not like the job. I was a college teacher in China for fifteen years; I have an MA in engineering. I want to do something more than be a smoking assistant, but I need qualifications here. It is very hard to work in our field; to fulfill our own hopes is almost impossible (Hien #5293).

As part of their effort to "break in" to an occupation or career, a number of the workers in this cluster were making a considerable investment in training that was not paid for by their workplace; twenty percent reported that they had taken more than fifty hours of unpaid training in the previous year. Hien told us that it was very difficult to add training to his responsibilities. He was taking courses over and above a full-time workweek to become a pharmacy assistant. He found the long hours hard to sustain because of his commitment to spend time with his family.

Others were involved in similar pursuits. One administrative assistant was taking property management courses in the hopes that her position in the company would improve and that both her wages and security would increase. Similarly, Scott, the real estate agent, had enrolled in teacher's college, hoping that a teaching career would be more stable than real estate. Another administrative assistant, Maggie, regularly took computer and systems upgrading courses during the years that she worked through a temporary employment agency, so that she would be as prepared as possible when a permanent position opened up.

A surprisingly high proportion of this cluster (fifty-eight percent) reported that they experienced discrimination as a barrier to getting work. Several attributed the discrimination to racism and sexism, although as Haru points out, it is often very difficult for individuals in short-term positions to pinpoint the problem. She said:

> Compared with people like us, original Canadians don't work as hard as us. That's true, right? I don't think I got enough pay for what I did. I think they pay other people more, but you can't ask ... No one will say it is discrimination, but you can feel but you cannot speak out, you understand what I mean? (Haru #5631)

Others attributed the difficulties they had getting the jobs they wanted to the discrimination of "insiders" erecting barriers to "outsiders"' rather than to human rights discrimination. That is, many felt they were discriminated against because they did not have permanent employment. Shawn told us that as a freelance events producer, he has learned that some people in his industry treat him differently than when he had a permanent position. This was painful for him, and he has learned to avoid situations where he might be in contact with certain people. "Some professional colleagues make it apparent that you're not as important" (Shawn #5317).

Cole, the casual retail worker we introduced earlier, was upset by how difficult it was to become permanent part-time in his company, and had to work hard at not interpreting the barriers he perceived as personal discrimination.

> Like I work so hard and diligent, and my cash is so good, and I'm just on top of everything, never late, never call in sick, never, you know, even if I am sick I go in and I'm like just do it you know – grin and bear it, whatever ... I do everything a PPT (permanent part-time) does, they just don't have to pay me any

benefits. I do everything; I do everything a PPT would have to do. I mean I should be getting PPT status (Cole #2698).

But of course, regardless of whether the source of discrimination is race, ethnicity, age, or gender, it is very difficult to challenge. Since hiring processes for contract and temporary positions are generally not as formal or transparent as permanent hiring procedures, the opportunities for discrimination are multiple and it is very difficult to establish whether discriminatory treatment is actually taking place. And few workers in insecure jobs, for short periods, are prepared to take the risk of challenging workplace violations. The stress that these workers experienced was compounded by their knowledge that how well they performed in one job or contract would likely affect their ability to find another and ultimately, a permanent one. Almost three-quarters said that employers' evaluations of their performance affected whether they would be offered more work. This, it must be emphasized, is not the same process undergone by most permanent workers. For contract workers, there is rarely a regularized process of performance appraisals. Less permanent workers face irregular but frequent, informal, often unspoken appraisals of their work. Not only do they face continuous evaluations, but this process and the criteria used to evaluate them and their work is largely invisible. Often, these assessments are only made known when workers apply for a new contract. This contributes to their sense that employers' decision-making process is inaccessible. For workers in this cluster, the challenge of negotiating for more work is further compounded by pressures from competitors.

Multiple Employer and Worksite Effort

Another source of stress in these workers' lives is the fact that many of them have multiple employers and worksites. Two of every five workers in the *on a path* cluster had more than one employer at a time, a higher proportion the other clusters. Consequently, many were dealing with conflicting demands from employers and the stress of working in more than one location. Almost three quarters worked in more than one location, and almost half experienced conflicting demands from each location.

Just under one-third of *on a path* workers spent more than two hours a day in unpaid travel, and this too was more than those in other clusters. Employment uncertainty, combined with having multiple work locations, meant that it was difficult for many to live close to all, or even any, of their jobs and consequently they faced long commutes. Rupert, for instance, had taken an intern position as an insurance adjuster. Not long after he was hired, his office was moved to a location that was not accessible by public transit and over an hour's drive from his home. He was uncertain whether he would last long in this job, and therefore was not prepared to move closer to this new location. For others, unpaid travel hours were built into their employment relationship. Haru was a middle-aged South Asian woman who was an administrative assistant for a group of property managers. She did not get paid for the time she spent driving to properties.

If you are part-time, you don't have benefits and then they counted by hours, they pay you by hours. But you know, what I did was more than what I got paid. I have a car, they don't pay me for transportation [time] or for gas … So, oh my God, the thing is in between I don't even have time for my lunch! I eat my lunch only when I'm driving (Haru #5631).

As will be discussed in more detail below, dealing with multiple employers and worksites affects the well-being of workers in several ways. The commuting time and energy, the effort exerted in each workplace in the hopes of securing future employment, and the stress associated with constant evaluation and worksite effort, all undermine workers' ability to relax and spend time with family and friends. Being in employment relationships that require significant amounts of unpaid time and training further erodes workers' free time.

Extra Effort and Low Pay: "Eating Hours"

A number of workers in this cluster worked long hours with low pay, often in competition with permanent workers or lower bidders on contracts. As Smith (2001) points out, it is to the advantage of employers to have a small core of desirable positions, and a hungry group of workers who are prepared to push themselves, over a long period of time, to increase their chances of getting one of the permanent jobs. It appears that many industries and corporations have adopted this strategy and many workers in this cluster were the victims of such a strategy.

Brent, an Asian man in his mid-twenties who was close to completing his Certified General Accountant program, clearly described the practice of "eating hours" among temporary accountants. He was working on three or four month sequential contracts for a large accounting firm, and would not qualify as a CGA without a certain amount of experience as a paid worker. He told us that many of his fellow accountants were in similar positions in temporary jobs and would:

> eat their time. You know with consulting or accounting you charge the time but you do the work but you don't charge the time … because of this people are competing with each other all the time. They stay late, but they don't charge their time so they look really good (Brent #227).

Several workers described being in short-term jobs where they were expected to work beyond the hours they were paid for. Gabe, who we introduced earlier, had a contract that specified the hours he was to be present at his school, and his pay was calculated on those hours, but he was also expected to work after those hours. Further, his future employment was based on his capacity to write proposals and take courses towards the completion of his graduate degree. Deepa was a South Asian administrative worker in her mid-twenties who felt that while her hours were similar to her co-workers, she was asked to do far more than other people on the job.

> The learning curve is just so huge and I think it seems to be this attitude, right, they seem to have with like young people who came out of university, like 'ah they're smart, they'll figure it out' (Deepa #2966).

Cole, the casual retail worker introduced earlier, did not exactly "eat his hours" but he invested unpaid hours in an effort to increase his wages and security. He liked what he did and wanted to become permanent staff. As we noted earlier, his employer, "awarded" permanent status only to a small number of workers. No one had permanent status at his store except the manager, although Cole thought some workers in other stores had at least part-time permanent status. He expended extra effort to be certain that his manager was happy with his performance. Cole handled the full range of cash transactions, he opened and closed the store, and he worked at least thirty-seven hours a week. Cole made himself available to come in if someone else didn't show up, or if they needed help unloading, and he spent time at home on the web learning about products partly because he wanted a recommendation from his manager to become permanent but also because he was just a helpful guy and enjoyed the work. He had been expending this kind of effort for a year, but it hadn't paid off. He had just been passed over for a promotion to part-time permanent when we talked. This promotion would have been a recognition of his efforts and would have resulted in a pay increase of four dollars an hour, plus benefits.

Maija had hit the limit as to how many hours she was prepared to "eat." She was the one person in this cluster who had slipped into an unsustainable work situation when we conducted the follow-up interview. In the three years since she graduated from a college web design program, heavy competition meant that there were very few full-time jobs and the amount she could charge for a contract had dropped by fifty percent. She estimated that she was earning approximately three dollars an hour after expenses in her most recent contracts. Maija decided that this effort was not leading anywhere, and she could not keep it up.

Hien had a unique observation that summed up his frustration about the inequalities in the difference between the time and effort he invests as a multiple job-holder and that which he sees invested by full-time workers in permanent employment.

The tax system needs to be improved because like we – a lot of people – are working two or three jobs, and get more income because lots of jobs, but we have to put in a lot of hours. But for most of people who have more pay, a higher salary, like $40,000, $50,000 a year, they just work eight hours a day. They are white collar and we are blue collar. We pay tax in the same way, according to your income but the government never considers that we have to work more hours (Hien #5293).

EMPLOYMENT RELATIONSHIP SUPPORT

Those in the *on a path* cluster had high levels of *employment relationship support*; almost as high as that reported by those in the *sustainable* cluster. Their support came particularly from family and friends. For many, such support included living with parents or other family members and reduced contributions to household expenses. In this cluster, only two individuals lived alone and without support from their families. The majority tended to be more dependent on their households than their households were dependent on them, in large part because their incomes were not very high. However, in direct contrast to the ongoing and fairly secure sources of support received by the *sustainable* cluster, support reported by those in the *on a path* cluster was limited, often quite short-term, and did not enable them to thrive. The support available to many *on a path* workers was often time-limited, or from a partner or family member who was also in less permanent employment. While this support made it possible for individuals to continue with their current employment, it also contributed to limiting their choices with regard to both their personal and work lives. Further, because this cluster of workers invested so much effort in their work, with little immediate return, they were aware that they might be depleting rather than building their assets.

For the younger workers in this cluster, support took the form of an extended period of financial or housing support from their parents. This phenomenon can be seen in the Canadian population: in 2001 forty-one percent of people aged twenty to twenty-nine lived with their parents, compared with twenty-seven percent in 1981 (Statistics Canada 2002). Many of the younger workers we interviewed wanted to get on with their lives – develop intimate partnerships, have children, own a home – and, at the same time, worried about how they would manage when their family's support ended. (Many families had provided support during post-secondary education, and often this support was extended into the young person's working life because of a substantial student debt.)

Deepa was an administrative worker in her mid-twenties who

worked on short-term contracts. She was living with her parents rent-free, and taking the highest paid administrative jobs she could find and even so, she estimated that it would take three years to pay off her student loan from university. She said, "If I didn't live at home, I'd be a wreck. I wouldn't know how I was going to pay my rent, especially you know living in Toronto, that's why I moved home" (Deepa, 2966). The limited and complicated aspect of this support stemmed from the fact that her mother was quite ill and she therefore felt more pressure to get her student loans paid off quickly and remain in the same city as her family. These issues made it more difficult for her to fully pursue the type of work she wanted.

> I feel like I'm a burden being at home and so, I think, in a lot of ways that affects the kind of jobs I do pick because ... like when people say to me you've got all this educational background, like why are you doing what you're doing, and I'm like, cause it pays my loans plain and simply, I get out of the home faster, I pay my loans faster. Because you know I'd love to take an internship and go to like the Sudan or something for a year, but I can't afford to (Deepa #2966).

Rupert was experiencing similar constraints. He was almost thirty, a kinesiology graduate who had worked as a physiotherapist and a physical fitness instructor. He was living with his parents, which was helpful to him because he did not pay rent. His mother had never worked outside of their home and his father had recently retired but was still taking on short-term jobs. Their household managed on a low fixed income from a small RRSP and from a government pension that was supplemented by Rupert's and his father's uncertain incomes. His parents had helped Rupert pay off his student loan, but were increasingly dependent on him, and were very concerned about whether he worked.

> As they get older it's going to be more so and I'll eventually have to support them, right? ... It is kind of strained and I've had some run-ins with my dad too like you know, if I even go a month without working you'll hear him start whining about hey, how he has to start carry the load. It's definitely important to be employed, you know (Rupert #5689).

Rupert really wanted a job as a sports coach, but there are very few of these and he could not afford to keep up the volunteer work and his own training that was necessary to create the networks that might lead him into this field. He also wanted to live on his own, so that he could have a bit more time to develop his own friendships and intimate relationships. The tension in his situation kept him single and forced him to take most available work, including a short stint in what appeared to be an opportunity for well-paid secure work as a full-time insurance adjuster. However, the predominantly computer work did not suit his strengths and he faced a commute of several hours a day. At the end of his probation period, he left to look for other work.

Several of our interviewees echoed Rupert's concern about not having the time or support to develop intimate partnerships or take personal risks, as have a number of recent studies. Wolbers (2007), in particular, has shown that in European countries, university graduates who go directly into insecure employment are less likely to leave their parents' home and establish a nuclear household and family than those who go into stable employment right after university or college. Liana, a graphic artist in her early thirties, had worked steadily as a temp for seven years and also had a weekend part-time job. She talked about how this worked in her life:

> With both jobs, it is closer to fifty-five (hours a week). Yeah, I think I've just gotten used to it; I'm an 'A-type' personality so I like to be busy, like the challenges. But it is hard to have a social life. I'm sure my love life has suffered – but I worked like this for so long, I worked so many hours that I don't know what a weekend is anymore (Liana #3049).

In our first interview with Liana she told us that she was living with another precariously employed graphic artist and that:

> Someday I'd like to have kids. And like you know, doing the contract thing would obviously not help that out at all ... So I mean obviously that's a big part of the reason I would like to have full-time is go in, be established, know I can do the maternity leave thing, come back and be secure (Liana #695).

And in fact she was one of the success stories among this cluster of workers. In our follow-up interview a year later, she told us that she had found one of the few available full-time jobs in her field, had just taken time off to get married, and hoped to have a child within the next year.

The middle-aged workers in this cluster tended to be in relationships with partners who were also in non-permanent positions. The support they provided for each other was enough to keep them in their current employment situations, but not enough to sustain personal risks. Suzanne told us that:

[Working like] this is not sustainable in the long-term; we'll never get a mortgage unless one of us gets a full-time job with a salary. You cannot plan or really even think about the future and future plans; as a freelancer, you're locked into the 'now' (Suzanne #2678).

In chapter 4 we introduced Julianne, a contract medical researcher, and Darryl, the construction manager. Their interviews provided a glimpse of the stress in households with two uncertain earners. While Darryl was learning the hard lesson that some clients in the construction industry do not pay invoices, Julianne had gone through a "dry spell" finding work in her field, although she had since picked up several contracts that were keeping her employed almost full-time. Darryl told us: "If it wasn't for my wife working we would have not been able to do it" (Darryl #2704).

Both periods of low income and assumptions about what kinds of support each partner needs can create tensions within households. Julianne talked about the decisions she needed to make as she became the primary earner in the household:

[H]is work situation was related to my work situation in a sense that when the jerks weren't paying, he had to take money from us personally in order to pay off what he needed to pay off. And I had been advised by people do not, do not mix personal and business. And so for quite a while I said to him No. No, you have to borrow money, small business loan, keep the business straight-up. But then, I just looked at him and he was

like totally stressed, and I looked at the percentages he was paying in interest ... and I just did not feel right (Julianne #5703).

EMPLOYMENT STRAIN AND HEALTH:
POSTPONED WELL-BEING

As indicated above, many workers in this cluster run the risk of
depleting sources of support due to their commitment to expend
effort in the hope of landing a permanent job. This same concern is
echoed when this cluster of workers discuss their health. While they
were not yet experiencing more symptomatic ill-health, they were
more likely to be exhausted after work than the other two clusters of
less permanent workers, and more likely to report that most days at
work were stressful. In our interviews, many made it clear that they
were not looking after themselves and were compromising their current health in order to improve their future employment situation.

Almost half of this cluster reported being exhausted after work
most days. Hien best described the exhaustion that was reported by
most in this cluster.

> I go home, the first thing I have to cook for my daughter, you
> know, do something. And after six o'clock I just lie down, sit
> down, relax. I can't do much more. Actually I want to, I am
> studying like pharmacy, pharmacy assistant, something like that,
> on weekends. But sometimes at six o'clock I cannot go. I feel
> tired; I am not doing very well in my studies (Hien #5293).

However, a key difference between workers in the *unsustainable*
cluster and those in the *on a path* cluster was the degree to which
on a path workers felt their exhaustion was high, but manageable.
Those in this cluster reported that they had high levels of stress and
worked long hours (doing both paid and unpaid work), and suggested that this stress was linked to feeling exhausted and having
little time to take care of themselves. Nevertheless, few workers in
this cluster reported that their overall health was poor, and most
said that they were able to manage their stress and other aspects of
their work that might have a negative consequence on their health
– but only for a limited amount of time. It seems that the stressors
linked to their employment situations were not yet impacting their

overall health, perhaps because they saw their employment situation as being short-term, and either a choice or a consequence of the "apprentice-like" aspects of their work and were hopeful about their future employment prospects.

Many of the *on a path* workers spoke about stress in relation to their health. Shawn drew on his musical sensibilities to reflect on the type of stress he experienced as a self-employed writer and musician compared to the stress he had known in a high profile permanent position. He said that the "tonality" or "melody" of his current stress was different than the stress of his previous work, but that it was by no means less significant.

> There is a lot of stress being a freelancer. I have a shorter fuse, my sleep is interrupted, it's harder to concentrate … Some people tell me that I look more relaxed than when I was running the event series. But this stress is more psychological (Shawn #5317).

Several workers in this cluster were trying to make conscious efforts to deal with tension, but they noted that taking time off from work to relax or exercise was often difficult. They had little time to unwind, largely as a result of unpaid training and other activities associated with *employment relationship effort*. Sheila, the self-employed editor, best captured the strategy adopted by a number of *on a path* workers. She was resolved to putting off taking care of herself until she had more permanent employment. Given that workers like Sheila hoped and expected more permanent employment, they felt they could put off dealing with any health issues that emerged until later.

> I don't really have any set time off, and I rarely take the weekend off. I know it would be good for my well-being if I took time-off … And my health? Well, I haven't been to the doctor or dentist in quite awhile. Sure I'm really stressed all the time, but I'm young and I generally feel fine … yeah, I should be going to the dentist for a check-up, I'm long overdue. In fact I haven't been in years, but the dentist is expensive and we really can't afford it. I'm putting off taking holidays or weekends off. I'm putting off going to the dentist … I guess I'm *postponing my well-being* [emphasis added] (Sheila #2678).

Scott, the real estate agent, was also conscious of the fact that he was compromising his health, even if only in the short-term. He told us:

> I haven't been to the doctor in years. I know I have a foot problem, it needs rest and elevation, but I can't really do that because I have to work. I can't really take time off, and my work requires me to be driving, so rest and elevation really isn't possible ... We have not had a family vacation in five years. The stress means that sleep and stomach issues keep creeping in. Because of my work schedule, I'm often away during dinner so I eat at fast food places ... I've gained thirty-five pounds since I got my realtor license ... I could manage the stress and financial worries better at the beginning, but I think it is catching up with me (Scott #2317).

Maggie, the administrative assistant we interviewed, had been hired into a permanent position after several years of temping with an in-house temporary agency. She was able to compare her ability to look after a stress-related chronic condition when she was a temp worker and now as a permanent worker.

> So needing time off and having to go to doctor's appointments and work all that out and knowing that you're not getting paid for those days off is stressful, and then the pay cheque comes and it's a lot less than what you normally need, like when you need every penny and all of a sudden there's three days off that you, you know, weren't able to be there for. ... Now I can pay to go to a specialist. Like now, I've gone back to my naturopathic doctor because I can; my benefits cover her and I avoided going to her before, I really shouldn't have, but I avoided going to her before because it would be cash out of my own pocket and I didn't get that back (Maggie #668).

ON A PATH:
MOVING INTO MORE SECURE EMPLOYMENT?

The sections above explored the specific ways in which *on a path* workers try to cope with less permanent employment relationships. Despite high levels of *employment relationship uncertainty*, two key factors appear to provide protection – if only temporary – from the negative effects of working without commitments: high levels of *employment relationship support*, and workers' strong belief that their situation was short-term and would – if they worked hard and acquired necessary skills and experience – lead to more stable, secure employment. In other words, those in the *on a path* cluster felt that what they were doing would pay off in the long term and that even if they were not taking proper care of themselves now, they would be able to in the future, once more stable employment was secured. As one worker put it, many in this cluster were "postponing their health and well-being."

So, according to our research findings and to workers' own views, their future health and well-being is dependent on them being able to move into more secure, permanent employment. But how likely is it that workers in this cluster will succeed? We fear that success is unlikely for most workers in this cluster. Three key labour market trends lead us to this conclusion. First, although certain temporary and contract positions in some occupations and industries are explicitly understood as entry level, training, or qualifying jobs, most forms of flexibility are not intended to provide routes into permanent jobs or to increase workers' employment security. Second, research suggests that non-permanent employment tends to be long-term rather than a way of entering the labour market. This is increasingly the case in most sectors and occupations. For instance, one study of the Canadian labour market showed that of the five million Canadian workers in non-permanent jobs in 1998, half were still in these types of jobs in 2001 (Kapasalis 2004). Third, as outlined in earlier chapters, workplace and employment changes in many core sectors are resulting in a rise of temporary and self-employment, thus making it more difficult for workers in these sectors to transition into permanent employment. Those we interviewed had witnessed these trends in the labour market, and correspond to broader changes that can be observed at the population level. For instance, six of Canada's twelve industrial sectors experienced growth in self-employment between 1995 and 2004. Self-employment increased from twelve percent to sixteen percent of jobs in professional, scientific, and technical services and from 12.5 percent to fourteen percent of jobs in construction. Finance, real estate and leasing, business and other support services, transportation and warehousing, and information and culture also experienced increases in self-employment (Webb 2004).

A fourth and less researched trend can also be noted: the growth in less permanent forms of employment in the not-for-profit sector and the often related use – or misuse – of temporary positions intended to serve as training positions for youth, students, or other entrants to the labour market or specific occupation. McMullen and Schellenber's (2003) research suggests that the incidence of contract work is growing in the non-profit sector. Scott's (2003) work supports this claim, and demonstrates that various funding changes for the non-profit sector, such as the shift from core funding to project-based and short-term funding, have contributed to the increased use of temporary staff in this sector. She suggests that not only do funding arrangements make it difficult for organizations to hire permanent employees, but subsidies available for internships and work placements encourage organizations to hire workers for shorter and fixed duration contracts. Indeed, research on this topic has shown that while the original mandate of positions such as internships or university co-op placements was to provide opportunities for hands-on work experience so that workers would be able advance into more permanent jobs, employers are increasingly exploiting these positions simply as a way to staff their workplaces with temporary workers. Data on labour market trends for new workers appears to support this finding. For instance, between 1989 and 2004, the percentage of new workers on temporary contracts in Canada more than doubled (Morissette 2005).

Our concern that few workers in the *on a path* cluster would move into more secure employment was born out when we followed up a year after the first interviews. Of the eighteen people that we re-interviewed, eleven were in the same or similar precarious positions. Two had moved into permanent full-time positions and were happy with their positions. Two had consolidated their consulting businesses and had a core group of clients – their security was in the networks they had created, rather than in a permanent job. Two others had taken permanent full-time positions that they did not want and were not happy with, but they remained in these jobs because they felt they needed the security. These two were still, however, looking for other work. The employment situation for one worker had deteriorated into what we would characterize as an *unsustainable, less permanent employment relationship* (see chapter 9). This worker had become very demoralized, and was relying on this low-paid on-call job only because she could not sustain her contract work. The situation for the remaining eleven did not seem likely to improve in the near future.

CONCLUSION

This chapter has explored the unique features of this cluster of workers in less permanent employment relationships: high levels of *employment relationship effort* and high – even if unstable and temporary – levels of *support*. We have shown that one of the key factors shaping their experience with less permanent employment is that they believe it will lead to more permanent, stable employment. As outlined in the chapter, workers in the *on a path* cluster are strongly motivated to work long hours, engage in training, and expend intellectual and creative effort while in unstable employment relationships, in large part because they see this as a way to secure more permanent work. And employers recognize the value of employing these workers; not only are they happy to take advantage of the workers' acceptance of long hours and hard work for low pay, they are able to benefit – without any costs to their business – from the training, education, and skills development activities that such workers complete on their own time. This is reflected, in large part, in the large pools of contract, temporary, and training positions that often surround a shrinking and restricted core of stable jobs. As other research also indicates, this is the dark side of the growing interest from employers in subsidized internships, experiential education, and co-op program at universities across North America.

Our own limited investigation suggests that at best, the path from less permanent to more permanent employment is a long one and for some, at least, unlikely to be realized. Our follow-up interviews with this group indicated that a year later, very few had made the transition to more permanent employment. However, the possibility of work in a chosen field, or of more stable work, keeps these workers – and their families and support networks – optimistic. Importantly, what this means for workers is that they delay taking care of themselves and moving forward in their own personal lives, and put up with poor treatment at work leading to high levels of stress and insecurity.

While this study suggests that these workers are not yet experiencing poor health and other negative consequences resulting from uncertainty and instability, the continuation of this employment situation is likely to lead to poor health. Indeed, our interviews show that there is a real concern that workers in this cluster are depleting rather than building personal assets as well as compromising their health, especially if their less permanent employment continues for many years. In addition, many do not have the time or resources to engage in intimate partnerships, marriage, childbearing, or home ownership, and thus are delaying them. Consequently, these workers have high levels of *employment strain,* and are likely jeopardizing their health as well as their personal lives. This is evident in the workers' own feelings that they are postponing their well-being and are putting themselves at risk of long-term health difficulties.

Finally, although workers in this cluster reported to having high levels of *employment relationship support,* we saw that this support was neither secure nor long-term. In contrast to those in sustainable, less permanent employment relationships, workers in the *on a path* cluster did not have ongoing sources of personal or employment support such as professional networks, or other employment support that replicate the type of support workers in permanent employment relationships with commitments are more likely to enjoy. Thus, if these *on a path* workers do not find the permanent work they seek fairly quickly, they risk falling into the *unsustainable* cluster described in the next chapter.

9

Unsustainable,
Less Permanent Employment

Oh it's stressful. I mean I'm, you know, I'm constantly thinking about it when I'm at work and I'm at home, you know. I mean I didn't go to university for four years to be doing this – you know what I mean? ... And, well, I think in the greater scheme of things, planning for the future, like down the road, I mean you can't. I mean I don't know where the money will be coming from, or if it's going to be there. Even from short-term, I mean planning's pretty hard. We're living day to day, and that's essentially what I do and I hate that (Dalton #5449).

INTRODUCTION

Individuals in what we have termed *unsustainable, less permanent employment relationships* provide a good illustration of the negative consequences of working without commitments. Workers in this cluster have high levels of *employment relationship uncertainty* (especially with regard to employment fragility) and earnings uncertainty, combined with high level of *employment relationship effort* and low levels of *employment relationship support*. As previous chapters have argued, the combination and interaction of *high uncertainty* and *high effort* leads to *high employment strain*. While workers in the *on a path* cluster discussed in the previous chapter did not all experience poor health as a consequence of their employment situation, almost all the workers in the *unsustainable* cluster report having very poor and deteriorating health. In addition, their *employment relationship effort* is unique, and contributes to their declining health and well-being. While other workers in less permanent employment relationships, especially those in the *sustainable* cluster, use various support structures to build up their client base and future employment options, workers in the *unsustainable* cluster exert effort sustaining multiple jobs and do not have the time, energy, or other resources necessary to carry out sustained job searches. They therefore appear to be trapped in *unsustainable* forms of less permanent employment.

Workers in *unsustainable, less permanent employment relationships* represent the largest cluster by far of the three categories of less permanent employment addressed in our study. As this chapter will outline, they are in relationships that are almost void of any commitment from employers beyond wage or contract payments and in which there is remarkable uncertainty. Consequently, these workers are forced to utilize, and often exhaust, their resources – their health, their social supports, and whatever financial assets are available to them. The interaction of high levels of *employment, income,* and *scheduling uncertainty* and low levels of *employment relationship support* result in high levels of *employment strain,* and poor, if not deteriorating health.

Of the three clusters we identified of workers in less permanent employment relationships, workers in this cluster suffer the most health problems. Our findings in this regard support claims made by other authors about the negative health consequences of precarious employment (see, for example, Burchell, Lapido, and Wilkinson 2002). This form of employment is also a key contributor to social exclusion. Workers with the fewest commitments from employers become increasingly isolated and marginalized the longer they remain trapped in less permanent employment. They have limited capacity to sustain their households and their households lack the resources necessary to buffer them against the uncertainty of their employment situation. The overall argument advanced in this chapter is that employment arrangements without commitments and with little support are simply *unsustainable*; these are toxic employment relationships, and workers and their families suffer negative consequences from them.

WORKERS IN UNSUSTAINABLE, LESS PERMANENT
EMPLOYMENT RELATIONSHIPS: A PROFILE

What differentiates this cluster from the two clusters discussed in earlier chapters is the almost complete lack of commitment from
employers, which is compounded for workers by limited support at
their jobs, from their households, and in the community. They share
six overall characteristics: dissatisfaction with their employment; the
desire to find more permanent employment but inability to secure
this type of work; low and unstable earnings; few employment benefits and limited access to social security benefits; scant workplace,
family, and community support; and an almost complete lack of control or power to negotiate terms and conditions of their employment.

The overall result is that individuals in this cluster report poor
and deteriorating health, largely as a result of chronic stress and
insecurity linked to their unstable and uncertain employment.
Before discussing these issues in more detail, we would like to introduce Devon, a fifty-three-year-old temporary agency worker whom
we interviewed in 2006 and again in 2007. Years of uncertain
employment and earnings were taking a toll on his health and overall well-being. His story is illustrative of the challenges and difficulties faced by workers in *unsustainable, less permanent employment relationships*.

PROFILING AN UNSUSTAINABLE, LESS PERMANENT
EMPLOYMENT RELATIONSHIP: DEVON'S STORY[1]

In 2001, Devon lost his permanent, full-time job in a furniture factory when the factory closed down. At that time he was in his late
forties, and had years of work experience in a range of manufacturing jobs. Devon felt qualified to work in many types of jobs and
began an intensive job search. However, in the context of a declining manufacturing sector in Ontario, it proved hard to find another permanent job. Eventually Devon registered with two employment agencies, both of which offered both permanent and
temporary placements. His hope was that he would either be placed

---

1 Devon, #5051.

in a permanent, full-time job, or that a temporary position acquired through one of the agencies would lead to a permanent employment relationship.

Five years later, Devon was *still* looking for a permanent, full-time job. He had been placed at a number of different companies in temporary placements, and had endured periods of unemployment between contracts. At the time of our first interview, he had just begun a new job in a plastics factory through one of the employment agencies. Although the position was not permanent, it was full-time and had an indefinite end date. He was told that after six months as a "temp," he could be considered for a permanent position. However, Devon was still a temporary worker at the same factory and had not heard whether his position would be converted into a permanent one when we next spoke with him, almost a year later. Although still hopeful, he was getting frustrated with his situation and was not confident that his position would become permanent, partly due to the fact that about half the entire workforce was temporary and few temporary workers that started before him had been converted into permanent employees. As he put it:

> I'm hanging on for the time being, but I'm becoming rather doubtful, the last word I had was over a month ago when the foreman said he was recommending me, but since then nobody has said anything, I don't know what's happening. I will hang on until they let me go, then I'll look for another job (Devon #5051).

Like other individuals in this cluster, Devon has seen his health and general well-being decline over the years. In addition to frequently feeling anxious about his situation, he has limited benefits and support, and feels like he is trapped. He has few sources of *employment relationship support* – workplace, community, or personal support – and is worried about his financial situation and his ability to save for retirement. Further, policy developments in Ontario have reduced his access to public support to buffer the impact of low wages and periods of unemployment. He no longer has a housing subsidy and he either does not work enough hours to qualify for unemployment benefits to cover periods of unemployment or, when he does qualify, he is unable to afford to be unemployed for the required waiting period before he can start collecting benefits. As he says:

Money issues are a big concern. When you work temp jobs, sometimes there is a gap between jobs and I've had problems paying the rent. And I can't save; I'm not saving at all. I don't have enough money to retire, not at all. I'm not making any RRSP contributions, I can't now. I recently went through four and a half weeks of unemployment, but I couldn't collect EI, so I didn't have any income for that period and I went deeper into debt on my Mastercard ... Mastercard bills, well, they're bad right now. It's a problem; it becomes very expensive to be unemployed (Devon #5051).

Although he felt that his health was "generally OK" at the time of the first interview, he did note that he constantly worried about his financial situation, and felt that the lack of health benefits associated with temporary work meant that he was unable to take proper care of himself. Indeed, one of Devon's biggest concerns was that his health would be negatively impacted if he remained stuck in temporary employment. He was right to be concerned; in the follow-up interview he reported that his stress levels were much higher and that his mental and physical health had deteriorated, as had his economic situation. As he said:

My health is important to me ... you're mortgaging your future if you don't take care of yourself. Now, I just don't feel as good as I used to, I don't think anyone should work in that kind of employment environment (Devon #5051).

Devon's situation was not unique. His inability to find full-time permanent employment, the stress and worry he regularly experienced as a result of insecure and unstable employment and income, and the limited sources of *employment relationship support* he could access to buffer the negative impacts of precarious employment were common experiences amongst individuals in this cluster.

Demographics and Occupational Categories

As with workers in the other two clusters of less permanent employment, those in *unsustainable, less permanent employment relationships* represented a diverse group in terms of education, occupation, sector, and employment arrangements. They included temporary, contract, part-time, and self-employed individuals. However, workers in temporary contracts of one year or less and those employed through temporary employment agencies were particularly concentrated in this cluster. In fact, those in the *unsustainable* cluster were three times more likely to be employed through a temporary employment agency than those in the *sustainable* cluster. Women were slightly more likely to be concentrated in this cluster, as were workers in mid-career, or at a later stage of their career. The workers in the latter stage of their career were not choosing employment options that would help them transition into retirement. Most were still far from retirement and none had chosen less permanent employment as a path to early retirement.

One commonality among workers in this cluster was their lack of choice. These individuals had not chosen to be employed in work that was not permanent or full-time. In fact, most reported a preference for permanent jobs. Despite this desire, most had been in a range of different jobs over several years, many of them precarious and low-paying, with few, if any, options of moving into more stable employment. Many workers were the casualties of restructuring; several workers had lost previous jobs (often permanent, full-time jobs) as a result of company closures or restructuring processes, still others had been unable to find permanent employment upon completion of university or college. A number of other individuals – particularly the women in the cluster – had been unable to find permanent employment after leaving another job for personal reasons or after being out of the labour market for several years due to child-rearing. In addition, several workers in this cluster were certain that they suffered from discrimination based on their race or ethnicity and others faced other constraints (e.g. family responsibilities, outdated training, a lack of time and resources to upgrade skills) that restricted their ability to move out of less permanent employment.

Workers in this cluster were spread across diverse sectors and occupations, and included retail workers, cleaners, a hospital orderly, computer programmers, web designers, manufacturing assemblers, a call centre worker, a translator, an HR manager and a senior-level worker in an oil company. A number of educators were also in this cluster, including sessional college teachers, supply teachers, a part-time child-care worker, and a self-employed private school teacher. Many were working in occupations that differed from their training and career aspirations. Many others were in sectors and occupations that have high levels of precarious employment, such as computer programming and education, and are exposed to downward pressure on wages and working conditions as a result of competitive international markets. For example, several web-designers reported that they were competing for contracts with workers based anywhere in the world through Internet employment sites. Others, such as the translators and college lecturers, were in occupations that are increasingly being filled with contract workers. These labour market conditions make it more difficult for these workers to exercise any control over their wages or working conditions.

EMPLOYMENT RELATIONSHIP UNCERTAINTY

For individuals in this cluster, working without commitments can serve as a significant barrier to day-to-day and long-term planning, and successfully transitioning between different stages of one's life.

Employment Fragility

Most individuals in the *unsustainable* cluster reported high levels of *employment fragility* and *earnings uncertainty*. For instance, many had jobs that lasted less than six months, and they were particularly likely to be on-call. The fragility of their employment relationships appears to be partly linked to the informality surrounding their employment relationships. Even the most basic commitment from employers – pay for work done – is not reliable for many in this cluster. Among our three interview clusters, they were most likely to report that their pay was often different than what they expected, and the least likely to receive a record of pay. Further, they were twice as likely as the *sustainable* cluster to not be paid on time.

Employment fragility and *earnings uncertainty* interfered with individuals' ability to transition from one stage of life to another.

Signing a rental agreement on an apartment, taking on a mortgage on a house, deciding to have children, or making financial decisions around retirement can be difficult without employment security or stability. Twenty-four-year-old Dalton reflected on his inability to make future plans with his girlfriend:

> In the greater scheme of things, planning for the future, like down the road, I mean you can't. I mean I don't know where the money will be coming from, or if it's going to be there (Dalton #5449).

Sheng, another man in his twenties, had similar frustrations. According to him,

> It is very hard to plan. I have a girlfriend but I couldn't get engaged until I knew about the job. I can't get engaged now because I don't have a job. I want to get married and move out of the house but I can't, I can't plan anything (Sheng #831).

An additional barrier to long-term planning was the fact that few individuals in this cluster had any advance notice whether their contracts would be renewed. Frank, a forty-nine-year-old working various temporary jobs, explained how abruptly his last job had ended. He had been teaching design courses on a contractual basis for about seven years when the college decided not to renew his contract.

> They failed to renew my contract without even telling me. I was teaching night school there and it was about the time they should be giving me a new contract. I said, 'So where's my contract?' [they said], 'Oh, didn't anyone tell you? We decided not to renew it' (Frank #2568).

Similarly, Sachi, a forty-eight-year-old administrative assistant who was employed through a temporary employment agency, had several temporary jobs end without notice. "Your boss asks you to go into the room and they say, 'OK, today is your final day. But there is no cause, we just send you home'" (Sachi #5492).

Devon had numerous experiences like those Sachi and Frank reported. Devon was given only a few minutes' notice that his contract was not being renewed at a job he'd had for several months in a retail warehouse in Toronto. This was not the first time he'd been given insufficient notice to plan ahead, however. At his previous job, a temporary contract at a steel plant that had been renewed several times over a few years, his foreman told him that his services were no longer needed and not to come back after he had punched out for the day. He felt poorly treated but did not have any recourse because technically, he had not been "fired": his contract simply had not been renewed.

A large proportion of the workers who felt their employment was unsustainable told us that they were frequently on-call, or had contracts that were short-term, and therefore could not count on continued employment. This uncertainty was a constant source of stress, partly because it made medium and longer term work, social, personal, and financial planning extremely difficult. Dalton's experiences were similar to many others in this cluster:

> It's basically, they'll call you and you go to work. You have no set schedule really. It's pretty hard to have a life when it's like that. They'll just call you whenever and harass you to go into work. I still get calls to go into work at some insane hour, like that day and I don't return their calls because I'm like 'this is ridiculous' you know? … It's irregular hours, I mean they could have you work the night shift. The one day I was in for a scheduled, I think ten-hour, twelve-hour shift, and they had me stay an extra two hours and it was like the most stressful like shift I, I've ever had in my life. I went home and I was like, 'I don't want to do this anymore,' but then you get up and you do it again (Dalton #5449).

Several other on-call and self-employed individuals described how difficult it was on themselves and on their family to be constantly available to employers or clients. One self-employed, forty-seven-year-old electronic engineer worked as an Internet technician for two companies for several years. His employment relationship remained very unstable, because neither company would hire him as an employee. They would only give him work on an on-call basis. He said:

> It becomes very tough to manage the time. I advertize twenty-four hours so people can call me anytime ... Because we have to take phone calls all the time, I have to stop doing whatever I'm doing and place the order for them; must just work when the call comes (Jiro #5120).

In addition to constantly working on-call, Jiro was often not paid on time or was paid a different amount than he expected. According to him, this employment situation was unsustainable for him and his family.

Earnings Uncertainty

A key component of the interaction that creates *high employment strain* for this cluster is their *earnings uncertainty*. Survey data revealed that most would lose pay if they missed work and many said that they were unable to anticipate that their income would be the same in six months. In addition, only a few individuals in the cluster reported that they were covered by long-term disability or company pensions. While these issues create stress in many workers' lives, it is the interaction of high *earnings uncertainty* with other characteristics of the employment relationship that make *earnings uncertainty* so problematic for workers in the *unsustainable* cluster. In particular, *earnings uncertainty* combined with *employment fragility* and low *employment relationship support* make it extremely difficult for these individuals to plan for the medium or longer term.

Three key themes emerged in the interviews with regard to *earnings uncertainty*: planning, risk taking, and financial instability. First, an important factor making these relationships unsustainable was that even for those individuals who had fairly regular work schedules, income uncertainty made it extremely difficult to make medium term or longer term plans. One twenty-six-year-old worker's comments summed up the feelings shared by many younger workers about the difficulties of planning their lives:

I never know how much I make in a month ... I have no idea, you know, because it's so different from month to month. It's so day-to-day ... The unpredictability, well, I feel like it doesn't give me very much flexibility to sort of move ahead in life (Gabi #2649).

Second, these workers reported that *earnings uncertainty* interfered with their ability to take risks or make big decisions in their lives. In some cases, the risks related to personal situations. Others had difficulty spending money on training or equipment that might improve their employment prospects in the future. For example Rachel, a fifty-three-year-old seamstress, needed to invest in an embroidery machine in order to expand her business. However, it had taken her so long to pay off the last loan she got from a family member that she felt uncomfortable asking for another one. According to her, being in ongoing precarious employment meant not taking risks:

You don't take risks. If I had more security, there are several things that I would have done in the past or now that would have possibly increased my employment. Things like investing in machines ... I had to get one beginning of December last year, $1,100 plus tax, sewing machines are like that these days ... She [mother] paid the whole price of my new machine and I'm paying it back to her over time ... All my free money, in other words, is still paying for this machine ... It's that working with machines that are on the edge of death and praying that they get you through one more run. If I had another steady day of work a week, I could risk an embroidery machine, which would expand the range of things I could do remarkably. You know, it's that kind of precariousness, you constantly have to juggle, if this, then what? You can't do anything (Rachel #2874).

Sachi's story illustrates the serious challenges these workers face with regard to making personal decisions or taking risks that come with increased financial responsibilities. Sachi immigrated to Canada in 1990. Shortly after arriving in Toronto, she found a permanent, full-time job. Her plan was to get settled, save some money, and then sponsor her mother to move from Hong Kong to Canada. After almost four years of stable, full-time employment, Sachi had the sponsorship paperwork all ready when her company went through a rough patch and laid off a number of people, including her. After several months failing to find work she registered with an employment agency, and has been doing temporary work ever since. She no longer has confidence that she will be able to save enough money to be able to sponsor her mother. Furthermore, the experience of getting laid off has made her doubt the stability of permanent employment. She said:

> I really feel very bad, actually, because I wanted to bring my mom over here but I got the form two days after I got the letter saying that you are laid off. And so, that's why I kind of have the feeling that I'm not feeling so secure after that job. And I'm not really that keen on getting like a job that doesn't give me security at all. But I needed a job ... still, if I have work, I have money and I can plan, like something that I wanted to do right ... you know, all kinds of things that I wanted to do. But if you don't have a secure job then it seems you cannot plan too much (Sachi #5492).

Third, financial insecurity was a key issue facing this cluster. Low incomes combined with a long history of precarious employment resulted in few workers in this cluster having personal savings, RRSPs, company pensions, investments, or any other alternative income. No one had any significant property and everyone, regardless of age, was living in rented accommodations. They all reported that financial insecurity was a constant source of stress. Jiro, a forty-seven-year-old self-employed male, said, "There is pressure, always pressure. If very slow, I have to find more work. I get scared. It becomes hard to go out, we don't go out, we don't make purchases" (Jiro #5120). Nabila, a thirty-four-year-old woman with computer and web-design training, took on-call translation work after being unable to find permanent employment in her field. She had been doing this job for about four years when we interviewed her, and was feeling very frustrated about her situation. She said, "You're not secure financially; it all depends on luck. I never feel like I have a real job. They don't hire interpreters full-time, so I can't really get more security" (Nabila #5494).

Another person who told us how difficult it was for him to live on his low and uncertain income was forty-one-year-old Allan. He had worked as an accountant for about ten years but lost his job in 2005 when the company closed down. Unable to get another accounting job, or any other type of permanent position, he had become self-employed doing people's income tax and had taken two other casual jobs, one of which was cleaning small apartment buildings. His experience of *earnings uncertainty* was this:

> It makes it difficult to do anything, like I like to go visit my sister and that, and I can't plan, I don't know if I'll have enough money to go and that, I don't know how I'm going to be able to keep my Internet going. You know I share that with one of my neighbours, she still needs money to pay for that. So if I lose Internet I can't try to find work because online is faster, it can save you so much time. So without frequent and regular income, I can't do anything really. I can't buy necessities, and I don't want to go to the food bank if I can help it, so that is why I try and stretch my food as much as possible (Allan #2493).

Dalton, the on-call security guard who works on a casual basis, expressed similar worries regarding covering current expenses and planning for his future. He noted that:

> Well, I think in the greater scheme of things, planning for the future, like down the road, I mean you can't. I mean, I don't know where the money will be coming from, if it's going to be there. Even from short-term, I mean planning's pretty hard. We're living day to day and that's essentially what I do and I hate that because, well, I want to know a week in advance what I'm going to be doing. I want to know when I'm going to the grocery store if I can go and buy that thing if it's not on sale; you know what I mean. I'm forever, well if soup's not on sale today so I'm not buying it. Or that's on sale so I'll buy four times as much, because I don't know when it'll be on sale again (Dalton #5449).

Several workers also talked about the impact their situation had on their families. Kata, a mother of two with a casual part-time job and a husband whose employment was also unstable, told us that if she had another part-time job and more certain earnings they would be happier and more secure as a family. She said:

> If we could secure our income yeah, I think then we maybe sometime we can go out, have a vacation, and you know get together, and that might help our relationship and can you know, have less stress (Kata #5478).

Scheduling Uncertainty

While *employment fragility* and *earnings uncertainty* impacts workers' ability to make long-term plans and decisions, *scheduling uncertainty* interferes with day-to-day and weekly planning. Almost a quarter of those in this *unsustainable* cluster reported that they have insufficient notice to plan their work week or their social activities. Many told us how difficult it is to organize leisure and domestic responsibilities around work when they have insufficient notice of their schedule. For instance, Kent was a twenty-four-year-old worker who was struggling to balance his volunteer activities with a part-time job as a sales clerk in a retail store, and in a full-time temporary position in a technical help call-centre. Despite the promises of flexibility in the jobs, Kent found the rotating shifts and limited notice of shift schedules made it impossible for him to continue his volunteer work, and made it difficult to continue working at his part-time Saturday job.

> They told me they need people to work weekends as well or to be flexible towards weekends. I told them okay I talked about my job on Saturday, and when I was signing my work contract I told them I could only work some Saturdays. On my availability sheet, I also told them only some Saturdays. But they crossed it off on my availability sheet and scheduled me for six consecutive Saturdays ... They have too many unexpected shift changes. They don't consult us before they post shifts to their liking. You can't normally say on your availability sheet that you want to work nine to five; I heard that would be rejected

for lack of flexibility. I didn't really like that I needed only two Saturdays off to do the Scouts Canada training, but I unfortunately I couldn't get that so it was pretty disappointing. I also am told that usually the policy is I'm only required to work one Saturday a month, and that they don't normally schedule employees over the weekends. But they did it to me ...I don't have enough flexibility in my schedule to be able to attend something (Kent #691).

Other workers said that irregular schedules made it hard for them to improve their employment prospects by enrolling in courses to upgrade their skills. Others noted that insufficient notice of work disrupted their social lives and limited their ability to participate in community activities. One twenty-seven-year-old woman, who had been hired on a short-term, part-time contract by a big box retail store, complained that she was frequently scheduled for full-time hours despite being paid at the part-time rate, and was expected to be available for work all the time. She felt that she could never count on a regular schedule and therefore was unable to plan any personal time for herself, her partner, or her family. According to her, scheduling uncertainty was the most stressful aspect of the job "just because you could never count on anything. If you made an appointment in advance you would always know that you would have to possibly reschedule it" (Kaitlin #867). Other individuals reported that they needed to be prepared for work at all times in case they were called in, and were therefore unable to relax during days off. Mala, a sixty-four-year-old who had been doing temporary work through an agency for approximately eleven years, told us that she always ironed clean clothes every night before she went to bed, just in case she got called into work on days she thought she had off. She never felt like she could relax properly at home.

Uncertainty made it difficult for workers to meet the multiple demands of work on the job and at home. Other researchers have argued that the problem of coping with domestic responsibilities such as childcare and eldercare tend to be more acute for women in precarious employment (Hyman, Scholarios, and Baldry 2005; Nelson, Burke, and Michie 2002). Our study supports these claims with regard to those in the *unsustainable* cluster. We found many women who were responsible for a disproportionate share of unpaid domestic tasks and therefore experienced work-life balance conflict. Women with primary responsibility for caring for an elderly parent found it extremely difficult to manage given their unpredictable work schedules, and told us about the stress this created for them and their families. For instance, one supply teacher bore sole family responsibility for her elderly mother, and noted that it was often difficult for her to accept work if she was not given enough notice to arrange alternative help for her mother.

Women with responsibility for childcare and most of the domestic tasks in their households experienced similar problems. They often had a hard time planning household activities around their uncertain work schedules or, alternatively, accepting last-minute employment opportunities when they were not given sufficient notice to make childcare arrangements. Nabila, the on-call translator, lived with her self-employed husband and their two young sons. She had primary responsibility for childcare and other domestic tasks and old us:

> I don't ever really know my schedule. You never know when you'll get called, and sometimes you don't get much notice. They might call in the morning and want you that same morning ... this is very difficult because if my husband isn't home, then I need to get a babysitter for my one-and-a-half-year-old and this can be difficult without notice ... And sometimes I have to refuse assignments because I can't get to it on time, then I don't make money ... and I don't like refusing, I never know about the next assignment, maybe they'll call someone else (Nabila #5494).

Other women we interviewed said they tried to deal with unpredictable work schedules by doing things like preparing meals ahead of time. A nanny told us that she never knew when her shifts would end, and that this had a negative impact on her family, their routines, and her relationship with both her son and her husband. According to her:

> They [her employers] never tell me when they're coming home. I have to wait. Sometimes they come home, but I have to stay

and look after the kids because they're busy. I must wait until they tell me I can go. I feel so bad; I have no idea when I'm off. They just do what they want. Like I told you, sometimes I won't get home until late, until maybe nine o'clock. I don't even know if I'll have supper with my family. So the only day to shop is Saturday, I shop on Saturday because I don't work. I always shop Saturday, most of the time I prepare supper the night before so there is supper for my family. I never know if I'll be home (Qing #5621).

In short, workers in this cluster have few, if any, commitments for set hours of work or future employment. *Scheduling uncertainty* creates difficulties for day-to-day planning, while uncertain future employment and earnings makes long-term planning extremely complicated. As these workers experiences reveal, key transitions in individuals' lives can be difficult or extremely risky without a stable job and predictable hours and income.

EMPLOYMENT RELATIONSHIP EFFORT

Earlier chapters drew attention to the significance of *employment relationship effort*, and argued that *employment strain* resulted from the combination of *uncertainty* and *effort*. Individuals in this cluster had high levels of *employment relationship effort*, especially with regard to *multiple employer* and *worksite effort*.

Effort Keeping Employed

Three key issues differentiate the effort experienced by this cluster relative to the other clusters of workers in less permanent employment: inadequate time and resources needed to look for employment; dwindling levels of emotional energy required to sustain job searches; and limited ability to challenge poor treatment at work or take other steps needed to improve employment options. In short, what differentiates this cluster from the others is not only the *level* of *employment relationship effort* but also the *nature* of that effort, and the *circumstances* that shape it.

Those in *unsustainable, less permanent employment relationships* often do not have the time, energy, or resources necessary to improve their situation by engaging in unpaid training or undertaking extended job searches for more permanent employment. Individuals in this cluster reported fewer unpaid training hours in comparison to other less permanent workers. Furthermore, these individuals are generally forced to accept the first jobs they are offered because they have so few sources of support and limited personal savings. This was certainly the case for Devon, whose situation had deteriorated in the year between interviews. Having taken a temporary position at a lower wage rate than his previous position, he was unable to meet his monthly expenses and was going further into debt. When asked why he accepted this position rather than looking for a higher paid job, he replied:

I had no money at the time; I had to take the first thing that I could get. I basically took this job because I need the money; I had to take the first thing I could get. I thought, OK, I'll try it. I couldn't afford to take much time to look for work, I had very little money to begin with ... Not being able to have a prolonged job search is a problem to getting a better job (Devon #5051).

Kamara was in a similar situation:

I mean I was desperate, because I've been looking for work since I left in March and I took a week or two off and had income tax returns so I was OK for a while. I was desperate; like I had to take anything that I got (Kamara #5178).

In addition to not having the time or resources to engage in extended job searches or unpaid training, this cluster experiences high levels of frustration leading to pessimism, which may result in them giving up. Allan, the self-employed accountant who took on other casual jobs to earn enough money to pay the rent, was very frustrated with his situation.

I just don't have any energy at the end of the week to look for work. I feel like I never have any energy to do anything. I don't want to look for another job. I don't want to look at the computer. I just get frustrated looking at it. And I can't look if the jobs aren't there (Allan #2493).

The frustration reported by this cluster stemmed from the fact that their job searches and retraining efforts had not paid off. One twenty-nine-year-old worker, Sheng, had been in a full-time contract position as a customer service agent at a licensing office for several years before he was given only five days notice that his contract was not going to be renewed. After failing to find another permanent job, he registered at a temporary employment agency. After several months waiting and sending out his résumé, he was bcoming pessimistic. He said:

I used to just look on the Internet sometimes, but when my job was ended I started looking all time, looking everywhere. I would send out my cv for jobs, I looked in the newspaper and on Workopolis, and I kept calling the agency. But nothing came. I got very frustrated and I'm not looking much now. I tell my dad I'm looking but the truth is, I'm not looking much now. I hope the agency will call me; it is very stressful not having a regular job (Sheng #831).

Many in this cluster felt trapped and isolated, and doubtful that any time and resources they might invest into additional training would pay off in terms of improving their employment options. As outlined in previous chapters, the *sustainable cluster* felt they had a high degree of control over future employment opportunities and could actively and consciously direct their future employment based on investments made in training, networking, and other activities. The *on a path cluster* believed that their hard work and unpaid training would pay off in the long run. In contrast, those in the *unsustainable* cluster were generally despondent about their future and felt that there was little they could do to improve their situations. According to one respondent:

After awhile, after looking for work all the time, I got frustrated. I have too many qualifications and I'm wasting them, I'm

doing this ... You dream and nothing comes of it ... I was looking for work for so long. I'm not really looking now; I just got
discouraged (Nabila #5494).

The experiences of these individuals demonstrate how employment flexibility impacts those individuals at the bottom rung of the
labour market. These are people who are, as one individual put it,
"expendable labour":

> I just seem to be in a state where basically all the tools I have
> are through a job site, through the newspapers, through things
> of that nature where you just have basically hoards of people
> applying and then they just, you know, they don't really check
> your résumé, they don't really care about your background and
> I think that because it's a, I call it like an employer's market
> where there's just so many, there's just so many of us. It's like
> they're sharks in the water and there's just hoards of fish, they
> don't, they just grab whatever one because there's so many of
> us, you know. Just pay them very little, don't have to offer them
> anything because, if they quit, well, there's like a million others
> they can get of us. We have no leverage, you know. And I just, I
> send this stuff out, you know (Dalton #5449).

Because of their sense of helplessness, workers in this cluster were
more likely to put up with poor treatment at work, or to do tasks
unrelated to their job in the hopes of securing future employment.
For many workers in this cluster, keeping employed seemed dependent on their not challenging or reporting harassment or poor treatment, and not refusing to do things unrelated to their work. Given
that many of these individuals were self-employed or working on
temporary contracts, discrimination and harassment were even
harder to prove than for those employed in more permanent relationships. If individuals refused to do things unrelated to their job,
or challenged harassment, their contracts could easily be terminated without any repercussions to their employers. This issue raises
concerns that discrimination and harassment are becoming more
difficult to address in the workplace and that they are "invisible"
amongst those working without commitments.

Multiple Employer and Worksite Effort

Most workers in this cluster worked at more than one location, and many struggled with having multiple employers and conflicting demands from those employers. They reported difficulty juggling multiple short-term, part-time contract jobs, and balancing the conflicting demands of clients and numerous temporary employment agencies. Forty-year-old Kamara had been a temporary worker for several years and was registered through several different agencies. She explained that if you register with more than one agency to improve your employment prospects, you frequently have to balance different contracts or possible contracts against each other, while trying not to get on any agency's "bad side." For example, when she was working on a temporary contact from one agency, she was offered another, higher paid contract with a different agency.

I was offered the other position so I had to lie to get out of the one I was currently working at, because the other one was a little bit more money and it was longer ... but they weren't sure if it was going to go long-term or not. So that, that I don't like at all. Because I don't know where I'm going to be, and plus it puts me in a bad position of having to turn down current work, and I was actually working at the head office of X Services so I was like, please don't find out, you know. If I get on their bad side they're not going to find work for me (Kamara #5178).

EMPLOYMENT RELATIONSHIP SUPPORT

In general, individuals in the *unsustainable* cluster had few sources of *employment relationship support* – limited financial buffers, no partner, parent or other family member to act as a buffer, and limited workplace support. They scored the worst on most survey indicators of *employment relationship support*, and were the least likely to have any support outside of work. They had the lowest individual incomes, were in households with the lowest average incomes, and were less likely to have any employment benefits. Further, these individuals were the most likely to be in households with other individuals in precarious employment relationships.

In terms of *workplace support*, most spoke about feeling isolated from other workers. Many said there were informal divisions between themselves and workers in more permanent employment relationships, and this made them feel like outsiders at work. Few had developed friendships or even close working relationships with colleagues, and none had been able to establish other kinds of work networks outside their workplaces. Nabila, the on-call translator, spoke of her relationship with the temporary employment agency in this way: "there is no one at work, they aren't co-workers" (Nabila #5494). Gabi, the young worker with two part-time casual jobs, expressed similar feelings of isolation. When asked about support at work, she told us about the challenges that she and other casual workers experience "there's a big divide, a wide divide, between the people who work there casual, part-time and the permanent, full-timers. Their offices are separate and we never really talk to them" (Gabi #2649).

Frank's reflections on the lack of relationship he felt during the seven years he worked as a casual teacher summed up the experiences of this cluster well:

> You don't have any relationship with the employer other than the person that you talk directly to. You know that they have virtually no relationship with you. They don't care if they fire you or whether you stay ... So you know, you would go in to this big large building, you are just one person in a large organization and unless there's a problem, you don't even necessarily talk to your employer or your manager or whatever. The only time you talk to him is when there's a problem. There is no sense of a relationship really; even though you see the same people every week. There's no sense of communal working towards some shared goal (Frank #2568).

This lack of support also meant that workers were often responsible for the tasks normally fulfilled by an human resources or accounting department; they were forced to spend their unpaid time and energy tracking down their wages, sorting out responsibilities, or ensuring they received payment for holidays and vacations. Sev-

eral individuals noted that they did not always have a desk or regular workspace, were not given supplies or much administrative
support, and often had to simply fend for themselves. Stella, a
forty-four-year-old who had been working as a contract lecturer for
many years, explained how she forced the college to give her some
resources and support.

> And because I'm a sessional, I often don't have workspace. I've
> got savvy now though, I go in on the first day and say 'OK,
> what computer can I use, what phone line can I use?' I go in
> now and tell them what I want and need. I use their paper now,
> and their ink – but it is still a problem (Stella #5093).

Having few sources of individual support compounded workplace isolation and vulnerability. Hardly anyone in this cluster
had family or friends they could count on, and few had support
in their community. Several were in households with another
individual in precarious employment so other household members could not help them. Their households are those discussed in
chapter 4, where none of the employed adults had a secure
income and there was little protection from the stress of precarious employment.

Several workers noted that their uncertain incomes and unreliable work schedules made socializing difficult. Some felt embar-
rassed about their employment situation; others simply did not
have the financial ability to go out and socialize. This meant that
they had fewer friends to turn to for support. For instance, a fifty-
seven-year-old casual worker, who had primary responsibility for
her elderly mother, said that she had neither the time nor the
money necessary to maintain friendships, and that this isolation
resulted in her having few sources of support. She told us with
sadness:

> I get lonely sometimes because I don't go out with my friends
> and after a while they stop calling, they're always going to be
> my friends but I just don't go, I don't go out for lunches
> because I don't want to spend, you know, twenty dollars for
> lunch with some of them who are in a comfortable space and
> don't have to worry about anything when they go out. So I'm

just always busy when they call. You manage to, you know.
I don't go to movies; I'm home all the time, actually (Polly
#703).

Allan, the accountant who had been in various contract jobs for
several years, had a dwindling circle of friends and only one family
member he could occasionally count on, largely because he limited
his socializing due to lack of time and money. He told us:

> We can't go to the movies because I can't join them. Or they
> want to go out to the bar and have a few drinks; I can't join
> them there either because I don't have the money to pay for
> the drinks. I get together with some classmates about every
> three months and what I basically mean is we sit in the bar
> and talk and buy a pitcher or two and I can't do it. I have to
> tell them, "well I can't join you because I can't pay for the
> beer." I have to either buy food or buy beer; I can't do both.
> So, like they offer to pay but I don't want to look like I'm
> relying on them for everything. So it's impossible to socialize
> sometimes. Or I want to go to the movies with somebody, I
> can't (Allan #2493).

Others had more friends or family members that they could ask for
help, but were reluctant to turn to them except in a real crisis. They
generally tried to cope on their own as much as they could.

The limited sources of support that the *unsustainable* cluster can
access is in sharp contrast to the other two clusters, especially the
sustainable cluster, who had established work networks outside regular employment relationships and had several sources of individual support that served as buffers to uncertainty. Without support,
workers have few buffers to protect them against the chronic stress
and insecurity associated with uncertain employment. And as will
be discussed in the section below, the overall result for them is poor
and deteriorating health.

EMPLOYMENT STRAIN AND HEALTH

Other studies have shown that job insecurity and work intensification are key causes of stress in workers, and that this stress can lead

to psychological and physiological strains (Burchell, Ladipo, and Wilkinson 2002). Our study supports these findings and provides additional information on the key causes of stress for workers in less permanent employment relationships. As we have shown in previous chapters, workers with high *employment relationship uncertainty* and high *employment relationship effort* had the poorest health. Almost all those in the *unsustainable* cluster fell into this quadrant.

Workers in the *unsustainable* cluster reported the worst health on four key indicators in comparison with those in *sustainable* and *on a path* precarious employment relationships. They were more likely to report their general health being poor, and much more likely to report that they worked in pain half the time or more. They had much worse mental health, were more likely to report having work-related sleep disorders, and were far more likely to report that "everything was an effort." The contrasts between the *unsustainable* and *sustainable* clusters are particularly noteworthy: the *unsustainable* cluster was six times more likely to report that they were "exhausted after work most days," almost twice as likely to say that "everything was an effort," and four times as likely to report that they had work-related sleep problems.

Chronic stress appears to be an important determinant of poor physical and mental health for workers in this cluster. As the discussion so far makes clear, *employment fragility*, *earnings uncertainty*, and *scheduling uncertainty* are constant sources of stress. *Multiple employer effort* and *multiple worksite effort* add to the stress. Harassment at work, poor treatment at work, and limited access to support all mean that precarious employment relationships are unsustainable for these workers, and lead to serious health problems. Workers in this cluster told us about digestive and other stomach problems, chronic headaches, ongoing sleeping problems and other anxiety-related issues. Several individuals also acknowledged that the constant stress and anxiety they felt about their employment situation made them short tempered with friends and family, and that these bad moods further isolated them from their few sources of support. Jiro, the engineer, told us that his sleep pattern was disrupted and his relationships with his wife and daughter were suffering as a result of *employment relationship uncertainty.* "Sometimes I can't sleep. Sometimes I have headaches. Scared about money all the time now. Sometimes I feel angry" (Jiro #5120).

Several workers reported that they were taking depression medication, most reported having stress-related health problems (such as sleeping problems, headaches, stomach problems), and many told us that they had noticed significant changes in their weight (often weight gain) because of their inability to exercise or do anything to take care of themselves. Like many others in this cluster, Allan told us that his health was suffering because of employment-related stress (Allan #2493). Frank, the contract teacher, told us how never knowing whether his contracts would be renewed until the last minute affected his mental health.

> Mentally and emotionally I would say I'm worried a lot of the time. So, I'd say I have probably a mild anxiety disorder in general, which is now on full alert. It's so hard to relax (Frank #2568).

Several people spoke about how their precarious employment eroded their self-confidence and had a negative impact on the entire family. Nabila summed it up in this way: "the family can't function like this. Not having work, not having a permanent job, well it impacts your own feelings, how you feel about yourself" (Nabila #5494).

A number in the cluster confessed that they were avoiding going to the doctor or dealing with health issues because they were afraid to find out how bad their health was. To quote Allan again:

> I don't get enough sleep because I don't know what happens from day to day. But I know I've got chest tightness sometimes from stress. I've got a friend who calls me every day to ask me how I'm doing but I say I'm OK. But you know deep down that you're not. You've got all this worry that you look for jobs and there's nothing there for you. I haven't seen a doctor in a number of years. Because I'm afraid to find out what a doctor might tell me. If he does find anything wrong I don't know how I'd pay for the medications (Allan #2493).

A number of workers with previous health conditions told us that their health was deteriorating as a result of living with chronic stress, or with not having health benefits or enough money to pay for medical treatments. For instance, a few individuals with minor health issues such as dental cavities acknowledged that their problems would require more extensive treatment later if they did not treat them now, but could not afford to take action. Others said that they were not taking medicine that had been prescribed for them because they didn't have the money and had no medical benefits. Other workers recognized the risks they were taking by ignoring their health, but felt limited in other ways: for instance, a temporary worker with carpel tunnel syndrome did not wear her wrist brace to work for fear she would not get promoted to a full-time, permanent job.

> That's true, I'm not [wearing the brace]. Because I'm afraid; because in this position, the other temp had to leave for an operation so I'm afraid they're unhappy because as soon as they offer people a job, they say 'oh by the way, I have to go for surgery,' because I know my mom had surgery on it. So I'm just trying to be so careful. Like if anybody sees me ... I do cry out in pain because it does hurt but I purposely am not going to wear the brace that I have. And as I said to my mom, even if I do go to the doctor and it does require something, I'm not going to be able to do it until I'm working full-time anywhere because then I need the benefits (Kamara #5178).

Other research has shown that one reason for a higher incidence of injury and illness in this group is that workers are at increased risk when a workplace is "disorganized" (i.e. when union presence is limited), when work processes are fragmented, and when workers move between multiple worksites and have limited awareness of procedures and process (Quinlan 2003; Quinlan, Mayhew, and Bohle 2001; Quinlan and Mayhew 2006). Our interviews support these observations. Several workers felt unprotected by labour legislation, health and safety legislation, and employment-linked public supports. As mentioned above, workers in this cluster were unlikely to have health benefits such as paid sick leave, and often could not access employment insurance because they either did not work enough weeks to qualify or could not afford to be unemployed long enough to collect benefits. Several individuals were aware of health and safety legislation, but had received limited training at work, or felt that they did not have the ability to exercise their rights. The experiences of one contract worker (a technician installing cable for a company that had jobs outsourced to them from a large phone company) highlights these issues:

> I needed ladder hooks to hook onto cables on the poles; they didn't have the hooks for the ladders. And they were supposed to have a safety harness for climbing up the poles and they didn't provide that either. There was a lot of safety equipment they didn't really provide, but we had to do the work. They would just say, just go out there and do the job. ... I was doing a house. I had my ladder up against a cable strand on the poles and one of the cables broke and almost fell. So that was very scary. It would have been a thirty-foot fall (Randy #5208).

Our study also provided some evidence that workers' health deteriorates the longer they are exposed to stress associated with high levels of *employment relationship uncertainty* and *employment relationship effort*, and low levels of *employment relationship support*. We conducted twelve random, follow-up interviews with individuals in this cluster a year later. Only one individual thought that his situation had improved. He had found a three-month contract that he hoped would become permanent, and his situation was now more like those in the *on a path* cluster. All the other workers we spoke to were worse off; often much worse off. In general, their health had deteriorated, their financial situation had worsened, and many reported feeling more socially isolated. In addition, a number of workers said that they had diminishing support. For instance, Polly, the supply teacher, was one of the only workers in this cluster who was a union member, and felt connected and supported by other teachers through her union activities. However, rising levels of stress over the year as a result of employment insecurity and difficulty balancing her unpredictable schedule with caring for her aging mother made her unable to participate in the union. "I used to go to union meetings, but I just don't have the energy anymore" (Polly #703).

Several people felt that the labour market situation was encouraging employers' to realize short-term cost-savings by offering temporary employment, and that finding full-time, permanent employment was getting more difficult. Jiro had seen competition for cell phone contracts increase and his commissions drop over the previous year.

> All the big companies outsource. When they outsource, they control costs and prices go down. They don't care about you. Business is not stable, you can't survive. We cannot survive working like this; before we could survive; now we can't (Jiro #5120).

Lance had similar observations after working as a self-employed graphic designer for almost a decade. His situation had also deteriorated over the year, partly as a result of increased competition from designers bidding on contracts from low waged countries. "It is hugely competitive. Far more competitive than when we started" (Lance #2747).

However, despite worsening health and fewer employment opportunities, some workers were not prepared to give up. Stella provides an excellent example of someone who had actually become *more* confident about fighting for better employment protection. Her situation had deteriorated quite significantly. Faced with escalating debt and continued insecurity about contract teaching at the college, she'd reconciled with her ex-husband – someone who had been abusive in the past – and had moved back in with him. Her situation went from bad to worse after the college cut back her courses and her relationship with her partner soured again. When he started showing signs that his anger was not under control and might erupt into abuse again Stella was forced to flee, and she had spent part of the year in a shelter. Nonetheless, she became active in a union fighting to improve contract lecturers' rights. She had recently moved into a small apartment on her own, and the support she was receiving from her activism and other contract lecturers in the cluster gave her the confidence to demand better treatment from her employer.

> I can't predict my schedule, or future work. It's not that I will be fired, but that I won't be rehired. The college doesn't have to have any accountability to us, they can use us from semester to semester, they don't have to worry about paying us benefits or, or just providing for us. They can just say 'bye, bye.' If we start to get expensive, they just hire someone else on contract ... I feel like I'm trapped in a cycle of uncertainty, a cycle of anxiety. My stress levels have gone up due to my inability to sustain myself financially, in that I am in an even more precarious situation because I have even less ability to predict my income. But, I'm trying to take some control back now. I decided that I didn't want this to happen anymore. It's not OK for me to become less than a marginal citizen anymore. I have hope, because I'm doing advocacy work. I have some buffer tools. Last year I thought my case was isolated, I thought it was an individual problem but I've gotten involved in the advocacy work so I see that it is a broader problem. This has helped. I don't feel as isolated (Stella #5093).

Many of the comments from interviewees offer insights into their vulnerability and how their employment situation has negatively impacted their health and well-being. As we have seen, workers in this cluster are in employment arrangements that are void of any type of commitment and they generally have scant forms of support. Prolonged exposure to the stress linked to such uncertainty means that these precarious employment relationships become toxic and workers and their families suffer negative consequences.

CONCLUSION

This chapter explored the employment experiences of the third and largest group of workers in less permanent employment relations: those in *unsustainable* relationships. What differentiates this cluster from the other two clusters discussed in the book is the almost complete lack of commitment from their employers, compounded by limited support at work, from their households, or in the community. As outlined in the chapter, those in the *unsustainable* cluster did not choose this type of employment relationship, are extremely dissatisfied with their employment, and desperately want to find more permanent employment. In addition, they have very low and unstable earnings, few employment benefits, limited access to social security benefits, and scant support of any kind. The overall result is that individuals in this cluster report poor and deteriorating health, largely as a result of chronic stress and insecurity linked to their unstable and uncertain employment.

Whatever the causes of their circumstances – market changes, regional shifts, outdated skills, or exposure to more competitive labour markets – it is clear that workers in unsustainable relationships suffer physically, mentally, economically, and socially. Survey and interview data demonstrate that those in this cluster have worse health as a result of working without commitments. Follow-up interviews suggested ongoing stress also contributed to workers' diminished hopes of ever finding more permanent jobs. Yet these workers did not believe that positive changes in the labour market were impossible; indeed, most felt that although the current situation was unacceptable, it could change if government and employers were willing to take action.

These workers were all too aware of their economic and social displacement. At best they felt left behind. At worst, they felt like their work only made others better off. As Daniel expressed it:

I think there is something very wrong with the idea, they seem to think that we have to make a more prosperous economy by having large numbers of people on low wages, that's not prosperity at all (Daniel #5051).

These workers' desire to find new jobs or create more certainty in their existing positions was often greater after being in precarious employment for a short period of time. But many had difficulty sustaining the drive to improve their situations in the long-run because they became worn out. In addition to trying to find ways to improve their own situations, those we interviewed also expressed a strong belief in the possibility of government policies helping them. Many felt that new policies, or the reform of existing policies and programs, might introduce more stability into their employment situations. This chapter points to the need for comprehensive policies that respond to the particular needs of those in *unsustainable, less permanent employment relationships*. The next chapter will explore some of the policy options that might be pursued by employers and governments to increase commitments between employers and employees. In particular, it will outline some innovative ways that policy-makers can reduce toxic employment relationships to keep citizens from feeling marginalized.

10

Creating Commitments in Less Permanent Employment: Policy Reforms to Address Rising Insecurity

Something needs to be done. Temporary agencies should pay their employees the minimum rate of eight dollars or more per hour; not less than eight dollars per hour. Temporary agencies should pay their employees the statutory holidays ... Companies and agencies should give enough or adequate notice to the temporary employees if they're not needed for the following day. And, if it happened that an employee/employees reported to work and were then sent back home, employees should be paid always a minimum three hours (Alex #563).

INTRODUCTION

This study found warning signs that the growth of employment flexibility, especially when it is unaccompanied by income security and employment support, is likely to contribute to diminished health among workers, and possibly even to a less efficient and more poorly trained workforce. Without any real public dialogue or awareness, Canadians have moved out of an era when we expected employers – sometimes with the help of unions – to handle responsibilities for hiring, training, health care insurance, pensions, and a range of other employment-related supports and benefits. Our study shows that the gradual transfer of these responsibilities and costs to individuals imposes new burdens on workers and their families. In the short run, many workers have to draw on assets, savings, and employment benefits accumulated in a more stable era of permanent employment. As well, their failing health will add to existing pressure on the public health care system and steadily increase health care costs. This dwindling of individual assets combined with increased worker health problems will mean that a more flexible labour market relying on people working without commitments is unlikely to be sustainable in the long run. What is required are comprehensive policies and new strategies that respond to workers' needs, especially the needs of those in *unsustainable, less permanent employment relationships*. As one survey participant commented, "something needs to be done" to address these problems. But what is that "something"?

To discover it, we need to re-think what is currently understood to be a "wage," and reconsider the security and support workers need not only to stay healthy but also to reproduce the next generation of workers. This study has shown that good health is based on more than the exchange of time for money. To stay healthy, workers cannot be traded on markets like commodities, as the ILO cautioned almost a century ago. Current policies, social programs, and labour legislation are increasingly inadequate for the contemporary workforce. Public policies and social programs are unable to offer workers the support they need to navigate contemporary labour markets or to buffer them while they work without commitments. This has become increasingly apparent as the financial crisis that began in 2008 deepens. More and more workers and their families are finding themselves without the security of permanent employment as a result of the shift from full-time employment in high-paying sectors to part-time employment, self-employment, and low wage positions (Tal 2009). Although it is too early to predict the longer-term outcomes of the current recession, even the short-term effects are cause for concern, given our findings.

Two related theoretical arguments are advanced in this book. First, following the work of Rubery et al. (2002), we offer an expanded notion of the employment relationship that takes into account the changing nature of work and employment. Our approach broadens the focus beyond the legal contract that shapes the exchange of time and/or services for remuneration. The concept of *employment relationship* developed in this book takes into account the employment-related effort of finding, securing, and keeping employment; control over the setting of future terms and conditions of employment; the costs and benefits of having multiple employers, work-sites, sets of co-workers, and supervisors; control over where and when work is done; and social relations at work, such as levels of support from employers and co-workers.

Second, we introduce the notion of "commitment" into our analysis of the employment relationship. Commitment represents a broad set of social factors that reflect the extent to which workers and employers have entered a mutual long-term relationship involving support and concern for the social and economic development of workers and the economic and social community of which they are members. Our study suggests that the commitments built into post-World War II permanent employment contributed positively to workers' health, and to the well-being of their households. Based on our expanded understanding of the employment relationship, we contend that high levels of *employment relationship uncertainty,* high levels of *employment relationship effort,* and low levels of *employment relationship support* are indicators of low levels of working with commitments and expose workers to *employment strain.* Workers whose relationships manifest these characteristics can be said to be in precarious employment. While our research is based on a single survey describing conditions at a particular point in time, we suggest that the prevalence of individuals in our sample whom we would describe as "working without commitments" is indicative of an increase in this form of employment and a possible harbinger of future developments.

Our research leads us to argue that in formulating a policy response, it is important not to merely associate precarious employment with low pay and limited social benefits and entitlements. Nor will the problems of those in less permanent employment be resolved by simply strengthening the existing health and safety regulatory system. Many of the health risks we have identified are related to stress, a condition against which existing regulatory systems provide relatively weak protection. More importantly, the risks we have identified are located mostly outside of the workplace itself. They are embedded in the ways by means of which workers find and keep work, and also in how they periodically renegotiate the terms and conditions of their employment. This is not to suggest that better health and safety regulations would play no role in improving the lives of workers. Rather, our study points to a need for a more comprehensive understanding of *how* and *why* the current regulatory framework and specific policies impact health.

The *employment strain model* provides a framework for such an analysis, and the basis for identifying the responses needed to bring a certain level of commitment and security back into employment relationships. As our study demonstrates, commitments are crucial to shaping health outcomes for workers. Turning workers back into commodities (as was the norm during the early capitalist labour markets and "free wage labour" discussed in chapter 2) is not only unpleasant for workers, but unhealthy for them and their families. Although we focus on the Canadian experience, experiences in other countries suggest that a similar shift towards flexible labour markets has taken place with similar results (Commission of the European Communities 2006; ILO 2006).

Permanent employment relationships are embedded in a set of social norms and practices which imply a level of commitment between employer and worker that goes beyond contractual securities. In relationships that still echo the old "standard employment" norm, employers invest in the development of their workers through a range of programs such as employer-supported training. They generally provide long-term security and protection for workers and their families through paid parental leaves, childcare subsidies, health plans, and other benefits. Staff parties and company-sponsored social events are other ways in which employers invest in the well-being of their workers and demonstrate their commitment. Workers in permanent employment relationships are more willing to invest in institutions such as trade unions that further advance their short-term and long-term interests. The combination of employer commitments to the long-term development of workers, and worker investment in their own collective organizations, make possible social networks between workers, and between workers and their employers.

In contrast, employers who have few or limited commitments to their workers tend to invest little in their training, career development, employment security, or protection. As a result, workers are required to use their own time and resources (and those of their family and friends, or other personal networks) for training, workplace health and safety preparation, educational courses, and other activities linked to career and skills development. Workers in relationships without commitments are generally forced to create and maintain the kinds of support networks of colleagues and services that are found in more permanent employment relationships. They are more responsible for insuring themselves against the costs of illness, economic dislocation, and old age. As employers weaken their commitment to their workforce, unpaid employment-related effort takes place, as workers search for work on their own time, engage in training, or perform tasks for employers beyond those defined in their contracts. The temporary nature of their own commitments to their employers makes investment in collective organizations less attractive and consequently denies these workers other sources of support. As a result, in addition to the stress associated with finding and keeping work, workers in relationships without commitments face greater uncertainty regarding their rights to future employment, and their control over workload, treatment at work, hours of work, and their wages.

Our study found that some workers – albeit a small and privileged cluster – had less permanent forms of employment that were sustainable and rewarding (see chapter 7). Their success depended on a unique set of circumstances: ongoing support inside and outside the workplace; access to health insurance; pensions; or other public supports from a family member or from previous employment; and work networks with core clients. Despite not having permanent employment, these workers had high levels of certainty surrounding future employment and had replicated other commitments that are associated with full-time, permanent employment relationships. For this small group, the transition to more flexible employment arrangements created new opportunities for self-realization. The question remains as to how, and to what degree, these same conditions can be extended to the majority of workers in our study who were not in *sustainable, less permanent employment relationships*.

Some analysts warn that strategies aimed at moving back to a model of employment based on mutual commitments and long-term job security are problematic, because our globalized and market-driven economy is no longer compatible with this type of employment (Cappelli 1999). Others argue that changing attitudes to work also mean that young workers are less committed to the "standard employment relationship" and its implicit trade-off of increased security for reduced personal flexibility (Gorz 2005). We agree that going back is unlikely. However, our study suggests that, at present, we are caught between the forces pushing us towards flexibility in labour markets and a set of social supports based on the "standard employment relationship." In particular, we face the reality that employers are not prepared to carry as many responsibilities as they have in the past, and are willing to pay only a portion of the social wage that workers need in order to live healthy productive lives, and that families and communities need to prosper. If this cannot be reversed, other social actors must become involved in putting commitments – and therefore security – back into economic relationships.

The remainder of this chapter explores two paths to improved health for those in less permanent employment. The first section looks at policy options and labour market regulations that can reduce income uncertainty, assist workers in finding employment, and provide social support. The proposals are not particularly radical; nor will they dramatically improve the situation of less permanent workers who are being buffeted by forces beyond the control of policy initiatives of individual states. Industrial relations systems designed in the 1930s to reduce social inequality are no longer working because employment has been reconfigured to avoid the constraints implicit in these systems, including collective bargaining.[1] It is unlikely we can put the genie back in the bottle and return to the system prevalent during the heyday of the "standard employment relationship." The proposals in this first section should be seen as simply a bridge to fundamentally new forms of employment relationship and labour market regulation. The second section explores more radical strategies; strategies with the potential to *reshape* the relationship between work and the individual. While we are not ready to go as far as some and declare that we are leaving the "work-based" society, we do agree with Gorz that less permanent work "must be civilised and recognised so that, rather than being a condition one reluctantly bears, this pattern of working can

1 We would like to thank Michael Quinlan for his comments on an early version of this chapter, and in particular for sharing his own assessment that returning to the world of employment characteristic of the post World War II period is highly unlikely.

become a mode of life one chooses, a mode that is desirable, one that is regulated and valued by society" (Gorz 2005: 53).

OPTIONS FOR A NEW LABOUR MARKET
POLICY FRAMEWORK

The contemporary debate over how to regulate labour markets is shaped by the dominant belief that flexibility – that is, increasing the responsiveness of labour markets – is the key to promoting economic activity and higher productivity (Commission of the European Communities 2006: ILO 2006). Two broad and opposing policy regimes dominate this debate. At one end is the neo-liberal market-driven system that dominates debates in North America and that promotes minimal intervention in labour markets. Advocates of this system argue that economic and labour regulations and statutory employment benefits lead to lower profits, reduced investment and innovation, and lower productivity gains. This approach therefore embraces de-regulation of labour markets, minimization of mandated benefits such as pensions and unemployment insurance, the weakening of trade unions, and free trade, in order to make firms more competitive internationally. In addition, this approach transfers more responsibility and costs onto individuals for training, retraining, health, and retirement. Some view this positively as a labour market made up of "free agents" (Pink 2001). Others describe this approach less glowingly as a "Gloves-off Economy" (Bernhardt et al. 2008). It is likely that pursuing this path will increase the polarization already underway in labour markets. One can expect a shrinking core of the workforce in full-time, permanent positions with benefits, a small group of highly paid flexible workers, and a large and growing group of workers in employment relationships with few benefits and decreasing levels of commitments. Reports sponsored by the European Union warn of the emergence of a labour market of "insiders" – those having permanent employment – and "outsiders," including the unemployed and those employed precariously (Commission of the European Communities 2006).

The findings of this study suggest that the market-driven approach described above is not a sustainable policy direction in the long run. This type of system downloads the risks and costs of flexibility onto workers. Not only will this policy option *not* prevent the health costs associated with flexible labour markets but these costs will likely increase, slowing economic growth and escalating social and health problems for a large and increasing number of workers and their families. While it is unclear when the breaking point will be, it does seem quite clear that at some point society will be forced to pay for the increase in toxic employment relationships.

A second policy regime aims to facilitate the coexistence of flexible labour markets with employment and social security for workers. While employment policies make it relatively easy to hire and fire workers, active labour market policies, training policies, and generous unemployment and social security benefits buffer the negative impact of employment insecurity. The goal is a set of policies that "regulates" flexibility (Sciarra 2008). The emphasis of these policies is not to recreate the "standard employment relationship" model of lifetime employment with a single employer but rather to focus on employability, and therefore facilitate easy movement between jobs. The ILO describes this as a shift from a model where labour-market flexibility leads to insecurity to one where security fosters greater flexibility (ILO 2006). Economic history provides some support for this hypothesis, suggesting that those nineteenth-century European economies that moved to regulate their labour markets so as to protect workers from some of the insecurity associated with the emerging industrial system also benefited from more stable industrial relations and improved productivity (Huberman and Lewchuk 2003). This type of policy regime, referred to as "flexicurity," has already been adopted in several European countries, and is being proposed and debated in other EU countries as a way to ensure that flexible labour markets are coupled with adequate social security (Commission of the European Communities 2006; European Expert Group on Flexicurity 2007; Philips et al. 2007; Keune 2008).[2] This approach embraces various types of labour market flexibility with active labour market policies, lifelong learning, and a strong social welfare program (including fair-

2 The European Union has issued framework agreements on Part-time Work and on Fixed-term Work that instruct member countries to enact regulations to ensure equal treatment of these groups relative to those in full-time permanent employment.

ly generous and long lasting unemployment benefits and social assistance). Other policies and programs may be introduced as well to encourage work-life balance and gender equity.

Two popular models of flexicurity, one in the Netherlands and one in Denmark, provide examples of how such an approach might work. The Dutch system places more emphasis on regulating the employment relationship of workers in less permanent employment relationships. It is sometimes referred to as an approach that seeks to "normalize" non-standard and precarious employment. Existing employment protection legislation was revised to lessen restrictions on employers releasing workers in "standard employment relationships" while simultaneously increasing protections for workers in non-standard and temporary employment relationships. Policies use a life-cycle model that allows workers to take time off for education and childcare, and guarantees them a steady income even when work hours are irregular. State support is provided to encourage voluntary saving schemes that spread earnings over non-work periods, and significant public resources are allocated to ease the transition between jobs (Viebrock and Clasen, 2009: 314–15). Under certain conditions, fixed term contracts are automatically converted into permanent contracts (Burri 2009). This is described as a "tenure track" model of labour markets, in which workers acquire increased security as their tenure with an employer or temporary employment agency increases (Wilthagen and Tros 2004: 174; European Expert Group on Flexicurity 2007: 35).

The Danish approach to flexible labour markets is often referred to as the "golden triangle": high levels of labour market flexibility, high levels of income security, and significant spending on active labour market policies. Its origin is a series of social compromises over the last hundred years, including a recognition of employers' right to hire and fire that dates back to the very end of the nineteenth century, the introduction of generous social welfare supports after World War II, and finally the loosening of employment protection legislation for permanent workers and the introduction of active labour market policies in the 1990s (Zhou 2007). Between one-quarter and one-third of Danes change jobs each year. Average job tenure in Denmark is eight years; slightly higher than in the US, but much lower than in most other European countries (Bredgaard et al. 2005: 10).

In the decade since the last component of the flexicurity model was implemented in Denmark, several studies have evaluated its effectiveness on a number of parameters. Bredgaard et al. (2005) suggest several advantages of labour market flexibility. It can support innovation, as firms will be more willing to employ new workers if there will be few penalties should those workers need to be laid off. It also facilitates the rapid reallocation of labour from low productivity to high productivity sectors. It is hypothesized that this makes employers more willing to create jobs. The disadvantage is that as employment relationships become increasingly short-term, employers have less incentive to train their workers and may also be less vigilant in protecting the health of their workers. Kvist and Pedersen (2007) report that most Danes view labour market activation as having a positive effect on their welfare: seventy percent report better daily life; fifty-eight percent better self-esteem, and about half improved labour market qualifications. Only one-quarter had a negative view of activation (Kvist and Pedersen 2007: 108).

Boeri and Garibaldi (2009) examined worker satisfaction over the decade that ended in 2005 in Denmark and other countries, using data from the European Survey of Working Conditions. They found an overall decline from about eighty-five percent to eighty percent in reported job satisfaction in the fifteen EU countries. Workers in Denmark were the most likely to report being satisfied with their jobs (greater than ninety percent), with only a marginal decline between 1995 and 2005. Another evaluation of the Danish system concluded: "Based on the above description of the Danish labour market as providing a rather insecure environment for the individual wage earner, one could suspect that Danish employees would regard their working life as unsafe and risky. The paradox is that the vast majority of studies of working-life satisfaction (and life-satisfaction in general) come to the conclusion that Danes are among the populations expressing the highest level of job-satisfaction and sense of stability in their working-life. With respect to life-satisfaction in general, the Danes are simply the happiest Europeans that one can find" (Madsen 2006: 148).

The flexicurity model goes a long way towards reducing *employment relationship uncertainty*, and *employment relationship effort*. Not only have policy developments in countries such as Denmark and the Netherlands meant that some groups of workers in flexible employment relations (e.g. fixed-term contract workers, workers on-call, or temp workers) now have better working conditions than in the past, but more workers are employed in full-time, permanent employment arrangement than is the case in Canada (Burri 2009: 127). While the laissez-faire system described above is based on deregulation, flexicurity is based on the re-regulation of the labour market. However, it emphasizes *employment* rather than job security. It does not try to recreate the "standard employment relationship" of the post World War II era. Variations on the flexicurity model are currently being proposed for other EU countries. Based on extensive research on the strengths and weaknesses of various European models, Wilkinson and Ladipo (2002) argue that we need to focus more on the security side by strengthening labour laws and labour market institutions, regulating technological developments, increasing the role of trade unions in policy development and workplace restructuring, and developing active labour market policies that combine high quality training, job creation, and measures to support labour mobility.

While these two approaches to policy reform – laissez-faire deregulation and flexicurity – have framed the debate, other courses of action exist. Two should be noted. One is to demand the restoration of the "standard employment relationship." This is unlikely in the current economic context and may be undesirable in markets where labour mobility is valued by employers and workers. In addition, as previous chapters have shown, while the "standard employment relationship" did provide secure, protected employment with benefits to workers in certain sectors, even at its height it benefited only a segment of the workforce – usually white male workers in core sectors of the economy. Some elements of the flexicurity model achieve this by making less permanent employment less attractive or by giving workers new rights as they accumulate service with an employer. While a wholesale return to the "standard employment relationship" is unlikely, there are certainly some sectors and some workplaces where policies should encourage its continuation, strengthening, and expansion as one way to restore working with commitments (Standing 2002; Benach et al. 2007; Benach and Muntaner forthcoming).

Another alternative is to abandon efforts to re-regulate labour markets and instead focus on improving social protection and compensation for those whose health suffers as a result of stress related to less permanent employment. Such strategies would increase *employment relationship support* for workers – a critical factor for reducing *employment strain*. This might include more generous worker compensation schemes, better public health resources, disability pensions, and early retirement. Such a strategy would be expensive and is therefore unlikely to be considered in the current economy. Moreover it would be a significant drag on the overall performance of any economy.

None of the approaches discussed above goes very far towards creating a model of working with commitments that would contribute to worker health. At best, they might mitigate the negative effects of less permanent employment or compensate workers for injuries. Flexicurity's emphasis on protective regulations, income support, and training begins to address some of the policy needs outlined above but does not fully address health problems resulting from *high employment strain* and working without commitments. As well, studies suggest that EU directives such as the one on Fixed-term Work or national legislation such as the Dutch Act on Flexibility and Security have had a limited effect on employer strategies (Larson 2008; Burri 2009). At their core, these are still labour market systems that individualize employment relationships and weaken the bond between employers and workers, and between workers themselves.

Interestingly, despite the shift towards flexible labour markets in Canada and elsewhere, there does seem to be widespread recognition of the need to have commitments built into employment relationships and an expectation that employers will provide some benefits to ensure a modicum of *employment relationship certainty* and *employment relationship support*. For instance, an annual competition ("Canada's Top 100 Employers") aims to identify the companies and organizations that lead their industries in attracting and retaining employees. This year, as in every previous year since the project's inception ten years ago, companies were selected based on their performance in eight key areas. Five of the eight areas (Health; Financial and Family Benefits; Vacation and Time Off; Work Atmosphere and Social; Training and Skills Development; and Community Involvement) implicitly accept and support the importance of working with commitments. With these general options and policy frameworks in mind, we will now explore some concrete areas for policy reform in the Canadian context. At the heart of these proposals is the importance of increasing commitments between employers and workers.

A POLICY AGENDA FOR POST-STANDARD EMPLOYMENT LABOUR MARKETS

The agenda for policy reform needs to be situated within the current context of the global financial crisis. Canadian employers have responded to the economic downturn by laying-off workers, reducing people to part-time status, and cutting wages and benefits. By October 2009, one year into the financial crisis, approximately 370,000 Canadian workers had lost their jobs (Hennessy and Yalnizyan 2009: 1). Analysts suggest the economy is continuing to shed permanent full-time jobs, many in sectors where the "standard employment relationship" has been the norm (Tal 2009). Thousands of Canadian auto-workers have lost their jobs or have been forced to accept wage and benefit cuts. Those finding new jobs are resorting to non-union temporary and part-time service sector employment. A significant proportion of jobs in the Canadian steel sector have been lost and production transferred off-shore. Print media workers are facing a contracting out of key tasks as the newspapers prune their workforce. Thousands of workers are facing major cuts to their pensions as firms with underfunded pension plans declare bankruptcy. Of course, these trends are not limited to Canada. There are numerous reports of workers in the United States being asked to take pay cuts and in the United Kingdom, the British Chamber of Commerce reported that, based on a survey from four hundred companies, fifty-eight per cent of businesses are planning wage freezes in the second half of 2009 and half are considering or certain to make redundancies in the next six months.[3]

Rising unemployment and wage cuts are not new or surprising during a recession. However, some current issues are unique, and should set off alarm bells for Canadian policy-makers. First, unlike in previous recessions, temporary shut-downs were not the cause of

---

3 http://www.britishchambers.org.uk/zones/policy/press-releases_1/majority-of-firms-plan-to-freeze-wages-as-recession-continues-to-bite.html

many of the jobs lost over the last year. More flexible production systems and weaker commitments from employers to their workforce have facilitated permanent shifts of jobs to other jurisdictions. Second, Canada entered this recession with greater social and economic problems than in the past. For instance, despite the economic boom between 2002 and 2007, income inequality increased (Hennessy and Yalnizyan, 2009). Most of the gains in economic equality associated with the rise of unions and the spread of social welfare programmes since the start of the twentieth century have been rolled back.[4] Third, not only is the social safety-net full of holes as a result of neoliberal policies introduced over the last several decades, research suggests that Canadians have never entered a recession with so much household debt (Hennessy and Yalnizyan 2009: 3). Personal and business bankruptcies have risen dramatically, as has the demand for services from food banks. Nearly 800,000 Canadians accessed a food bank in March of 2009.[5]

While the long-term impact of the recession on employment relationships and employment security is difficult to predict, the massive job losses that have taken place in the last year, especially amongst men in their prime working years (that is, aged twenty-five to fifty-five) and the parallel rise in part-time work and self-employment, when added to the lack of social assistance for unemployed workers, will take a significant toll on families and communities across Canada. A growing number of unemployed Canadians are in urgent need of retraining, as well as of unemployment benefits and other social security supports, but they are less likely to receive such assistance than during earlier downturns (Osberg 2009). While politicians applaud the recent rise of self-employment as an indica-

---

4 Canada is not unique in this sense. For example, by 2005, the share of total US income going to the richest ten percent of Americans was higher than it was in 1917 and had increased by almost one-third since 1967 (McNally 2009: 40).

5 Food banks in Canada provide emergency food assistance. Research from food banks across Canada suggests that people with low-waged, insecure jobs constitute a large and growing group of food-bank clients. Food Banks Canada has noted a twenty percent national rise in people using food banks over a one-year period, while the Salvation Army Food Banks across Canada reported a seventy-two percent increase in users and forty percent decrease in donations (Food Banks Canada 2009).

tor of economic recovery, the evidence of rising poverty and inequality across the country demonstrates that this growth in self-employment is little more than a survival strategy for most individuals. The current study confirms this fact, and suggests the need for immediate action. Even as the financial crisis exposes the weakness in the existing policy framework, it also opens up possibilities for restructuring the employment relationship and reducing employment insecurity. What is required, we believe, is a policy framework that is less focused on life-time employment with a single employer and more cognizant of the stress associated with new forms of employment and their impact on health and productivity.

As Thomas and others point out, there is a need to re-regulate the labour market from the bottom up, and to re-think labour market regulation in light of current employment realities. "Improvements to specific standards will not be sufficient to adequately address the structural transformations that have reshaped labour markets over the past several decades, however, as they remain rooted in a system of labour market regulation built upon the norm of the standard employment relationship. A much more thorough process of labour market re-regulation may be required to reflect the proliferation of non-standard employment relations and labour market precariousness" (Thomas 2009: 161). A first step towards addressing these concerns is to review what can be done to reduce *employment relationship uncertainty* and *employment relationship effort* and to increase *employment relationship support,* the three factors contributing to *employment relationship strain.* Employers argue that they need increased flexibility in labour markets to operate competitively in the global environment, but regulations that facilitate flexibility must not allow them to abandon their obligations to their workers or expose them to unhealthy levels of stress. New strategies are needed to deal with increased employment fragility, income security, and gaps in employment benefits. Workers need more help finding jobs and training for new careers, and they need to be supported in their day-to-day work lives. Existing unions and other worker organizations need to develop new strategies so that collective organization may be brought to those working without commitments.

One important component of these reforms is the need to broaden the scope of labour legislation to cover more workers in less permanent employment relationships. For instance, the existing common law distinction between "employee" and "independent contractor" is not a useful basis for delineating the personal scope of labour and employment laws (Fudge, Tucker, and Vosko 2002: 107; ILO 2006). In the absence of a consistent test to determine who is an employee and who is an independent contractor, labour laws are applied and interpreted in an ad hoc manner. We agree with others who suggest that workers should be defined as "persons economically dependent on the sale of their working capacity, unless there is a compelling reason for not doing so" (Fudge, Tucker, and Vosko 2002: 109).

As well as broadening the coverage of existing regulations, there needs to be a greater understanding of the vulnerability of workers in short-term positions and their reluctance to exercise their rights for fear of repercussions or of compromising future employment prospects. Introducing new regulations will have little impact if workers are afraid to take advantage of them. This will require new, and more comprehensive, enforcement programs and the agencies responsible will need to be more focused on the vulnerability of workers in less permanent employment relationships (Fudge, Tucker, and Vosko 2002; Quinlan 2003; Bernstein et al. 2006; Bernstein 2006). They will have to be willing to enforce standards on behalf of workers, and to defend those workers who claim employers are not renewing contracts in response to their efforts to exercise their rights.

PROPOSALS TO REDUCE EMPLOYMENT
RELATIONSHIP UNCERTAINTY

The keys to reducing *employment relationship uncertainty* are to make employment less fragile and informal, to make income more secure, and give workers more control over the scheduling of work. Proposals forcing employers to convert temporary and short-term jobs into permanent positions would go some way to improving the situation, but it is unclear if there is the will in Canada to move down the path of tenure-based employment rights as implemented in European countries adopting "flexicurity" models. The other way insecurity can be reduced is through "formalizing" short-term and temporary placement contracts. Common complaints of those in our study was that they did not have written contracts, were paid in cash with no formal record of how their pay was calculated, and their pay was often different from what they expected. Requiring employers to provide written contracts setting out the terms and conditions of employment and assignment end-dates, plus employing a formal system for recording hours worked and calculating pay, would go some way to removing this insecurity. Another problem for workers in our study was that they received little or no notice of work assignments. This issue could be solved if employers were required to provide advance notice of work assignments or pay workers a premium for undertaking work at short notice. Paying a premium for overtime hours is a well-established practice, introduced originally to discourage the use of overtime. A similar program requiring employers to plan work schedules in advance or pay a wage premium might also discourage the current practice of last-minute work assignments.

As well, workers need a more effective avenue of recourse if their job descriptions turn out to have been misleading or their employers do not living up to current labour standards. Recent changes in Ontario provide workers with a little more protection in this area. The province now requires employers to provide temporary agency workers with details of their work assignments and gives workers the right to seek remedy from both their placement agency and the company that employs them should their rights be violated. In addition, agencies can no longer block the conversion of a temporary position into a permanent one. This has reduced some employment uncertainty for this class of worker.[6] However, there is still a need for an external agency that can take up issues like these as they arise, and can also defend workers if reporting problems at work results in retribution by employers.

Enhancing severance payments for short-term contract workers would create an incentive for employers to provide longer-term contracts as well as a financial buffer for workers having to regu-

---

6 The Ontario provincial government has gone some way towards ensuring this is the case for temporary agency workers by introducing new labour regulations in November of 2009. For details about these regulations, see the Ontario Ministry of Labour web site at http://www.labour.gov.on.ca/english /es/pubs/guide/tempagencies.php.

larly search for new jobs. Austria has adopted a life-cycle approach to severance entitlements where workers employed on short-term contracts are paid severance out of a central fund to which employers contribute. Rather than severance being calculated on the basis of each *individual* contract, worker entitlements are based on their continuous employment pattern, and as long as there is no break in employment they continue to accumulate additional severance entitlements.[7] This is another area where Ontario has already introduced changes, giving temporary agency workers the right to severance payments; however, the current rate of payment is minimal. A worker on a contract lasting less than one month would receive no severance and someone on a one-month contract earning $2,000 a month would be entitled to less than $14.00 severance.[8]

More can be done in the short term to reduce income uncertainty. A universal and accessible unemployment insurance system that bridges workers between job assignments would be a good start. Rather than simply providing insurance to permanent workers who occasionally face periods of unemployment, the system needs to recognize the needs of those regularly employed on short-term contracts. We recommend the creation of a special category for temporary, short-term, and seasonal workers with reduced hours eligibility requirements, shorter waiting periods, and more generous income replacement levels, to reflect that workers in less permanent relationships are likely to have more frequent bouts of short-term unemployment. The costs of these benefits would be funded by a levy on those employers who use less permanent forms of the employment relationship. In this way the cost of labour market flexibility would be transferred to *employers* benefiting from employing workers on short-term contracts rather than being borne exclusively by workers, as it is in the current situation. A further improvement would be eliminating the waiting period for workers engaged in approved training.

Even when workers in precarious employment are regularly employed, they are still likely to experience gaps in employment, and variability of earnings creates a need for income smoothing

---

7 See the Austrian Severance Act (*Abfertigungsrecht*) 2002, as discussed in Commission of the European Communities 2006: 10.

8 http://www.labour.gov.on.ca/english/es/pubs/guide/tempagencies.php.

policies. Research on income stability in the United States has shown that earnings show greater variability from year to year (Hacker 2006b). While the increase in volatility is greatest for women, workers from racialized groups, and the less educated, men, whites, and even the well educated have also experienced increased income volatility. One way to deal with this is through simple changes to the tax system that would allow workers to average their income over several years. The Alliance of Canadian Cinema, Television and Radio Artists (ACTRA), has recently proposed that the federal government consider implementing wage-averaging for self-employed actors (ACTRA 2009). Their proposal is based on tax measures already taken in Quebec (since 2004) that permit income-averaging for artists.[9] These tax measures allow individuals to defer the tax on a portion of their income, and spread their income over a maximum period of seven years. Income-averaging for cultural professionals such as artists and performers is also practiced in several European countries, including Germany and France. The Income Tax Assessment Act in Australia allows artists with fluctuating incomes to average their income for tax purposes for a period of up to five years (ACTRA 2009). We suggest that these tax measures introduced in Quebec and various European countries be used as a model for developing a system of income-averaging over a multi-year period for *all* precariously and self-employed workers in Canada. Policy-makers may want to consider even more ambitious schemes that allow workers in less permanent employment, with a history of earnings, to "borrow" from future earnings as a way of bridging periods of low earnings. This might include low interest loans repayable from future earnings.

A more substantial change would be the implementation of a Universal Insurance program as proposed by Hacker (2006b). His plan would partially protect workers from income loss of more than twenty percent in one year. It would be available to all families below the 95th percentile of income. Hacker's model would see families cover the first twenty percent of any income loss. Insurance would cover a potion of the remaining income starting at twenty percent for families between the 95th and 75th income percentiles

9 See www.budget.finances.gouv.qc.ca/budget/2004-2005/index-en.asp for more information on the Quebec model.

and rising to fifty percent for families below the 25th percentile. It would be financed by insurance premiums related to earnings. Hacker estimates that this would cost about 0.6 percent of payroll to fund.

Kling (2006) proposes a similar scheme composed of wage-loss insurance to compensate job-losers who end up in lower-paying jobs. He suggests that workers create individual accounts funded by voluntary savings so that if they lose their jobs, they can apply for relief. Those who failed to save, or did not save enough, could still borrow against future earnings. Workers with low wages would have all or part of their debt forgiven, and debt would also be forgiven if their account was still in deficit at their retirement. Any surplus at retirement would be returned to the worker with interest. The income insurance portion of the plan would work much like Hacker's proposal. Existing unemployment insurance premiums would be redirected to fund the income loss insurance scheme that would top-up the wages of unemployed workers who end up taking a job at a lower wage. The top-up would be equivalent to twenty-five percent of the difference between the old wage (maximum $15.00) and the new wage. Employers would fund this insurance program, and premiums would be experience-rated based on a company's layoff history. Kling argues this would give firms an incentive not to engage in temporary layoffs, and would simultaneously encourage the return to work of the unemployed, because they would have an incentive not to draw down their accounts and would still have some support if the jobs they took paid a lower wage than those they had lost.

More radical solutions to the income uncertainty facing those in precarious employment have been debated in Canada and elsewhere (Chancer 1998). The idea of a generic, universal income-security program that is underwritten and administered by government – the guaranteed annual income – has recently re-appeared in Canadian policy discussions. This idea was endorsed by two Royal Commissions in the 1970s and 1980s, but was rejected by subsequent governments. During the anti-poverty debates of the mid-2000s, the idea for such a program resurfaced with a proposal by a Conservative senator for a $30,000 a year minimum, with payments made to those who earn less through the existing tax system. This program would replace all existing government social security, old age, disability, and employment insurance programs (Monse-braaten 2007). Guaranteed annual income proposals may have other potential drawbacks, but they do have the singular advantage of removing basic earning insecurity from the concerns of all workers. They are a central plank of reforms proposed by various authors looking for ways to humanize work and give workers more freedom to refuse sub-standard jobs (Gorz 2005; Standing 2002).

Recent unpublished research by Forget (2010) provides a new insight into the potential of guaranteed annual income policies to mitigate the health effects of insecure employment. Forget examines the social and health effects of MINCOME, a social experiment conducted during the 1970s in the small Manitoba community of Dauphin. Her research shows that during the years when residents were provided with cheques to assure they all had a minimum income, young members of the community stayed in school longer, hospitalizations – particularly hospitalizations for accidents and injuries and mental health diagnoses – declined, and physician contacts for mental health diagnoses fell relative to a comparator group matched by age, sex, geography, family type, and family size. Forget concludes, "These results would seem to suggest that a Guaranteed Annual Income, implemented broadly in society, may improve health and social outcomes at the community level" (Forget 2010: 2).

An alternative to a Guaranteed Annual Income policy is a "living wage" strategy (Rathke 2009). Here the onus is on employers to offer a wage that is sufficient to sustain a minimum standard of living. "Living wage" campaigns have become popular across the US and Canada in recent years, and the Canadian Centre for Policy Alternatives (CCPA) recently advocated such a strategy to reduce poverty in Canada. The CCPA discusses a "living wage" campaign in Victoria that saw a number of employers voluntarily raise their wages closer to the $14.88 per hour minimum recommended by the Community Social Planning Council of Greater Victoria (CCPA 2009).

One of the advantages of the "standard employment relationship" was the adoption of an employment benefits program based on long-term commitment to a single employer. Workers came to expect adequate employer-funded pensions to cover expenses as they aged, income replacement programs when they were ill or unable to work, and coverage of medical expenses not funded by public health insurance. As fewer workers find themselves in permanent employment relationships, major gaps have emerged in employment benefits; gaps that compound the income insecurity associated with low and variable earnings. One solution to this problem is to fund benefits such as pensions, sick leave, vacations, and health coverage from a central fund to which employers make contributions. In this way, workers employed on short-term contracts with multiple employers could have greater access to the benefits received by workers in permanent employment relationships. This is a model that has long been in use in the Canadian construction sector and is similar to the Austrian severance plan discussed above. Several proposals have emerged for dental care that range from the delivery of services for particularly disadvantaged citizens through public health facilities to full public coverage for all citizens (MISSWA 2006).

The entire pension system (Old Age Security, the Canada Pension Plan (CPP) and employer-sponsored pension plans) needs to be reviewed and reformed in light of the growing gaps in employer-based plans described above. An important reform would be to enhance the Canada Pension Plan so that it replaces a larger percentage of earnings in retirement, thus making workers less dependent on employer-based schemes. The CPP has the advantage that workers earn credits even when employed on short-term contracts. This would also have the advantage of reducing administrative costs and reducing risks when individual employers declare bankruptcy and leave an unfunded pension liability. One of the most critical areas for reform is to make pensions portable so that workers in less permanent employment arrangements and those with multiple employers (e.g. temporary workers working for multiple employers simultaneously) can be covered. Sectoral employer-funded plans are one way to achieve greater coverage. Reforms in this direction would help to reverse the trend of recent decades away from collective responsibility and concern for workers' retirement income.[10] Indeed, the International Labour Organization (ILO) has called for countries to re-think their pension systems and contends

---

10 For a discussion of some of these issues and recommendations, see the Ontario Federation of Labour's submission to the Ontario Expert Commission on Pensions (2007).

that providing for the aged is a collective social obligation, with public pensions being fundamental to this obligation.

PROPOSALS TO REDUCE
EMPLOYMENT RELATIONSHIP EFFORT

The increased frequency of job changes, combined with the critical link this study found between *employment relationship effort* and *employment strain,* suggests there is a need for policies and programs to assist workers looking for work by retraining them for new positions and helping them keep jobs once they find them. Such programs would include employment counseling to more effectively link individuals' abilities and aspirations with available or emerging jobs.

As we noted in the previous chapter, the choices in training for occupations outside of tightly defined professions have become bewildering and expensive, with the costs being borne increasingly by individuals. The issue of who pays for training has always been contentious, and recent trends have shifted more of this cost onto individual workers and away from the companies that hire them. It is unclear what incentive firms have to invest in the training of less permanent employees. Governments, in cooperation with other labour market stakeholders, must play a larger role in facilitating training and in making it an essential part of economic policy at all levels of government. Much like basic training for young people is seen as a public expense, so must retraining become a collective responsibility. In Denmark, the recognition that employers are' becoming a less effective source of training led to a decision to make training – and retraining – publically funded activities (Bredgaard et al. 2005). The province of Quebec took a significant initiative in this regard by instituting a one percent payroll training tax in the mid-1990s (although its exemption for companies with payrolls smaller than one million dollars may be negatively affecting workers in less permanent positions).

Other initiatives have attempted to involve government, labour, business, and trainers themselves in efforts to design training and credentials that are industry- or region-specific. Over thirty Sector Human Resource Councils operate in Canada, more than half of which are in industries where employment is not permanent (trucking, agriculture, food production, textiles, and others). In Quebec, the "Institut de tourisme et d'hôtellerie du Québec" provides training for individuals pursuing careers in the restaurant and hotel sectors: sectors with a high percentage of workers in less permanent employment relationships. A similar initiative has been launched in Las Vegas called the "Culinary Training Academy." Some unions, including construction unions, have taken responsibility for the development of their members' skill sets by setting up training centres.[11]

Workers employed through a series of short-term contracts with different employers need some formal recognition of their skills to assist in job searches. At the moment, only apprentices and those completing formal training programs have access to certificates. Sectoral councils could play a larger role in developing skills certificates that included prior learning assessments and that would be recognized beyond a worker's immediate employer. Proposals such as the Automotive Manufacturing Foundations Certificate advanced by the Canadian Automotive Workers and the Automotive Parts Sectoral Training Council in the mid-1990s, would have formally recognized skills acquired through on the job training and provided a tool for workers searching for employment and companies looking for qualified workers (Rutherford 1998). While those initiatives failed, they could still be used as models to promote broader skill recognition and reduce the effort workers spend looking for new jobs.

Having largely withdrawn from assisting workers looking for employment, the current publicly available employment-counseling and assistance programs are limited. In some provinces, government-supported worker adjustment centres are established for large scale lay-offs; however, these mainly serve workers leaving permanent full-time employment, with the result that workers in less permanent employment turn to private employment services or temporary employment agencies for help finding work. Sectoral councils should play a larger role in assisting job-seekers through electronic bulletin boards and regional job fairs. Public labour market intermediaries and workforce intermediaries that will be dis-

---

11 One of the most successful of these initiatives has been the LIUNA Local 183 Training Centre in Southern Ontario.

cussed in more detail in the next section can play a central role in this area and further reduce *employment relationship effort.*

PROPOSALS TO INCREASE EMPLOYMENT
RELATIONSHIP SUPPORT

One of the most glaring needs created by the growth of less permanent employment relationships is in the area of support. Workers in both the *on a path* and the *unsustainable, less permanent employment* classifications noted a lack of support at work, weak representation by unions, and limited support from other household members. This last point reflects the reality that many households are now made up of multiple individuals, each of whom is in a precarious employment relationship. Increasingly, those in employment relationships that we describe as "working without commitments" must navigate through the day-to-day challenges of making a living on their own. Closing this gap in household support will require new institutional forms and enhanced welfare benefits. In contrast to existing employment agencies, which offer little more than temporary job placement services, these new institutions should provide some of the services which workers in relationships with commitments have historically been able to access in their workplace. As Osterman put it, new labour market institutions should "construct better pathways through the labour market" to reduce the negative impact of job mobility (Osterman 1999: 132). They can provide employment support, training, and networking opportunities for workers while also helping to improve firms' competitiveness.

In a similar vein, Giloth (2004) proposes the creation of labour market intermediaries to serve both employers and workers, while giving priority to providing services for low-income and less skilled workers. According to Giloth, workforce intermediaries (wis) creatively package a complex set of policies, programs, and tax incentives to create jobs and services. However, he suggests that the creation of wis are dependent on several related actions, including securing sustainable financing for the myriad roles that wis perform and having workplace development and training as an essential part of economic policy at all levels of government (Giloth 2004: 399–401). Such institutions would need to perform a range of functions, such as supporting the development of new adult education programs; providing employment and on-site job training; offering career support and advice; providing information about health and safety, employment standards, and other employment rights; and giving workers opportunities to network and access support from unions and other workers by, for example, providing meeting spaces and computer access.

Historically, unions have played a central role in providing support, information, career/employment networks, and other important services to workers, especially workers in permanent full-time employment. Declining union strength vis-à-vis management, combined with declining union density[12] and related problems unionizing the growing number of workers in less permanent employment, have made it increasingly difficult for unions to support workers. In addition, the type of tripartite system that emerged in Canada in the post-war period has not worked very well, and most unions currently play a very limited role in workplace training or in broader processes associated with restructuring, hiring, and career development. At a minimum, unions need to re-think their current structures and strategies in order to become more responsive to and representative of the growing number of workers in non-traditional employment forms. Although defending job security with a single employer should be a key priority for all unions, there is a need for a more pro-active approach to address broader employment insecurity and uncertainty issues faced by workers in less permanent employment. Reforms to labour laws will be needed to reduce the focus of union organizing and collective bargaining on a single workplace and move towards sectoral bargaining. Some progress has been made in terms of organizing and representing workers in less permanent employment relationships. However, membership drives have tended to be quite instrumental, focusing simply on increasing membership without any deeper inquiry into union structures, policies, methods, or bargaining priorities and (Ross

---

12 Although union membership in Canada has been growing at a steady pace for the past twenty-five years, union density (the proportion of the workforce who are union members) has been slowly declining. The decline is most pronounced and pervasive in the private sector, where privatization and other processes of restructuring have eroded union strength.

2004) the unique needs of workers in less permanent employment. Key to being successful in this endeavour is becoming more inclusive of *all* workers, and redirecting their activities beyond the workplace (Heery and Abbott 2000).

Broader changes are needed. The re-thinking of union strategies and priorities should be accompanied by other changes which would give unions a stronger role in a wide range of employment processes and practices. For example, among the most significant stressors reported by study participants was the insecurity associated with regular changes in employers, and the corresponding uncertainty as to how this would affect the terms of employment. Unions can help to develop and implement new workplace or sector-specific policies to guarantee casual workers a certain number of hours and entitlements to future employment while defending wage rates when they change employers. In addition, unions can work to influence government policies (including training policies) and secure changes in labour laws and regulations to increase employment security for all workers (Heery and Abbott 2000).

As part of the overhaul of labour regulation, there is a pressing need to introduce reforms to occupational health and safety (OHS) legislation so that workers feel they are not on their own. Both the government and employers need to be sensitized to the health costs associated with increased labour market flexibility. As our research demonstrated, workers in less permanent employment arrangements face more health risks than other workers, partly due to "disorganized workplaces" and lower levels of support, but also due to higher stress levels associated with *employment strain*. Workers in precarious employment relationships often change employers and workplaces. Incomplete understanding of the hazards associated with a new workplace can increase the risk of workplace injuries or poorer health. Policies and workplace practices need to help workers adjust to new duties, equipment, environments, and co-workers, through, for instance, targeted training regarding health and safety risks, and practices aimed at promoting greater inclusion of all workers so that precarious workers are less isolated.

Of course, one of the key issues with regard to workers' health and safety is the monitoring and enforcement of legislation. Workplace inspection and compliance practices need to be strengthened by including components such as the development and introduction of new enforcement measures and more substantial financial penalties for non-compliance; the adoption of proactive and regular inspections and spot-checks; and an increase in the number of workplace inspectors. In much of Canada, the first line of compliance is the internal responsibility system. While this sometimes works for those workers with unions to back them, it is ineffective for those in temporary positions who lack union support and have limited workplace power. And we have shown elsewhere that those in precarious employment are unlikely to exercise their existing occupational health and safety rights for fear of compromising future employment prospects (Lewchuk, Clarke, and de Wolff 2009).

The health of all workers could be improved by making companies at the top of extended supply chains liable for injuries and illness caused by the activity of firms to whom they have contracted out work (Weil and Mallo 2007). There is growing pressure to make temporary agencies and companies jointly liable regarding payment of wages and benefits (HRSDC 2008). Ontario has recently moved in this direction and in both Quebec and Saskatchewan, a client employer is deemed liable for any unpaid wages due and owing to agency workers (HRSDC 2008: 67). Other countries, such as South Africa, have gone further. Recent amendments to the country's labour laws have deemed the temporary employment agency and client jointly and severally liable in respect of breaches of collective agreements and arbitration awards regulating terms and conditions of employment (Clarke 2006). What is needed is an extension of this principle to include contraventions of labour legislation which could result in a client being held responsible for, amongst other things, the unfair dismissal of an employee by the temporary employment agency itself, as well as liability for injury and illness.

RESTORING COMMITMENTS INTO LESS PERMANENT
EMPLOYMENT RELATIONSHIPS

The previous section outlined a number of policy initiatives with the potential to reduce *employment strain* by providing workers with more certainty over job prospects and income, and increasing support, thus reducing the effort needed to find and maintain employment. Such initiatives would greatly improve conditions for those in less permanent employment, but should not be viewed as long-term solutions to the problems created by the decline of the "standard employment relationship." They will not restore commitment, or the sense of belonging that we argue is an important factor contributing to workers' health. They represent, at best, a bridge to a very different form of social organization: one whose characteristics we can only begin to imagine.

Others have grappled with this issue. Gorz has turned the question on its head by arguing that what is needed is not a set of regulations and institutions that facilitate flexible access to labour for employers, but rather a system that permits flexible access to work for workers (Gorz 2005). Working from the assumption that work is becoming increasingly scarce,[13] Gorz proposes a transition from a "work based" society to a "multi-activity" society where work for pay is only one component of activity. This system would be designed to give workers greater freedom when to work while still being dependent on a company for security of income and status. It would create an environment where workers have continuous income for discontinuous work (Gorz 2005: 76). This new mode of social organization is described as one where "For multi-activity to develop, society will have to organize itself to achieve it through a range of specific policies. Social time and space will have to be organized to indicate the general expectation that everybody will engage in a different range of different activities and modes of membership of the society ... (and) to encourage each member to refresh and surpass him/herself ever anew in competitive co-operation with the others, this pursuit of excellence by each being a goal common to all" (Gorz 2005: 78).

---

13 The assumption that we will reach a stage in social development where productive activity will allow everyone to have a high standard of living with minimal work effort runs through a number of scholarly and literary works. Keynes, in an essay titled "Possibilities for our Grandchildren," put his faith in a world of abundance when "we shall be able to rid ourselves of many of the pseudo-moral principles which have hag-ridden us for two hundred years, by which we exalted some of the most distasteful of human qualities into the position of the highest virtues" (Keynes 1972: 329). William Morris described a similar utopia in his novel "News from Nowhere," as did Edward Bellamy in "Looking Backward."

Standing also proposes a fundamental reordering of society organized around a guaranteed basic income, or Citizenship Income, leaving individuals free to take added work at the going price. In his words: "The Good Society of the twenty-first century will be based on the right of occupation, or occupational security, where increasing numbers of people will be able to combine competencies to create their own occupation, with varying work statuses, and moving in and out of economic activity. In one sense, this will be an extension of individuality, with a growth in the realm of autonomy. In another, the individuality will only flourish if there is a sense of collective security, a sense of community to which an individual belongs" (Standing 2002: 275).

Hodgson (1999) takes the analysis even further, suggesting that the shift to a more knowledge-intensive economy will undermine the existing contractual form that gives the owners of physical capital control within most employment relationships. Hodgson sees workers engaged in long-term relationships to facilitate the development of human capital, especially in organizations where an "ethos of community and obligation to others" is stressed (Hodgson 1999: 260–1). He argues that the increasing importance of human capital, which cannot easily be divested from the individual who has acquired it through training or natural selection, will empower labour and lead to a different form of social organization, one that he suggests will represent the end of capitalism as we know it.

These visions are attempts to make discontinuous employment desirable. They represent advanced forms of what we uncovered in interviews with those in the *sustainable, less permanent employment* group, individuals who had income security without the need for continuous employment, individuals who had reconstructed a work community without having a permanent attachment to a single employer.[14] To achieve this goal for all will require a re-evaluation not only of how we regulate employment but also of a range of social norms and customs. It will require a revolution to fill the gaps this study has identified as resulting from the decline in the prevalence of the "standard employment relationship" and the spread of working without commitments. At the end of the nine-

---

14 For a discussion of institutional innovations that support this class of employee see Pink (2001).

teenth century, the first wave of individualized employment relationships gave birth to what Jacoby described as "Modern
Manors." This study has identified similar stresses linked to a new
wave of employment individualization, so new employment relationships need to be formed in response to them.

It is clear that a range of activities and supports that used to be
provided by employers to workers in permanent full-time employment are no longer being provided. This should be seen as an
opportunity for unions to fill as they move to become supporters of
workers, places to facilitate training and job searches, and
providers of workplace benefits. There are historical precedents in
early unions, such as the craft unions or the Knights of Labor, for
whom bargaining for wages was but one aspect of a broader support for workers that gave them security, community, and identity.
In some ways, one can see the period from the end of World War II
until the mid 1980s, when unions focused on collective bargaining,
as a deviation from unions' more typical concern with the development of the individual and the creation of a community that hon-
oured labour. More recently, particularly in the construction trades,
unions have acted as hiring halls and taken over responsibility for
administering employment benefits on behalf of their members. We
see in new labour initiatives proto-organizations with the potential
to become centres for co-ordinating and supporting workers with
multiple employers. The Workers Action Centre[15] in Toronto has
positioned itself to represent workers who are mainly employed in
precarious positions. In Calgary, the Workers Resource Centre[16]
and in Hamilton, the fledgling Migrant Workers Family Resource
Centre[17] are both providing a home for workers working outside of
the "standard employment relationship."

CONCLUSION

This study shows that workers' lack of control over whether they
will be employed, the terms and conditions of such employment,

---

15 For details on the activity of WAC see, http://www.workersaction
centre.org.

16 See, http://www.calgaryworkers.org.

17 See http://www.migrantresourcecenter.org/members.

and their work schedules, are key components of the *employment strain* that leads to poor health. Our results also highlight the capacity of employment-related support networks to buffer the ill effects of this lack of control. They suggest the need for a new policy framework that is less focused on lifetime employment with a single employer. However, the reality is that while changes to the regulatory framework are needed and would improve the situation of many workers, they cannot be expected to fully compensate for what is being lost with the decline of the "standard employment relationship." We are likely on the cusp of a fundamental reordering of our society similar to that experienced in the first half of the twentieth century with the rise of the family wage and the single wage-earner household. All of these institutions are under stress. What will replace them is beyond the scope of this project. We have suggested that new forms of support are necessary, and that unions and emerging worker's organizations are likely to play an important role in future developments. These emerging institutions may be rooted in current organizations, but it is unlikely that they will look anything like they look today. They will need to help workers navigate a changing labour market and provide them with support and community. If the employer-based systems of the twentieth century can be described as "modern manors" then those of the next century are likely to be "workers' manors" – sites of mutual support and security.

Methods

THE SURVEY

The inspiration for this project came from the work of Robert Karasek, whose research explored the interaction between workload and control. The "Job Strain" model was developed during a period when the standard employment relationship and permanent full-time employment were the norms in North America. The recognition that things were changing led our research team to explore the applicability of the control/workload/support trilogy to different issues such as how people find and keep employment, and the relationships between employers and workers in less permanent employment. The concept of Employment Strain had its origins in a series of articles by the authors using a small pilot data set (Lewchuk et al. 2003; 2006a; 2006b). Insights from this research led to revisions in the survey instrument and the sampling strategy. The survey was designed to measure levels of uncertainty over future employment prospects, effort expended searching for work, and actions workers take to keep the jobs they have. It also explored support from employers, co-workers in the community and households, the physical conditions of work, and health outcomes. The data were collected through a fixed response self-administered survey conducted in the fall of 2005 and winter of 2006.

SURVEY PARTICIPANTS

A population-based sampling strategy was used. Our goal was to obtain a representative sample from areas of Toronto with a high percentage of individuals in precarious employment relationships. We identified census tracks where the percentage of employed people normally working full-time was less than eighty percent and the median household income was less than $70,000. This produced sixty Toronto area census tracts representing 145,109 households who reported an individual working at the time of the 2001 census.

All households in the selected census tracts received a multilingual postcard inviting members of the household over the age of eighteen who had worked in the previous month to participate. The postcards included information on how to obtain a copy of the survey. Participants were offered $10.00 for completing the survey which they could mail in, submit by e-mail, or complete online.[1] Surveys were available in English, Chinese, and Tamil. Posters with tear-off information sheets were posted in public spaces in the targeted areas to encourage more individuals to participate. We anticipated between a one and two percent response rate. Those who completed the survey were asked to distribute additional postcards to people they thought might be interested in completing the survey.

A total of 3,244 surveys were received. Of these, 1,959 (60.4 percent of all surveys) were from the targeted postal drop area. This represented 1.4 percent of all households in the postal drop area. Another 689 (21.1 percent of all surveys) were from regions adjacent to the postal drop area. Together, the surveys from the postal drop area and the adjacent area are referred to as the Greater Toronto Area (GTA) sample and are the basis of the analysis that follows.[2] The remaining 596 surveys from outside the Toronto region are not included in what follows.[3] Comparison of the sample data with census data indicates that the GTA sample is reasonably representative of the area. Our sample is marginally over-represented in employed women (51.0 versus 47.1 percent) and has marginally

---

1 84.2% of all surveys, and 80.9% of GTA surveys, were returned electronically.

2 The GTA includes a region approximately fifty kilometres either direction from the centre of Toronto and is bounded by Oshawa to the east, Hamilton to the West, and Barrie to the north.

3 We are reasonably confident that the GTA sample is representative of the GTA population. We are less confident that the other 596 surveys from outside of the GTA area are representative of the Canadian labour market, and hence have opted to drop them from the analysis.

more individuals who completed college or university (63.0 versus 55.4 percent). It has fewer individuals working more than thirty hours (72.9 versus 83.8 percent). The percentage of part-time employees (16.2 versus 15.5 percent) and median individual incomes (30,653 versus 30,013) were almost identical.

We excluded full-time students from our analysis, recognizing that full-time employment is difficult for them. Our interest is in the connection between the employment relationship and the health of those who are available to work full-time. The full-time students in the sample were less likely than non-students to be in a permanent position, less likely to be working more than thirty hours a week, and less likely to be receiving employment benefits. But of course, students were less likely to *want* more permanent employment. We also dropped the eleven individuals who reported they were self-employed and had employees of their own. This left us with a sample of 2,117 employees who were not full-time students and who lived in the Greater Toronto Area.

CONSTRUCTING THE INDICES

Data from questions representing the three core dimensions of the Employment Strain model were subjected to factor analysis.[4] Survey questions that failed to load on any of the factors were dropped from the analysis. The results of this exercise identified multiple factors strongly associated with each of the three core dimensions. The resulting factors were interpreted, resulting in the more detailed Employment Strain model presented in chapter 3. The reliability of the indices was tested by calculating Cronbach's alphas.[5]

---

4 The entire non-student data set (n=2,636) was used in the factor analysis. Factor analysis was conducted using the principal component estimation procedure. Varimax rotation was applied to help interpret the factors. Factors with eigenvalues greater than one were retained and variables with loadings of at least .40 were included in each factor. The exception was Unpaid Work-Related Training which loaded on the Effort Keeping Work index marginally below .40. It was retained on the basis of strong theoretical reasons to suspect that unpaid training is an important strategy for keeping employment and the limited variance in the responses to the question as designed.

5 Further discussion of the survey methodology and the development of the indices can be found in Lewchuk, Clarke, and de Wolff 2008.

Table A.1
Components of the employment strain model and individual indices

EMPLOYMENT RELATIONSHIP UNCERTAINTY (alpha=.82; mean=26.3; std. dev.=18.1)

Employment fragility
(alpha=.63; mean=14.1; std. dev.=15.8)

* Jobs last less than 6 months on average
* Insufficient notice to accept work
* On-call worker
* Receive record of pay
* Often not paid on time
* Pay often different from expected

Earnings uncertainty
(alpha=.74; mean=48.8; std. dev.=33.2)

* Unable to plan income 6 months in advance
* Not covered by disability insurance in household
* Not covered by pension in household
* Not paid if miss work

Scheduling uncertainty
(alpha=.89; mean=20.4; std. dev.=24.4)

* Difficult to plan work week
* Difficult to plan household responsibilities
* Difficult to plan social responsibilities

EMPLOYMENT RELATIONSHIP EFFORT (alpha=.79; mean=18.9; std. dev.=14.1)

Effort keeping employed
(alpha=.77; mean=13.3; std. dev.=16.2)

* Time spent looking for work
* Discrimination a barrier in getting work
* Asked to do things not related to work
* Experience harassment at work
* Experience discrimination at work
* Unpaid work-related training

Multiple employers
(alpha=.81; mean=12.4; std. dev.=25.2)

* More than one employer
* More than one employer same time
* Conflicting demands from more than one employer

Multiple locations
(alpha=.67; mean=20.9; std. dev.=22.4)

* More than one location
* Work at more than one location causes conflicts
* Unpaid travel more than two hours per day
* Work in unfamiliar locations regularly

Constant evaluation effort
(alpha=.78; mean=33.5; std. dev.=28.4)

* Evaluations affect kind of work offered
* Evaluations affect amount of work offered
* Evaluations affect rate of pay

Table A.1 (*continued*)

EMPLOYMENT RELATIONSHIP SUPPORT (alpha=.72; mean=51.6; std. dev.=17.9)

Household economic support (alpha=.82; mean=34.6; std. dev.=29.8)	* High individual income * High household income * Some household employment benefits * Probability of major employment benefits
Union support (alpha=.90; mean=18.5; std. dev.=32.6)	* Union member * Union will help at work
Individual support (alpha=.71; mean=54.8; std. dev.=22.5)	* Help with work * Friends with co-workers * Someone to help in crisis * Support from friends and family * Support from community

PHYSICAL RISKS (alpha=.78; mean=21.7; std. dev.=19.8)

* Work awkward positions
* Work standing
* Poor air quality
* Uncomfortable temperature
* Noisy work environment
* Exposed to toxic materials

Table A.1 lists the questions represented by the various indices. The raw data for most questions was categorical on a scale of 1–5. All questions were normalized to take values between 0 and 1. Indices were calculated by summing these values and then converting each index value on a scale of 0–100 with 0 representing low uncertainty, low effort, low support, and low physical risks. All questions were weighted equally in calculating the indices.

The survey is available from the authors.

INTERVIEW PARTICIPANTS
PHASE ONE INTERVIEWS

A number of survey respondents were selected for further interviews during 2006, approximately six months after completing the survey. We limited interviews to individuals who reported being in less permanent employment on the survey or those in full-time employment but reporting *high employment relationship strain*. We also limited interviews to individuals who were not full-time students and who had indicated on their survey they were willing to be interviewed. We used a stratified sampling technique to select interview participants at different stages of their careers and in different types of employment relationships (See Table A.2). All individuals who completed the survey and met the criteria for one of the categories of individuals to be interviewed were included in a list of potential candidates. Names were randomly selected from this list until either the list was exhausted or the target number to be interviewed was reached.

The interviews were conducted face to face. The interviews were open ended using a standard questionnaire to insure basic issues were covered with each individual. Most interviews lasted from forty-five to ninety minutes. All interviews were recorded and transcribed.

PHASE TWO INTERVIEWS

A second round of interviews was conducted in the spring of 2007 with a sample of those interviewed in 2006. We focused on those we had identified as in the *unsustainable* and *on a path* categories. We wanted to understand more clearly the long-term implications of being in *unsustainable, less permanent employment* and to what extent the optimism of those in the *on a path* category was realized. All thirty-seven individuals in the *unsustainable* category were contacted, and twelve agreed to a second interview. This was an open-ended face to face interview lasting approximately one hour. The focus of the interview was whether their employment relationship had changed, whether their health had changed, and how they were coping with the situation in which they found themselves. Efforts were made to contact all twenty-six individuals in the *on a path* category by phone. We were successful in reaching eighteen in this group to complete phone interviews. The focus of these interviews was whether their employment relationship had changed since being interviewed the previous year.

Table A.2
Interview Sample

	Target number to be interviewed	Number interviewed	Contacted and refused or unable to schedule interview	Unable to contact
Mid-career workers 25-50	40	30	15	7
Younger workers (<25)	10	8	10	12
Older workers (50+)	10	10	9	6
Temporary agency workers	15	15	26	21
Own-account, self-employed	10	12	4	3
Full-time (high employment strain)	10	7	6	3
TOTAL	95	82	80	52

THE EMPLOYMENT RELATIONSHIP CATEGORIES

Allocating individuals to the different employment relationship categories was critical to our understanding of how less permanent employment was affecting health outcomes. As indicated above, individuals were selected for interviews from a pool of survey participants indentified as being in less permanent employment. We constructed the interview sample with the goal of including a range of individuals in less permanent employment with different characteristics. During the interviews we paid particular attention to whether individuals wanted to remain in a precarious employment relationship and, if they did not, what their medium-term goals were. We asked if they expected they would move to something more permanent or if they expected to remain in their current employment relationship. It was only after conducting the interviews that we were able to define the three core categories, *sustainable, less permanent employment,* "*on a path*" *less permanent employment,* and *unsustainable, less permanent employment.*[6]

---

6 Further discussion of the three categories can be found in Clarke, Lewchuk, and de Wolff 2007.

These categories were developed during multiple discussions by the research team and analysis of the interview transcripts. While any such categorization has limitations, we believe it captures key differences that help to explain the different experiences of individuals in less permanent employment, as well as the pathways from less permanent employment to health.

Bibliography

ACTRA. 2009. Alliance of Canadian Cinema, Television and Radio Artists (ACTRA), Written Submission to The House of Commons Standing Committee on Finance, Pre-budget Consultations 2010. Toronto: ACTRA. http://www.actra.ca/actra/images/documents/2010-ACTRA-Pre-budget-submission.pdf

Allen, John and Nick Henry. 1996. "Fragments of Industry and Employment: Contract Service Work and the Shift towards Precarious Employment." In *Changing Forms of Employment: Organisations, Skills and Gender*, ed. Rosemary Crompton, Duncan Gallie, and Kate Purcell, 65–82. London: Routledge.

Anderson, John. 1998. "Public and Private Sector Unions in the Delivery of Training: The 1998 CLC Protocol," *Training Matters: Works In Progress WIP #1*. Toronto: Centre for Research on Work and Society, York University.

Armstrong, Pat. 1996. "The Feminization of the Workforce: Harmonizing Down in a Global Economy." In *Rethinking Restructuring: Gender and Change in Canada*, ed. Isabella Bakker, 29–54. Toronto: University of Toronto Press.

Aronson, Jane, and Sheila M. Neysmith. 1997. "The Retreat of the State and Long-Term Care Provision: Implications for Frail Elderly People, Unpaid Family Careers and Paid Home Care Workers," *Studies in Political Economy* 53: 37–66.

Aronsson, Gunnar. 1999. "Contingent Workers and Health and Safety," *Work, Employment and Society* 13 (3): 439–59.

Artazcoz, Lucía, Joan Benach, Carme Borrell, and Imma Cortès. 2005. "Social Inequalities in the Impact of Flexible Employment on Different

Domains of Psychosocial Health," *Journal of Epidemiology and Community Health* 59: 761–7.

Arum, Richard, and Walter Müller, eds. 2004. *The Re-emergence of Self-Employment: A Comparative Study of Self-Employment Dynamics and Social Inequality*. Princeton: Princeton University Press.

Bakker, Isabella, ed. 1996. *Rethinking Restructuring: Gender and Change in Canada*. Toronto: University of Toronto Press.

Baragar, Fletcher, and Mario Secarecia. 2008. "Financial Restructuring: Implications of Recent Canadian Macroeconomic Developments," *Studies in Political Economy* 82: 61–83.

Bardasi, Elena, and Marco Francesconi. 2004. "The Impact of Atypical Employment on Individual Wellbeing: Evidence from a Panel of British Workers," *Social Science and Medicine* 58: 1671–88.

Baron, Ava. 1987. "Contested Terrain Revisited: Technology and Gender Definitions of Work in the Printing Industry, 1850–1920." In *Women, Work and Technology: Transformations*, ed. B. Wright, 58–83. Ann Arbor: University of Michigan Press.

Bartley, M. 2005. "Job Insecurity and its Effect on Health," *Journal of Epidemiology and Community Health* 59: 717–18.

Bauman, Zygmunt. 1998. *Globalization: The Human Condition*. New York: Columbia University Press.

– 2005. *Work Consumerism and the New Poor*. Maidenhead: Open University Press.

Beck, Ulrich. 1992. *Risk Society: Towards a New Modernity*. London: Sage Publications.

– 2000. *The Brave New World of Work*. Cambridge: Polity Press.

Beder, Sharon. 2000. *Selling the Work Ethic: From Puritan Pulpit to Corporate PR*. London and New York: Zed Books.

Benach, Joan, M. Amable, C. Muntaner, and F.G. Benavides. 2002. "The Consequences of Flexible Work for Health: Are We Looking in the Right Place?" *Journal of Epidemiology and Community Health* 56: 405–6.

Benach, Joan, D. Gimeno, and F.G. Benavides. 2002. *Types of Employment and Health in the European Union*. Dublin: European Foundation for the Improvement of Living and Working Conditions.

Benach, Joan, D. Gimeno, F.G. Benavides, J.M. Martínez, and D.M. Torné. 2004. "Types of Employment and Health in the European Union: Changes from 1995–2000," *European Journal of Public Health* 14: 314–21.

Benach, Joan, C. Muntaner, and V. Santana (Chairs). 2007. *Employment Conditions and Health Inequalities.* Final Report to the WHO Commission on Social Determinants of Health.

Benach, Joan, and C. Muntaner. 2007. "Precarious Employment and Health: Developing a Research Agenda,"*Journal of Epidemiology and Community Health* 61: 276–7.

– (forthcoming). *Employment, Work and Health Inequalities: A Global Perspective.*

Benavides, F. G., and J. Benach. 1999. *Precarious Employment and Health-Related Outcomes in the European Union.* Dublin: European Foundation for the Improvement of Living and Working Conditions.

Benavides, F. G., J. Benach, A.V. Diez-Roux, and C. Roman. 2000. "How Do Types of Employment Relate to Health Indicators? Findings from the Second European Survey on Working Conditions," *Journal of Epidemiology and Community Health* 59: 494–501.

Benavides, F.G., J. Benach, C, Muntaner, G.L. Delclos, N. Catot, and M. Amable, 2006. "Associations between Temporary Employment and Occupational Injury: What Are the Mechanisms?" *Occupational and Environmental Medicine* 63: 416–21.

Bernhard-Oettel, Cluaida, Magnus Sverke, and Hans de Wittte. 2005. "Comparing Three Alternative Types of Employment with Full-time Work: How Do Employment Contract and Perceived Job Conditions Relate to Health Complaints?" *Work and Stress* 19 (4): 301–18.

Bernhardt, Annette, Heather Boushey, Laura Dresser, and Chris Tilly, eds. 2008. *The Gloves-Off Economy: Workplace Standards at the Bottom of America's Labor Market.* Urbana-Champaign: Labor and Employment Relations Association.

Bernstein, Stephanie. 2006. "Mitigating Precarious Employment in Quebec: The Role of Minimum Employment Standards Legislation." In *Precarious Employment: Understanding Labour Market Insecurity in Canada,* ed. Leah Vosko, 221–40. Montreal and Kingston: McGill-Queen's University Press.

Bernstein, Stephanie, Katherine Lippel, Eric Tucker, and Leah Vosko. 2006. "Precarious Employment and the Law's Flaws: Identifying Regulatory Failure and Securing Effective Protection for Workers." In *Precarious Employment: Understanding Labour Market Insecurity in Canada,* ed. Leah Vosko, 203–20. Montreal and Kingston: McGill-Queen's University Press.

Bezanson, Kate. 2006. "The Neo-Liberal State and Social Reproduction:

Gender and Household Insecurity in the Late 1990s." In *Social Repro-
duction: Feminist Political Economy Challenges Neo-Liberalism*, ed.
Kate Bezanson and Meg Luxton, 173–214. Montreal and Kingston:
McGill-Queen's University Press.

Black, Clementina. 1915. *Married Women's Work: Being the Report of
an Enquiry Undertaken by the Women's Industrial Council*. London:
G. Bell and Sons.

Boeri, Tito, and Pietro Garibaldi. 2009. "Beyond Eurosclerosis," *Economic Policy* 24 (59): 411–61.

Bohle, Philip, Michael Quinlan, David Kennedy, and Ann Williamson.
2004. "Working Hours, Work-Life Conflict and Health in Precarious
and Permanent Employment," *Revista de Saude Publica* 38 (Supp):
19–25.

Bradley, Harriet. 1989. *Men's Work, Women's Work*. Minneapolis: University of Minnesota Press.

Brandes, Stuart. 1984. *American Welfare Capitalism, 1880–1940*. Chicago: University of Chicago Press.

Braverman, Harry. 1974. *Labor and Monopoly Capital: The Degrada-
tion of Work in the Twentieth Century*. New York: Monthly Labor
Review.

Bredgaard, Thomas, Flemming Larson, and Per Kongshoj Madsen. 2005.
"The Flexible Danish Labour Market: A Review," CARMA Research
Papers 1: 1–43.

Brody, David. 1968. "The Rise and Decline of Welfare Capitalism." In
Change and Continuity in Twentieth-Century America: The Twenties,
ed. John Braeman et al., 147–78. Columbus: Ohio State University
Press.

Broom, Dorthy H., et al. 2006. "The Lesser Evil: Bad Jobs or Unemployment? A Survey of Mid-Aged Australians," *Social Science Medicine* 63:
575–86.

Burchell, B., D. Ladipo, and F. Wilkinson, eds. 2002. *Job Insecurity and
Work Intensification*. London: Routledge.

Burgard, S., Jennie Brand, and James House 2005. *Job Insecurity and
Health in the United States*. Ann Arbor: Population Studies Centre,
University of Michigan.

Burgess, J., and A. De Ruytner., 2000. "Declining Job Quality in Australia: Another Hidden Cost of Unemployment," *Economic and
Labour Relations Review* 11 (2): 246–69.

Burke, Ronald. 2002. "Men, Masculinity and Health." In *Gender Work*

Stress and Health, ed. Debra Nelson and Ronald Burke, 35–54. Washington: American Psychological Association.

Burri, Susanne D. 2009. "The Netherlands: Precarious Employment in a Context of Flexicurity." In *Gender and the Contours of Precarious Employment*, ed. Leah Vosko, Martha MacDonald, and Iain Campbell, 127–42. London: Routledge.

Cameron, Barbara. 2006. "Social Reproduction and Canadian Federalism." In *Social Reproduction: Feminist Political Economy Challenges Neo-Liberalism*, ed. Kate Bezanson and Meg Luxton, 45–74. Montreal and Kingston: McGill-Queen's University Press.

Campbell, Iain, and John Burgess. 2001. "Casual Employment in Australia and Temporary Employment in Europe: Developing a Cross-National Comparison," *Work, Employment and Society* 15: 171–84.

Campbell, Iain, Gillian Whitehouse, and Janeen Baxter, 2009. "Australia: Casual Employment, Part-Time Employment and the Resilience of the Male-Breadwinner Model." In *Gender and the Contours of Precarious Employment*, ed. Leah Vosko, Martha MacDonald, and Iain Campbell, 60–75. London: Routledge.

Canadian Centre for Policy Alternatives. 2009. *The View from Here: How a Living Wage Can Reduce Poverty in Manitoba*. Ottawa.

Cappelli, Peter. 1999. *The New Deal at Work: Managing the Market-Driven Workforce*. Boston: Harvard University Press.

CCPA. 2009. *Municipal taxation needs reforming*. http://www.policyalternatives.ca/editorials/2005/03/editorial1073/?pa= 2005 [retrieved November 3 2009].

Challenge, Q.O.L. 2007. *A Bold New Way for People in BC's Capitol Region to Work Together. Report of Phase One, 2003–2006*. Victoria, B.C.: Social Planning Council.

Chancer, Lynn. 1998. "The Case for Guaranteed Income in Principle." In *Post-Work: The Wages of Cybernation*, ed. Stanley Aronowitz and Jonathan Cutler, 81–127. New York: Routledge.

Chaykowski, Richard. 2005. "Non-Standard Work and Economic Vulnerability," Vulnerable Worker Series – No. 3. *Work Network*. Ottawa: Canadian Policy Research Netword (CPRN).

Cherlin, Andrew J. 2005. "American Marriage in the Early Twenty-First Century," *The Future of Children* 15 (2): 33–55.

"China Strengthens Labour Protections," *Globe and Mail*, 29 June, 2007, A12.

Chirumbolo, Antonio, and Johnny Hellgren. 2003. "Individual and

Organizational Consequences of Job Insecurity: A European Study,"
Economic and Industrial Democracy 24 (2): 217–40.

Christie, Nancy. 2000. *Engendering the State: Family, Work, and Welfare in Canada.* Toronto: University of Toronto Press.

Clarke, Marlea. 2006. *"All the Workers"? Labour Market Reform and Precarious Work in Post-Apartheid South Africa, 1994–2004.* Ph.D. dissertation. Political Science Department, York University, Toronto.

Clarke, Marlea, Wayne Lewchuk, Alice de Wolff, and Andy King. 2007. "'This Just Isn't Sustainable': Precarious Employment, Stress and Workers' Health," *International Journal of Law and Psychiatry* 30 (6): 311–26.

Cooper, C.L. 2002. "The Changing Psychological Contract at Work," *Occupational Environment Medicine* 59: 355.

Commission of the European Communities. 2006. *Green Paper: Modernising Labour Law to Meet the Challenges of the 21st Century.* Brussels.

Corman, June, and Meg Luxton. 2007. "Social Reproduction and the Changing Dynamics of Unpaid Household and Caregiving Work." In *Work in Tumultuous Times: Critical Perspectives*, ed. Vivian Shalla and Wallace Clement, 262–88. Montreal and Kingston: McGill-Queen's University Press.

Cranford, Cynthia, Leah Vosko, and Nancy Zukewich. 2003. "Temporary Employment in the Canadian Labour Market: A Statistical Portrait," *Just Labour* 3: 46–59.

Cranford, Cynthia, Judy Fudge, Eric Tucker, and Leah Vosko, eds. 2005. *Self-Employed Workers Organize.* Montreal and Kingston: McGill-Queen's University Press.

Cranford, Cynthia, and Leah Vosko. 2006. "Conceptualizing Precarious Employment: Mapping Wage Work across Social Location and Occupational Context." In *Precarious Employment: Understanding Labour Market Insecurity in Canada*, ed. Leah Vosko, 43–66. Montreal and Kingston: McGill-Queen's University Press.

Crompton, Rosemary, ed. 1999. *Restructuring Gender Relations and Employment: The Decline of the Male Breadwinner Model.* Oxford: Oxford University Press.

– 2006. *Employment and the Family: The Reconfiguration of Work and Family Life in Contemporary Societies.* Cambridge: Cambridge University Press.

Crompton, Rosemary, Suzan Lewis, and Clare Lyonette, eds. 2007.

Women, Men, Work and Family in Europe. London: Palgrave MacMillan.

Cummings, Kristin J. 2008. "Contingent Workers and Contingent Health: Risks of a Modern Economy," *Journal of the American Medical Association* 299 (4): 448–50.

Daubas-Letourneux, V. and Thébaud-Mony, A. 2003. *Work Organization and Health at Work in the European Union*. Dublin: European Foundation for the Improvement of Working and Living Conditions.

De Witte, H. 1999. "Job Insecurity and Psychological Well-Being: Review of the Literature and Exploration of Some Unresolved Issues," *European Journal of Work and Organizational Psychology* 8: 155–77.

de Wolff, Alice. 2006a. "Bargaining for Collective Responsibility for Social Reproduction." In *Social Reproduction: Feminist Political Economy Challenges Neo-Liberalism*, ed. Kate Bezanson and Meg Luxton, 93–116. Montreal and Kingston: McGill-Queen's University Press.

– 2006b. "Privatizing Public Employment Assistance and Precarious Employment in Toronto." In *Precarious Employment: Understanding Labour Market Insecurity in Canada*, ed. Leah Vosko, 182–99. Montreal and Kingston: McGill-Queen's University Press.

Department of Trade and Industry. 2007. Employment Status and Employment Rights of Agency Workers. http://www.gov.im/lib/docs/dti/employmentrights/guides/agencyworkersandemploymentstatus.pdf, accessed 22 November, 2008.

Doogan, K.. 2001. "Insecurity and Long-term Employment," *Work Employment and Society* 15 (3): 419–41.

– 2005. "Long-term Employment and the Restructuring of the Labour Market in Europe," *Time and Society* 14 (1): 65–87.

D'Souza, R.M., L. Strazdins, L.L-Y. Lim, D.H Broom, and B. Rodgers. 2003. "Work and Health in a Contemporary Society: Demands, Control, and Insecurity," *Journal of Epidemiology and Community Health* 57: 849–54.

Duxbury, Linda, and Chris Higgins. 2001. *Work-Life Balance in the New Millennium: Where Are We? Where Do We Need to Go?* Ottawa: Canadian Policy Research Network.

Edwards, Richard. 1979. *Contested Terrain: The Transformation of the Workplace in the Twentieth Century*. New York: Basic Books.

Ellingsæter, Anne Lise. 1999. "Dual Breadwinners between State and Market." In *Restructuring Gender Relations and Employment: The*

Decline of the Male Breadwinner Model, ed. Rosemary Crompton, 40–59. Oxford: Oxford University Press.

Elson, Diane. 1999. "Labor Markets as Gendered Institutions: Equality, Efficiency and Empowerment Issues," *World Development* 27 (3): 611–27.

European Expert Group on Flexicurity. 2007. *Flexicurity Pathways: Turning Hurdles into Stepping Stones.* Brussels.

Farber, Henry S. 2005. "What Do We Know about Job Loss in the United States? Evidence from the Displaced Workers Survey, 1984–2004," *Federal Reserve Bank of Chicago: Economic Perspectives Issue Q II:* 13–28.

– 2008a. "Job Loss and the Decline of Job Security in the United States," *Princeton University Industrial Relations Section Working Paper* no.520, at http://www.irs.princeton.edu/pubs/pdfs /520revised.pdf.

– 2008b. "Short(er) Shrift: The Decline in Work Firm Attachment in the United States." In *Laid Off, Laid Low: Political and Economic Consequences of Employment Insecurity*, ed. Katherine S. Newman, 10–37. New York: Columbia University Press,

– 2008c. "Employment Insecurity: The Decline in Worker-Firm Attachment in the United States," *Princeton University Working Paper* 530. Princeton, New Jersey.

Farber, Henry S., John Haltiwanger, and Katharine G. Abraham. 1997. "The Changing Face of Job Loss in the United States 1981–95," *The Brookings Papers on Economic Activity, (Microeconomics Supplement)*: 55–142.

Ferguson, Niall. 2008. *The Ascent of Money: A Financial History of the World.* New York: Penguin Press.

Ferrie, J.E. 2001. "Is Job Insecurity Harmful to Health?" *Journal of the Royal Society of Medicine* 94: 71–6.

Ferrie J.E, W.H., G. Oxenstierna, and T. Theorell. 2007. "The Impact of Moderate and Major Workplace Expansion and Downsizing on the Psychosocial and Physical Work Environment and Income in Sweden," *Scandinavian Journal of Public Health* 35 (1): 62–9.

Ferrie, J.E, M.J. Shipley, M.G. Marmot, S.A. Stansfeld, and D. Smith, 1998. "The Health Effects of Major Organizational Change and Job Insecurity," *Social Science Medicine* 46 (2): 243–54.

Ferrie, J.E., M.J. Shipley, S.A. Stansfeld, and M.G. Marmot. 2002. "Effects of Chronic Job Insecurity and Change in Job Security on Self

Reported Health, Minor psychiatric Morbidity, Physiological Measures, and Health Related Behaviours in British Civil Servants: The Whitehall II Study," *Journal of Epidemiology and Community Health* 56: 450–4.

Ferrie, J.E, M.J. Shipley, K. Newman, S.A. Stansfeld, and M.G. Marmot. 2005. "Self-Reported Job Insecurity and Health in the Whitehall II Study: Potential Explanations of the Relationship," *Social Science and Medicine* 60: 1593–1602.

Fevre, R. 2007. "Employment Insecurity and Social Theory: The Power of Nightmares," *Work, Employment and Society* 21 (3): 517–35.

Food Banks Canada. 2009. *Hunger Count 2009*, http://www.cafb-acba.ca/documents/HungerCount2009NOV16.pdf, accessed 16 November, 2009.

Forget, Evelyn L. 2010. "The Town with No Poverty: Using Health Administration Data to Assess Outcomes of a North American Guaranteed Annual Income Field Experiment," *Working Paper*. Winnipeg: University of Manitoba.

Frade, Carlos, and Isabelle Darmon. 2005. "New Modes of Business Organization and Precarious Employment: Towards the Recommodification of Labour?" *Journal of European Social Policy* 15 (2): 107–21.

Fraser, Jill Andresky. 2001. *White Collar Sweat-Shop: The Deterioration of Work and Its Rewards in Corporate America*. New York: Norton.

Fudge, Judy. 1997. *Precarious Work and Families*. Toronto: Centre for Research on Work and Society, York University.

Fudge, Judy, Eric Tucker, and Leah Vosko. 2002. *The Legal Concept of Employment: Marginalizing Workers, Report for the Law Commission of Canada*: 1–141.

Galarneau, Diane. 2005. "Earnings of Temporary versus Permanent Employees," *Perspectives* 6 (1) : 5–18.

Galbauzi, Grace-Edward. 2004. "Racializing the Division of Labour: Neoliberal Restructuring and the Economic Segregation of Canada's Racialized Groups." In *Challenging the Market: The Struggle to Regulate Work and Income*, ed. Jim Stanford and Leah Vosko, 175–204. Montreal and Kingston: McGill-Queen's University Press.

Ganage, Charlene. 1986. *Double Day Bind*. Toronto: The Women's Press.

Garrahan, Philip, and Paul Stewart. 1992. *The Nissan Enigma: Flexibility at Work in a Local Economy*. London: Mansell.

Giatti, L., S.M. Barreto, and C. Comini Ceaser. 2008. "Household Context and Self-Rated Health: The Effect of Unemployment and Informal Work," *Journal of Epidemiological Community Health* 62: 1079–85.

Giloth, Robert, ed. 2004. *Workforce Intermediaries for the Twenty-first Century*. Philadelphia: Temple University Press in association with The American Assembly Columbia University.

Gindin, Sam. 1995. *The Canadian Auto Workers: The Birth and Transformation of a Union*. Toronto: James Lorimer and Co.

Golsch, Katrin. 2005. *The Impact of Labour Market Insecurity on the Work and Family Life of Men and Women*. Frankfurt: Peter Lang.

Gordon, David, Richard Edwards, and Michael Reich. 1982. *Segmented Work, Divided Workers: The Historical Transformation of Labor in the United States*. Cambridge: Cambridge University Press.

Gornick, Janet, and Marcia Meyers. 2003. *Families that Work: Policies for Reconciling Parenthood and Employment*. New York: Russell Sage Foundation.

Gorz, André. 2005. *Reclaiming Work: Beyond the Wage-Based Society*. Cambridge: Polity Press.

Gottfried, Heidi. 2009. "Japan: The Reproduction Bargain and the Making of Precarious Employment." In *Gender and the Contours of Precarious Employment*, ed. Leah Vosko, Martha MacDonald, and Iain Campbell, 76–91. London: Routledge.

Goudswaard, A., and F. Andries. 2002. *Employment Status and Working Conditions*. Dublin: European Foundation for the Improvement of Working and Living Conditions.

Graham, L. 1995. *On the Line at Subaru-Isuz*. Ithaca: ILR Press.

Green, Francis. 2006. *Demanding Work: The Paradox of Job Quality in the Affluent Economy*. Princeton: Princeton University Press.

Greenglass, Esther R. 2002. "Work Stress, Coping, and Social Support: Implications for Women's Occupational Well-Being." In *Gender Work Stress and Health*, ed. Debra Nelson and Ronald Burke, 85–96. Washington: American Psychological Association.

Grnell, Marianne. 2001. "Job Losses and New Rules on Employment Conditions in Temporary Work Agencies." European Foundation for the Improvement of Living and Working Conditions. http://www.eurofound.europa.eu/eiro/2001/11/feature/nlo111102f.htm, accessed 22 November, 2008.

Guadalupe, Maria. 2003. "The Hidden Costs of Fixed Term Contracts: The Impact on Work Accidents," *Labour Economics* 10: 339–57.

Haber, William, and Wibur Cohen, eds. 1948. *Readings in Social Security*. New York: Prentice-Hall.

Hacker, Jacob S. 2006a. *The Great Risk Shift: The Assault on American Jobs, Families, Health Care and Retirement and How You Can Fight Back.* Oxford: Oxford University Press.

– 2006b. *Universal Insurance: Enhancing Economic Security to Promote Opportunity.* The Hamilton Project, Washington: The Brookings Institution.

Hallock, Kevin F. 2009. "Job Loss and the Fraying of the Implicit Employment Contract," *Journal of Economic Perspectives* 23 (4): 69–93.

Hebson, Gail, and Irena Grugulis. 2005. "Gender and New Organizational Forms." In *Fragmenting Work: Blurring Organizational Boundaries and Disordering Hierarchies,* ed. Mick Marchington, Damian Grimshaw, Jill Ribery, and Hugh Willmott, 217–37. Oxford: Oxford University Press.

Heery, Edmund, and Brian Abbott. 2000. "Trade Unions and the Insecure Workforce." In *The Insecure Workforce,* ed. Edmund Heery and John Salmon, 155–80. London: Routledge.

Heery, Edmund, and J. Salmon, eds. 2000. *The Insecure Workforce.* London: Routledge.

Hennessy, Trish, and Armine Yalnizyan. 2009. Canada's "He-cession," *Behind the Numbers.* Ottawa: CCPA: 1–3.

Hochschild, Arlie Russell. 1997. *The Time Bind: When Work Becomes Home and Home Becomes Work.* New York: Metropolitan Books.

Hodgson, Geoffrey M. 1999. *Economics and Utopia: Why the Learning Economy Is Not the End of History.* London: Routledge.

HRSDC. 2008. Discussion Paper on the Review of Labour Standards in the Canada Labour Code. Ottawa: Human Resources and Social Development Canada (HRSDC) Labour Program.

Huberman, Michael, and Wayne Lewchuk. 2003. "European Economic Integration and the Labour Compact, 1850–1913," *European Economic History Review* 7: 3–41.

Hyman, J., D. Scholarios, and C. Baldry. 2005. "Getting On or Getting By? Employee Flexibility and Coping Strategies for Home and Work," *Work Employment and Society* 19 (4): 705–25.

International Labour Organisation. 2003. *Report V: The Scope of the Employment Relationship* (Report prepared for the International Labour Conference, 91st Session). Geneva: International Labour Organisation.

– 2006. *Report V (1) The Employment Relationship.* Geneva: International Labour Office.

– 2007. *The Employment Relationship: An Annotated Guide to ILO*

Recommendation No. 198. Accessed 15 July, 2008, from http://www
.ilo.org/public/english/dialogue/ifpdial/downloads/guide_rec198.pdf

Jacoby, Sanford. 1997. *Modern Manors: Welfare Capitalism since the
New Deal.* Princeton: Princeton University Press.

Jackson, Andrew. 2004. "Gender Inequality and Precarious Work:
Exploring the Impact of Unions through the Gender and Work Data-
base." Paper read at Gender and Work: Knowledge Production in
Practice Conference, at York University, North York, Ontario.

Johnson, Jennifer. 2002. *Getting By on the Minimum: The Lives of
Working-Class Women.* New York: Routledge.

Jonsson, Inger, and Anita Nyberg. 2009. "Sweden: Precarious Work and
Precarious Employment." In *Gender and the Contours of Precarious
Employment,* ed. Leah Vosko, Martha MacDonald, and Iain Camp-
bell, 194–210. London: Routledge.

Kahn, Joseph, and David Barboza. 2007. "China Passes a Sweeping
Labor Law," *New York Times,* 30 Jun 2007. http://www.nytimes.com
/2007/06/30/business/worldbusiness/30chlabor.html

Kapsalis, Costa, and Pierre Tourigny. 2004. "Duration of Non-standard
Employment," *Perspectives* 5 (12): 5–13.

Karasek, R., and T. Theorell, 1990. *Healthy Work: Stress, Productivity
and the Reconstruction of Working Life.* New York: Basic Books.

Kaufman, Bruce E. 2008. *Managing the Human Factor: The Early Years
of Human Resource Management in American Industry.* Ithaca: Cornell University Press.

Keune, Maarten. 2008. "Flexicurity: A Contested Concept at the Core of
the European Labour Market Debate," *Intereconomics* March/April:
992–8.

Kivimaki, M., J. Vahtera, J. Pentti, and J.E. Ferrie. 2000. "Factors
Underlying the Effect of Organisational Downsizing on Health of
Employees: Longitudinal Cohort Study," *British Medical Journal in
Health* 320: 971–5.

Kivimaki, M., J. Vahtera, J. Pentti, L. Thomson, A. Griffiths, and T. Cox.
2001. "Downsizing, Changes in Work, and Self-Rated Health of
Employees: A 7-Year Panel 3-Wave Panel Study," *Anxiety, Stress and
Coping* 14: 59–73.

Kivimaki, Mika, Jussi Vahtera, Marianna Virtanen, Marko Elovainio,
and Jaana Pentt. 2003. "Temporary Employment and Risk of Overall
and Cause-Specific Mortality," *American Journal of Epidemiology*
158: 663–8.

Kling, Jeffrey R. 2006. *Fundamental Restructuring of Unemployment Insurance, Wage-Loss Insurance, and Temporary Earnings Replacement Accounts.* Washington. Brookings Institution, Discussion Paper 5.

Knowledge Socialization Project at IBM Research http://www.research .ibm.com/knowsoc/stories_IBMHistory.html, accessed 4 June, 2007.

Krahn, Harvey. 1995. "Non-Standard Work on the Rise," *Perspectives on Labour and Income* 7 (4): 35–42.

Krantz, Gunilla, Leeni Berntsson, and Ulf Lundberg. 2005. "Total Workload, Work Stress and Perceived Symptoms in Swedish Male and Female White-Collar Employees," *The European Journal of Public Health* 15 (2): 209–14.

Kumar, Pradeep. 2008. "Is the Movement at a Standstill? Union Efforts and Outcomes," *Our Times* 27 (5): 11.

Kvist, Jon, and Lisbeth Pedersen. 2007. "Danish Labour Market Activation Policies," *National Institute Economic Review* 202: 99–111.

Larson, Jeffry H., Stephan M. Wilson, and Rochelle Beley. 1994. "The Impact of Job Insecurity on Marital and Family Relationships," *Family Relations* 43 (2): 138–43.

Larson, Trine. 2008. "EU Fixed-Term Work Directive Has Limited Effect at Local Level," http://www.eurofound.europa.eu/eiro/2008/08 /articles/dk0808039i.htm_, accessed 9 November, 2009.

Lazonick, William. 2009. "The New Economy Business Model and the Crisis of U.S. Capitalism," *Capital and Society* 4 (2): 1–67.

Leeson, R.A. 1980. *Travelling Brothers: The Six Centuries' Road from Craft Fellowship to Trade Unionism.* London: Granada.

Letourneux, V., 1998. *Precarious Employment and Working Conditions in the European Union.* European Foundation for the Improvement of Living and Working Conditions. Luxembourg: Office for Official Publication of the European Communities.

Lewchuk, Wayne. 1993. "Men and Monotony: Fraternalism at the Ford Motor Company," *Journal of Economic History* 53 (4): 824–56.

Lewchuk, Wayne, and D. Robertson. 1996. "Working Conditions under Lean Production: A Worker-based Benchmarking Study," *Asia Pacific Business Review* 2 (Summer): 60–81.

– 1997. "Production without Empowerment: Work Reorganization from the Perspective of Motor Vehicle Workers," *Capital and Class* 63: 37–64.

Lewchuk, Wayne, Alice de Wolff, and Andy King. 2006a. "The Hidden Costs of Precarious Employment: Health and the Employment Relationship." In *Precarious Employment: Understanding Labour Market Insecurity in Canada*, ed. Leah Vosko, 141–62. Montreal and Kingston: McGill-Queen's University Press.

– 2006b. "Employment Strain and Temporary Employment." In *Work and Labour in Tumultuous Times: Critical Perspectives*, ed. Vivian Shalla and Wallace Clement, 98–130. Montreal and Kingston: McGill-Queen's University Press.

Lewchuk, Wayne, Marlea Clarke, and Alice de Wolff. 2008. "Working Without Commitments: Precarious Employment and Health," *Work Employment and Society* 22: 387–406.

– 2009. "Precarious Employment and the Internal Responsibility System: Some Canadian Experiences." In *Workplace Health and Safety: International Perspectives on Worker Representation*, ed. Theo Nicholls and David Walters, 109–33. London: Palgrave Macmillan.

Lindsay, Colin. 2008. "Are Women Spending More Time on Unpaid Domestic Work than Men in Canada?" *Component of Statistics Canada*, catalogue no. 89-630-X. Ottawa: Statistics Canada.

Lippel, Katherine. 2006. "Precarious Employment and Occupational Health and Safety Regulation in Quebec." In *Precarious Employment: Understanding Labour Market Insecurity in Canada*, ed. Leah Vosko, 241–55. Montreal and Kingston: McGill-Queen's University Press.

Louie, A., A.S. Ostry, M. Quinlan, T. Keegel, J. Shoveller, and A.D. LaMontangne. 2006. "Empirical Study of Employment Arrangements and Precariousness in Australia," *Relations Industrielles/Industrial Relations* 61 (3): 465–89.

Lowe, Graham. 2007. *21ˢᵗ Century Job Quality: Achieving What Canadians Want*. Ottawa: Canadian Policy Research Networks, Research Report W/37.

Lundberg, Ulf, and Marianne Frankenhaeuser. 1999. "Stress and Workload of Men and Women in High-Ranking Positions," *Journal of Occupational Health Psychology* 4 (2): 142–51.

Luxton, Meg. 1990. "Two Hands for the Clock: Changing Patterns in the Gendered Division of Labour in the Home." In *Through the Kitchen Window: The Politics of Home and Family*, ed. M. Luxton, 17–36. Toronto: Garamond Press,

Luxton, Meg, Harriet Rosenberg, and Sedef Arat-Koc, eds. 1990. *Through the Kitchen Window: The Politics of Home and Family*. Toronto: Garamond.

Luxton, Meg, and June Corman. 2001. *Getting by in Hard Times: Gen-*

dered Labour at Home and on the Job. Toronto: University of Toronto Press.

Madsen, Per Kongshej. 2006. "Labour Market Flexibility and Social Protection in European Welfare States: Contrasts and Similarities," *Australian Bulletin of Labour* 32 (2): 139–62.

McBride, Stephen. 1998. "The Political Economy of Training in Canada," *Centre for Research on Work and Society Training Matters: Working Paper Series #98-07*. Toronto: York University.

McKay, Ian. 2008. *Reasoning Otherwise: Leftists and the People's Enlightenment in Canada, 1890–1920*. Toronto: Between the Lines.

McNally, David. 2009. "Inequality, the Profit System and Global Crisis." In *Bankruptcies and Bailouts*, ed. Julie Guard and Wayne Antony, 32–45. Halifax: Fernwood Publishing.

Malenfant, R., A. LaRue, and M. Vezina. 2007. "Intermittent Work and Well-being: One Foot in the Door, One Foot Out," *Current Sociology* 55 (6): 814–35.

Marchington, Mick, Damian Grimshaw, Jill Ribery, and Hugh Willmott, eds. 2005. *Fragmenting Work: Blurring Organizational Boundaries and Disordering Hierarchies*. Oxford: Oxford University Press.

Marglin, Stephen. 2008. *The Dismal Science: How Thinking Like an Economist Undermines Community*. Cambridge: Harvard University Press.

Marmot, Michael, Sharon Friel, Ruth Bell, Tanja A.J. Houweling, and Sebastian Taylor. 2008. "Closing the Gap in a Generation: Health Equity through Action on the Social Determinants of Health," *Lancet* 372: 1661–9.

Marshall, Katherine. 2003. "Benefits on the Job," *Perspectives on Labour and Income* 4 (5) *Statistics Canada Catalogue no. 75-001-X*. Ottawa: Statistics Canada: 5–12.

– 2006. "Converging Gender Roles," *Perspectives on Labour and Income* 7 (7) *Statistics Canada Catalogue no. 75-001-X*. Ottawa: Statistics Canada: 5–17.

– 2009. "The Family Work Week," *Perspectives on Labour and Income* 10 (4): 5–13. *Statistics Canada Catalogue no. 75-001-X*. Ottawa: Statistics Canada.

May, Martha. 1982. "The Historical Problem of the Family Wage: The Ford Motor Company and the Five Dollar Day," *Feminist Studies* 8 (Summer): 399–424.

McKeen, W. 2004. *Money in Their Own Name: The Feminist Voice in*

Poverty Debate in Canada, 1970–1995. Toronto: University of Toronto Press.

– 2006. "Diminishing the Concept of Social Policy: The Shifting Conceptual Ground of Social Policy Debate in Canada," *Critical Social Policy* 26 (4): 865–87.

McKeen, W., and A. Porter. 2003. "Politics and Transformation: Welfare State Restructuring in Canada." In *Changing Canada: Political Economy as Transformation*, ed. Wallace Clement and Leah F. Vosko, 109–34. Montreal and Kingston: McGill-Queen's University Press.

Melman, Seymour. 1958. *Decision Making and Productivity.* Oxford: Blackwell.

Menéndez, María, Joan Benach, Carles Muntaner, Marcelo Amble, and Patricia O'Campo. 2007. "Is Precarious Employment More Damaging to Women's Health than Men's?" *Social Science Medicine* 64: 776–81.

Meyer III, Stephen. 1981. *The Five Dollar Day: Labor Management and Social Control in the Ford Motor Company, 1908–1921.* Albany: State University of New York Press.

Milkman, Ruth. 1997. *Farewell to the Factory: Auto Workers in the Late Twentieth Century.* Berkeley: University of California Press.

Mills, C. Wright. 1956. *White Collar. The American Middle Classes,* New York: Oxford University Press.

MISSWA. 2006. *Time for a Fair Deal, Report of the Task Force on Modernizing Income Security for Working-Age Adults.* Toronto: St Christopher House and Toronto City Summit Alliance.

Monsebraaten, Laurie. 2007. "Guaranteed Income, Guaranteed Dignity." *Toronto Star* 5 March, 2007.

Morissette, R., Johnson, A. 2005. *Are Good Jobs Disappearing in Canada?* Statistics Canada, Business and Labour Market Analysis Division (11F0019MIE — No. 239): 1–52.

Murray, Jacqueline, ed. 2007. *Employment Conditions and Health Inequalities: Final Report to the Commission on Social Determinants of Health (CSDH).* Geneva: Employment Conditions Knowledge Network (EMCONET).

Nelson, Daniel. 1975. *Managers and Workers: Origins of the New Factory System in the United States, 1880–1920.* Madison: University of Wisconsin.

Nelson, Debra L., Ronald J. Burke, and Susan Michie. 2002. "New Directions for Studying Gender, Work Stress, and Health." In *Gender, Work Stress and Health*, ed. D.L Nelson and R.J. Burke, 229–42. Washington: American Psychological Association.

Newman, Katherine S., and Victor Chen. 2007. *The Missing Class: Portraits of the Near Poor in America*. Boston: Beacon Press.

National Union of Public and General Employees (NUPGE), 2007a. *Pensions Backgrounder #2, A Brief History of Pensions in Canada, National Union's Pensions Manual*, 4th ed. [accessed 28 November, 2008]. Available from http://www.nupge.ca/publications/Pensions%20Documents/History_of_Pensions.pdf.

– 2007b. *Pensions Backgrounder #6, Workplace Pension Plans*. [accessed 3 December, 2008]. Available from http://www.nupge.ca/publications/Pensions%20Documents/ Workplace_Pension_Plans.pdf.

OECD. 1994. *The OECD Jobs Study: Facts, Analysis, Strategies*, Paris: Organisation for Economic Co-operation and Development. http://www.oecd.org/dataoecd/42/51/1941679.pdf

– 1997. OECD *Employment Outlook 1997*, Paris: Organisation for Economic Co-operation and Development. http://www.oecd.org/dataoecd/19/17/2080463.pdf

– 2000. OECD *Employment Outlook 2000*, Paris: Organisation for Economic Co-operation and Development. http://www.oecd.org/dataoecd/10/44/2079593.pdf

– 2006. OECD *Employment Outlook 2006*: Boosting Jobs and Incomes, Paris: Organisation for Economic Co-operation and Development.

– 2009. *Overview: Data on Informal Employment and Self-Employment From "Is Informal Normal? Towards More and Better Jobs in Developing Countries,"* Paris: Organisation for Economic Co-operation and Development. http://www.oecd.org/dataoecd/4/49/42863997.pdf (Oct 22, 2009).

– nd. OECD. *Stat Extracts*, Paris: Organisation for Economic Co-operation and Development. http://stats.oecd.org/wbos/Index.aspx

Ontario Federation of Labour. 2007. Brief to the Ontario Expert Commission on Pensions. Toronto: OFL.

Origo, Federica, and Laura Pagani. 2008. "Flexicurity and Workers' Well-Being in Europe: Is Temporary Employment Always Bad?" University of Milan-Bicocca Working Paper 141, Milan: 1–41.

Osberg, Lars. 2009. *Canada's Declining Social Safety Net: The Case for EI Reform*. Ottawa: CCPA.

Osterman, Paul. 1999. *Securing Prosperity: The American Labor Market: How It has Changed and What to Do about It*. Princeton: Princeton University Press.

Palmer, Bryan. 1979. *Culture in Conflict: Skilled Workers and Industrial*

Capitalism in Hamilton, Ontario 1860–1914, Montreal and Kingston: McGill-Queen's University Press.

Parker, Sharon, Mark Griffin, Christine Sprigg, and Toby Wall. 2002. "Effect of Temporary Contracts on Perceived Work Characteristics and Job Strain: A Longitudinal Study," *Personnel Psychology* 55 (3): 689–719.

Pedersen, H.H., C.C. Hansen, and S. Mahler. 2003. *Temporary Agency Work in the European Union*. Dublin: European Foundation for the Improvement of Living and Working Conditions.

Pfau-Effinger, Birgit. 1999. "The Modernization of Family and Motherhood in Western Europe." In *Restructuring Gender Relations and Employment: The Decline of the Male Breadwinner Model*, ed. Rosemary Crompton, 60–79. Oxford: Oxford University Press.

Philips, Kaia, Raul Eamets, with Janika Alloja Kerly Krillo, and Anne Lauringson. 2007. *Approaches to Flexicurity: EU models*. Dublin: European Foundation for the Improvement of Living and Working Conditions.

Picchio, Antonella. 1992. *Social Reproduction: The Political Economy of the Labour Market*. Cambridge: Cambridge University Press.

Pink, Daniel H. 2001. *Free Agent Nation: The Future of Working for Yourself*. New York: Warner Business Books.

Pocock, B. 2005. "Work-Life 'Balance' in Australia: Limited Progress, Dim Prospects," *Asia Pacific Journal of Human Resources* 43 (2): 198–209.

Presser, Harriet B. 2003. *Working in a 24/7: Challenges for American Families*. New York: Russell Sage Foundation.

Pupo, Norene, and Anne Duffy. 2003. "Caught in the Net: The Impact of Changes to Canadian Employment Insurance Legislation on Part-time Workers," *Social Policy and Society* 2 (1): 1–11.

Pupo, Norene, and Mark Thomas, eds. 2010. *Interrogating the New Economy: Restructuring Work in the 21st Century*. Toronto: University of Toronto Press.

Purcell, Kate. 2000. "Gendered Employment Insecurity." In *The Insecure Workforce*, ed. Edmund Heery and John Salmon, 112–39. London, Rutledge.

Putnam, Robert. 2000. *Bowling Alone: The Collapse and Revival of American Community*. New York: Simon and Schuster.

Quinlan, Michael. 1999. "The Implications of Labour Market Restructuring in Industrialized Societies for Occupational Health and Safety," *Economic and Industrial Democracy* 20: 427–60.

- 2003. "Flexible Work and Organisational Arrangements – Regulatory Problems and Responses." *Working Paper #16*. Canberra: National Research Centre for OHS Regulation, Australian National University, Australia.

Quinlan, Michael, and Chris Mahew. 1999. "Precarious Employment and Workers' Compensation," *International Journal of Law and Psychiatry* 5–6: 491–520.

- 2000. "Precarious Employment, Work Re-Organization and the Fracturing of OHS Management." In *Systematic Occupational Health and Safety Management: Perspectives on an International Development*, ed. Kaj Frick, Per Langaa Jensen, Michael Quinlan, and Ton Wilthagen, 175–98. Oxford: Pergamon Science.

- 2006. "Economic Pressure, Multi-Tiered Subcontracting and Occupational Health and Safety in the Australian Long Haul Trucking Industry," *Employee Relations* 28 (3): 212–29.

Quinlan, Michael, Chris Mahew, and Philip Bohle. 2001. "The Global Expansion of Precarious Employment, Work Disorganization, and Consequences for Occupational Health: A Review of Recent Literature," *International Journal of Health Services* 31 (2): 335–414.

Rathke, Wade. 2009. *Citizen Wealth: Winning the Campaign to Save Working Families*. San Francisco: Berrett-Koehler Publishers.

Robinson, Peter. 2000. "Insecurity and the Flexible Workforce: Measuring the Ill-defined." In *The Insecure Workforce*, ed. Edmund Heery and John Salmon, 25–38. London: Routledge.

Rodriguez, Eunice. 2002. "Marginal Employment and Health in Britain and Germany: Does Unstable Employment Predict Health?" *Social Science and Medicine* 55: 963–79.

Rogers, G. 1989. "Precarious Work in Western Europe: The State of the Debate." In *Precarious Jobs in Labour Market Regulation: The Growth of Atypical Employment in Western Europe,* ed. G. Rodgers and J. Rodgers, 1–16. Geneva: International Institute for Labour Studies.

Rose, Sonya. 1992. *Limited Livelihoods: Gender and Class in Nineteenth-Century England*. Berkeley: University of California Press.

Ross, Stephanie. 2004. "Social Unionism and Membership Participation: What Role for Union Democracy?" Paper read at the annual conference of the Canadian Political Science Association, Political Economy Section, in Winnipeg, Manitoba.

Rubery, Jill, and Jane Humphries. 1984. "The Reconstitution of the Supply Side of the Labour Market: The Relative Autonomy of Social Regulation," *Cambridge Journal of Economics* 8: 331–46.

Rubery, J., J. Earnshaw, M. Marchington, F.E. Cooke, and S. Vincent. 2002. "Changing Organizational Forms and the Employment Relationship," *Journal of Management Studies* 39 (5): 645–72.

Rutherford, Tod D. 1998. "'Still in Training?' Labor Unions and the Restructuring of Canadian Labor Market Policy," *Economic Geography* 74: 131–49.

Salami, Reihan. 2009. "The Death of Macho," *Foreign Policy* July/August: 1–4.

Saloniemi, A., P. Virtanen, and J. Vahtera, 2004. "The Work Environment in Fixed Term Jobs: Are Poor Psychosocial Conditions Inevitable?" *Work, Employment and Society* 18: 193–208.

Sangster, Joan. 1995. "Doing Two Jobs: The Wage Earning Mother, 1945–1970." In *A Diversity of Women*, ed. Joy Parr, 98–134. Toronto: University of Toronto Press.

Sassen, Saskia. 2001. *The Global City: New York, London, Tokyo.* 2nd ed., Princeton: Princeton University Press.

Saunders, R. 2006. "Making Work Pay: Findings and Recommendations," *Research Highlights, Canadian Policy Research Networks* 6 (May): 10.

Schomann, Klaus, Ralf Rogowski, and Thomas Kruppe. 1998. *Labour Market Efficiency in the European Union: Employment Protection and Fixed-Term Contracts.* London: Routledge.

Sciarra, Silvana. 2008. "Is Flexicurity a European Policy?" URGE Working Paper 4, Florence: Research Unit on European Governance.

Scott, H.K.. 2004. "Reconceptualizing the Nature and Health Consequences of Work-Related Insecurity for the New Economy: The Decline of Workers; Power in the Flexible Regime," *International Journal of Health Services* 34: 143–53.

Seifert, Ana Maria, Karen Messing, Jessica Riel, and Céline Chatigny. 2007. "Precarious Employment Conditions Affect Work Content in Education and Social Work: Results of Work Analyses," *International Journal of Law and Psychiatry* 30: 299–310.

Sennett, Richard. 1998. *The Corrosion of Character: The Personal Consequences of Work in the New Capitalism.* New York: W.W. Norton.

Shalla, Vivian, and Clement Wallace, eds. 2007. *Work in Tumultuous Times: Critical Perspectives.* Montreal and Kingston: McGill-Queen's University Press.

Sidel, Ruth. 1990. *On Her Own: Growing Up in the Shadow of the American Dream.* New York: Viking.

Smith, Vicki. 2001. *Crossing the Great Divide: Worker Risk and Opportunity in the New Economy*. Ithica, NY: Cornell University Press/ILR Press.

Standing, Guy. 2002. *Beyond the New Paternalism: Basic Security as Equality*. London: Verso.

Statistics Canada, 2001. "Income: Low Income Cut-offs," *2001 Census Dictionary*. Ottawa: Government of Canada.

– 2002. *Profile of Canadian Families and Households: Diversification Continues, 2001 Census*. Catalogue no. 96F0030SIE200100, Ottawa: Statistics Canada.

– 2006. "Study: Canada's Labour Market at a Glance," *The Daily*, Thursday, 1 June, 2006. http://www.statcan.ca/Daily/English /060601/d060601a.htm

– 2008. *Earnings and Incomes of Canadians over the Past Quarter Century, 2006 Census*. Catalogue no. 97-563-X, Ottawa: Statistics Canada.

Stevenson, Betsey, and Justin Wolfers. 2008. "Marriage and the Market," *CATO Unbound* January 18.

Sverke, Magnus, J. Hellgren, and K. Naswall. 2002. "No Security: A Meta-Analysis and Review of Job Insecurity and Its Consequences," *Journal of Occupational Health Psychology* 7: 242–64.

Tal, Benjamin. 2009. *Canadian Employment Quality Index: Employment Stabilizing-Quality Falling*, Canadian Imperial Bank of Commerce. http://research.cibcwm.com/economic_public/download/eqi-cda-20091102.pdf

Thomas, Mark P. 2009. *Regulating Flexibility: The Political Economy of Employment Standards*. Montreal and Kingston: McGill-Queen's University Press.

Tilly, Louise A., and Joan W. Scott. 1987. *Women, Work and Family*. New York: Routledge.

Tompa, Emile, H. Scott-Marshall., D. Dolinschi, S. Trevithick, and S. Bhattacharyya. 2007. "Precarious Employment Experiences and their Health Consequences: Towards a Theoretical Framework," *Work* 28: 209–24.

Townson, Monica. 2000. *Reducing Poverty among Older Women: The Potential of Retirement Incomes Policies*. Ottawa: Status of Women Canada Policy Research Fund.

– 2006. "The Impact of Precarious Employment on Financial Security in Retirement." In *New Frontiers of Research on Retirement*, edited by L.O. Stone, Chapter Nineteen. Ottawa: Statistics Canada.

US Department of Labor. 2005. *Contingent and Alternative Employment Arrangements, February 2005*, Washington: Bureau of Labor Statistics.

Vallée, Guylaine. 2005. *Towards Enhancing the Employment Conditions of Vulnerable Workers: A Public Policy Perspective*. Ottawa: Canadian Policy Research Network (CPRN).

Valletta, Robert G. 1999. "Declining Job Security," *Journal of Labor Economics* 17 (4, part 2): S170–S197.

– 2007, "Anxious Workers," *Federal Reserve Bank of San Francisco, Economic Letter* 13: 1–3.

van Dresser, Steve. 1999. "The Employment Rights of Repeatedly Renewed Private Sector Contract Workers" http://www.debito.org /rightsofrepeatedlyrenewed.htm, accessed 22 November, 2008.

Vidal, Matt, and Leann M. Tigges. 2009. "Temporary Employment and Strategic Staffing in the Manufacturing Sector," *Industrial Relations* 48 (1): 55–72.

Viebrock, Elke, and Jochen Clasen. 2009. "Flexicurity and Welfare Reform: A Review," *Socio-Economic Review* 7: 305–31.

Virtanen, P., J. Vahtera, M. Kivimaki, J. Pentti, and J. Ferrie, 2002. "Employment Security and Health," *Journal of. Epidemiology and Community Health* 56: 569–74.

Virtanen, P., J. Vahtera, M. Kivimaki, V. Liukkonen, M. Virtanen, and J. Ferrie. 2005. "Labor Market Trajectories and Health: A Four-Year Follow-up Study of Initially Fixed-Term Employees," *American Journal of Epidemiology* 161: 840–6.

Virtanen, M., M. Kivimaki, M. Joensuu, P. Virtanen, M. Elovainio, and J. Vahtera. 2005. "Temporary Employment and Health: A Review," *International Journal of Epidemiology* 34: 610–22.

Vosko, Leah. 2000. *Temporary Work: The Gendered Rise of a Precarious Employment Relationship*. Toronto: University of Toronto Press.

– ed. 2006. *Precarious Employment: Understanding Labour Market Insecurity in Canada*. Montreal and Kingston: McGill-Queen's University Press.

– 2006. "Precarious Employment: Towards an Improved Understanding of Labour Market Insecurity." In *Precarious Employment: Understanding Labour Market Insecurity in Canada*, ed. L. Vosko, 3–42, Montreal and Kingston: McGill-Queen's University Press.

– 2007. "Gendered Labour Market Insecurities: Manifestations of Precarious Employment in Different Locations." In *Work in Tumultuous*

Times: Critical Perspectives, ed. V. Shalla and W. Clement, 52–97. Montreal and Kingston: McGill-Queen's University Press.

Vosko, Leah, Nancy Zukewich, and Cynthia Cranford. 2003. "Precarious Jobs: A New Typology of Employment," *Perspectives on Labour and Income* 4 (10): 16–26.

Vosko, Leah, Martha MacDonald, and Iain Campbell, eds. 2009. *Gender and the Contours of Precarious Employment*. London: Routledge.

Vrankulj, Sam. 2010. "CAW Worker Adjustment Tracking Project: Preliminary Findings." unpublished.

Wagner, Alexandra. 2005. "Services and the Employment Prospects of Women." In *Working in the Service Sector*, ed. Gerhard Bosch and Steffen Lehndorff, 103–30. London: Routledge.

Wallulis, Jerald. 1998. *The New Insecurity: The End of the Standard Job and Family*. Albany: University of New York Press.

Watkins, Emily. 2006. *Joe Job, McJob, Not a Real Job: A Study of Working Post-Secondary Students in the Greater Toronto Area*. MA Thesis (Work and Society), McMaster University.

Webb, M. 2004. *Canada's Self Employment – On the Rise Again*. Global Economic Research, Scotiabank Group: 4.

Weil, David, and Carlos Mallo. 2007. "Regulating Labour Standards via Supply Chains: Combining Public/Private Interventions to Improve Workplace Compliance," *British Journal of Industrial Relations* 45 (4):791–814.

Whyte Jr., William H. 1956. *The Organization Man*. New York: Simon and Schuster.

Wilkinson, Frank, and David Ladipo. 2002. "What Can Governments Do?" In *Job Insecurity and Work Intensification*, ed. B. Burchell, D. Ladipo, and F. Wilkinson, 172–84. London: Routledge.

Wilson, S., S. Silver, and J. Shields. 1998. *Involuntary Job Loss in Canada*. Ottawa: Statistics Canada.

Wilthagen, T., and F. Tros. 2004. "The Concept of 'Flexicurity': A New Approach to Regulating Employment and Labour Markets," *TRANSFER – European Review of Labour and Research* 10 (2): 166–87.

Wolbers, M. 2007. "Employment Insecurity at Labour Market Entry and Its Impact on Parental Home Leaving and Family Formation: A Comparative Study among Recent Graduates in Eight European Countries," *International Journal of Comparative Sociology* 48 (6): 481–507.

Wood, Ellen Meiksins. 1995. *Democracy against Capitalism: Renewing Historical Materialism*. Cambridge: Cambridge University Press.

Yeandle, Sue. 1999. "Women, Men and Non-standard Employment: Breadwinning and Caregiving in Germany, Italy, and the UK." In *Restructuring Gender Relations and Employment: The Decline of the Male Breadwinner Model*, ed. Rosemary Crompton, 80–104. Oxford: Oxford University Press.

Zhou, Jianping. 2007. "Danish for All? Balancing Flexibility with Security: The Flexicurity Model," *IMF Working Paper* 36. European Department. Washington.

Zuboff, Shoshana, and James Maxmin. 2002. *The Support Economy: Why Corporations Are Failing Individuals and the Next Episode of Capitalism*. New York: Penguin Books.

Index